Karl Barth in North America

Karl Barth in North America

The Influence of Karl Barth in the Making of a New North American Evangelicalism

JOHN P. LEWIS

RESOURCE *Publications* · Eugene, Oregon

KARL BARTH IN NORTH AMERICA
The Influence of Karl Barth in the Making of a New North American Evangelicalism

Resource Publications
A division of Wipf and Stock Publishers
199 W. 8th Ave., Suite 3
Eugene, OR 97401

www.wipfandstock.com

ISBN 13: 978-1-49825-229-4

Manufactured in the U.S.A.

Contents

For Charlotte and Christian

Preface

THEOLOGICAL APPROACH IS A component of all theological systems, whether they are Roman Catholic, Anglican, Protestant, conservative, or liberal. Each has its own particular characteristics. Evangelical approaches to theology are particularly influenced by the theology of the Reformation, and those subsequent movements that have carried its heritage. The emphasis is on the exegesis of particular texts, and the use of historical sources that stand in the Reformation tradition. Usually, philosophical constructs are avoided in preference to what is regarded to be 'a straight reading of the text.' This view has often led to simplistic theological outcomes, that appear to be unaware of the actual influences and sources that have contributed to the construction of their discourses. In the past few years there have been a small number of attempts to address this issue. However, a number of theologians have agreed that there remains a scarcity of work dedicated to this important area.

The aim of this book is to produce a study of the effect that the influence of Karl Barth has had in the theological structures of new evangelicals. While previous works have done well in describing Barth's influence in various theologies, none have made a comprehensive *study* of their works. This contribution, therefore, is chiefly concerned with an investigation of those theologians who made an appreciative response to Barth. The *form* the analysis of this thesis takes is also new. Never before has Barth's influence in North American evangelicalism been studied in terms of *how* Barth came to be an *influence* in the theologian's thinking, before discussing the results of this influence.

The approach taken by this thesis will be in considering: (1) the *influences* that have come to bear on these theologians, which subsequently led to Barth becoming a *source* in their theologies; (2) the *motifs* that emerged as a result of the influence of Barth; (3) the theological *agendas* which arose; and (4) the *common agenda* they all shared.

Method

THE STUDY OF THEOLOGICAL approaches is an important undertaking since every theologian has an approach, whether consciously or unconsciously, that determines the final shape of his or her theological concepts. As Clark Pinnock has put it theologians are like cooks, they use ingredients in a certain manner, follow procedures, appeal to sources, place them in order and weigh their importance.[1] However, theology can no longer be said to amount to the rightful ordering of knowledge. In recent times there has occurred a necessity for theologians, as indeed for all social scientists, to reflect more upon the methods they employ in the pursuit of their discipline. Indeed, there has been a shift in thinking from modernism to postmodernism that has resulted in the need for theologians to approach theology differently.

What was known as modernism followed a rationally based approach that usually culminated in a series of objective propositional statements. The postmodernist approach, however, is more attuned to the reality that many of our assertions are subjective and that, consequently, experience and narrative are preferred contexts in which theology is to be understood and written.[2] Because of the experiential nature of postmodernism this thesis will examine the biography of the theologian as the key to unlocking the meaning of his or her writings, and a valuable tool for a thorough investigation of their work. Here we will focus on the biography of Karl Barth and how this relates to his theological writings. Attention will then be turned on a group of North American theologians to analyze how Barth's theology has influenced their personal experiences and corresponding theologies. Biography fits well into our current intellectual climate for a number of important reasons.

1. Pinnock, "New Directions in Theological Method," 197.

2. See Grenz, *A Primer on Postmodernism*; Hicks, *Explaining Postmodernism*; Penner, *Christianity and the Postmodern Turn*; Shepherd and Arisian, *Humanism and Postmodernism*; Ward, editor, *Blackwell Companion to Postmodern Theology*.

The personal experience of the theologian provides the background to the theological judgments she or he makes, and therefore provides valuable insight into what they have written. John Macquarrie, Emeritus Professor of Divinity in the University of Oxford, gave sound direction when he pointed out that "some experience of the life of faith precedes theology and may indeed be said to motivate it."[3] This "life of faith" constitutes a formative context from which theology is written. It determines the reason that the theology stands as it does, with its particular motifs, approach and issues that are explored and discussed. Experiences in the theologian's life determine how he or she forms and communicates the ideas that the experiences have given rise to. Just as a grieving parent may write on the dynamics of grief from his or her own experiences and therefore connect dynamically and profoundly with the reader, so do theologians profoundly connect with readers as they write theology as an expression of their experiences of faith. It is this process that this book seeks to study and analyze.

Theological communities also encounter formative experiences that guide, direct, form, and define their characteristics, shared beliefs and common sense of identity and vision. In the context of postmodernism the emerging theologies of these individuals and communities are to be seen as transient and conditional on one's environment, instead of stagnant, subservient to reason alone, and unconcerned with its human origins. Indeed, a biographical approach considers the subjective nature of knowledge and belief. One must also note the postmodern emphasis on the journey to understanding as being the key to one's personal truth, as distinct from modernism's belief in a final and definitive objective truth. Therefore this thesis contends that there is a necessary connection that is to be made between the theologian as a person and the theology that emerges out of her or his unique biographies. Indeed, it will be argued that theology is born out of the lived encounters of the theologian that develop into the kind of personal convictions, passions, concerns, questions and a motivation to connect with others, that is evident in their writings. Consequently, theology and theologian are inseparable. Indeed, theology is written in the context of a church tradition that upholds certain assumptions, a society that has a unique culture, and a faith community that perpetuates norms and traditions. Added to all this is the separate

3. Macquarrie, *Principles of Christian Theology*, 5.

family environments that contain their own unique histories, personalities, thoughts and beliefs. Therefore an approach to reading theology in the context of the author and the particular influences that shaped her or his thinking is both reasonable and necessary. We will seek to uncover the precise nature of these experiences and show how these contributed to the theology produced. Indeed, our new contextual world-view would have us comprehend theology as a subjective expression of the religious self. As Macquarrie pointed out, "the personal quality of such expressions vary widely and amount to what has been called the varieties of religious experience."[4] Dermot Lane wisely added to this argument by asserting that we "do not come into the world with a ready-made self. Rather we enter life with a capacity to become which is shaped by our experiences of reality . . . especially the reality of the human community composed of other selves."[5]

Previously the study of a theologian's work was carried out within the terms of a single philosophical paradigm; seen in Donald Bloesch's description of his own theology as "Fideistic Revelationism."[6] Such a method, however, appears to the postmodernist mind as being far too prescriptive and inflexible. A single approach based on a philosophical theory can only serve to compress a body of work into a tight conceptual framework that distorts its true meaning. However, theology that is read in the context of the biography of the author, and that takes account of factors such as personalities, experiences, sources, motifs and agendas, will deliver richer insights and appear, to the post-modern mind, to have greater depth as it rightly presents a theology as an expression of the life the author. Indeed, it changes as people and societies do by taking on new forms in response to changing circumstances. This is a subject that has attracted few investigations. There are three works that point in this new direction; those being James McClendon's groundbreaking work: *Biography as Theology: How Life Stories Can Remake Today's Theology,*[7] Bernhard Lohse's, *Martin Luther's Theology: Its Historical and Systematic*

---

4. Ibid.

5. Lane, "Experience, God and Theology," 10.

6. Grenz, "Fideistic Revelationism" 35.

7. McClendon, *Biography as Theology*, 1990.

Development,[8] and Scott Hendrix's essay, "Luther," in *The Cambridge Companion to Reformation Theology*.[9]

McClendon made deliberate and penetrating connections between the theology of Martin Luther King and his biography. The author pointed to "King's boyhood, his upbringing in which church and home were virtually indistinguishable, his calling to the ministry and his decision for graduate studies in theology, his choice of the Black Baptist church in the South and his enduring commitment to that church after fame had opened other options."[10] These influences, some determined by the circumstances of birth and others according to personal choice, formed the context in which King's theology developed and took shape. These formative influences found in his biography also gave rise to his approach to political activism that followed after the pattern of his Black Southern church meetings, with their "revivalist and Spirit-filled" fervor and passionate illusions to biblical imagery of freedom and liberation. Furthermore King, in his famous "I have a dream" speech, rallied the consciousness of a nation in a declaration that was primarily influenced by his Black Southern religion. McClendon concluded that it was the influence of numerous sermons, camp meetings, prayer groups and Scripture readings that shaped King's approach, language and agenda. This is clearly seen as King drew upon the language of the prophet Isaiah for the imagery of "freedom from every hill," and the lines of the old Negro spiritual, "free at last," to advocate for civil liberties. From McClendon's work one can rightly assert that King's beliefs were a product of the influences that shaped him as a person and became a valuable storehouse of sources that served his motifs of liberation and freedom, together with his agenda to bring justice via civil rights to the forefront of the American psyche. Indeed, McClendon believed that it "would require a high order of cynicism to suppose that the man who so eloquently spoke and so profoundly moved his hearers was not speaking from the depth wells of his own being, was not then truly declaring his own dream, his own faith."[11]

Bernhard Lohse has also significantly contributed to this discussion in his review of Luther's biography and its contribution to the study

---

8. Lohse, *Martin Luther's Theology*.

9. Hendrix, "Luther," 39–56.

10. Ibid., 55.

11. McClendon, *Biography as Theology*, 58.

of his theological development. In a chapter entitled "Luther's Personal Development" Lohse discussed the guiding influences in Luther's life that shaped him into the person and theologian he became. Lohse pointed to Luther's parental home, particularly the influence of his father, his student years, where he became indebted to "the philosophical orientation of the School of Arts in late medieval Occamism,"[12] his crisis in a storm during which he vowed to enter monastic life, and his challenges in the cloister. It was the influence of Occamism, Lohse contended, that intensified Luther's inner conflict and produced his search for a gracious God, and which ultimately led to his personal crisis.[13] Without these influences Luther would not have become the man he was, and the theological revolutionary who changed world history.

Scott Hendrix adds to this discussion by providing a detailed outline of the dominant influences in Martin Luther's early life that contributed to the formation of his theology. Hendrix made the important link between biography and theology as he observed that "Luther was subject to a number of influences, which can be identified in his writings."[14] In developing this theme Hendrix cites Luther's personal reflections on his experiences and how these contributed to the pursuit of his theological writings. In addition to the influence of personal experience Hendrix also noted Luther's acknowledgement of literary influences, evident in his early work. Importantly, Hendrix noted Luther's reference to the influence of Augustine of Hippo (354–430), who became a significant source in Luther's writings, particularly in his lectures on the Book of Romans (1515–1516).[15]

This contribution to the study builds on the examples of some sections within the work of McClendon, Lohse and Hendreix, by discussing the biographies of theologians who were ultimately influenced by a single source that predominated over a variety of other sources, and guided them in the writing of their works. The connection between influence and source will be an important part of our study. By analyzing the theologian's writings links are to be made between the sources used and the influences in their lives that led to these sources being utilized in the

12. Lohse, *Martin Luther's Theology*, 32.

13. Ibid., 33.

14. Hendrix, "Luther," 41.

15. Ibid.

way that they were. That is, if Barth is seen to be a significant source in a particular theological work the question must be asked as to the reason for its presence. As the author's biography is studied connections will be made between influences in life and the presence of the source in the extract under investigation. We will seek to uncover how Barth came to be such an important influence by identifying key moments in their lives. This will be determined by linking the author's biography with a study of the author's writings about Barth as a theologian of importance, studying their incorporation of Barth as a significant reference in their works, and identifying Barthian theological motifs they pursued. We will seek to discover what exactly took place when the influence of a single source was incorporated into the body of a distinct theological tradition. That is, we will seek to determine what kind of theology was produced when Barth's theology influenced North American evangelicalism. Therefore this thesis will seek to uncover what theological themes were explored as a result of Barth's influence and how the great Swiss scholar was used as a source to expound these themes. We contend that the study of theological approach from this perspective will promote a better understanding of how theology is written and will therefore enhance the significance of future contributions.

In the writings of Donald Bloesch, for example, one can draw distinct lines of connection between his biography and the theology he produced. The process that will clearly define these connections is two-fold. Firstly, it will involve a detailed analysis of his work that will use his biography as the key that unlocks the connection between his writings and formative influences in his life. Secondly, comparisons will be made between Bloesch's theology and Barth's life and work. The approach used to analyze the connections between Bloesch, Barth and biography, will involve an *identification* of those aspects of Bloesch's theology that display indebtedness to Barth. Indebtedness will be identified by Bloesch's personal reflections, his positive references to Barth's work, and themes that bear his distinct influence. Also, a *discussion* of these theological extracts will determine the nature and extent of Barth's influence. Other influences in Bloesch's biography will need to be weighed up with the influence of Barth in order to determine the extent nature of the influence that was made. Therefore this thesis will seek to determine the context in which Bloesch interpreted Barth's theology and will analyze the kind of theology that ensued. These discussions will then follow a process of *assessment*.

That is, we will seek to ask why Barth's influence has given meaning to Bloesch's theology, in what manner he has appealed to Barth, and how this has contributed to his theological arguments.

Throughout it will become evident that theology can be studied carefully, precisely and accurately from this new perspective. Indeed, the approach undertaken here is intended to provide helpful guidance to others seeking to understand the works of theologians and will thereby contribute to more thoughtful, honest and introspective work in the future. The implications for the future study of theological approaches among evangelicals in North America are significant. As the rationalism of the modernist era fades in significance, and dominant new thought patterns of the post-modern age create a new environment with its own set of assumptions, models for future work will need to be established, defined and promoted if moderate evangelicalism is to avoid the designation: "relic of the past." Indeed, the emergence of a new evangelicalism indebted to Barth may well be seen to be a survival mechanism that allows this theological culture to re-cast itself so as to find its place in the new order. While the older modernist mind set was dominated by the need for reasoned propositions the post-modern mind seeks to engage with narratives and explore the experiences that unfold within them. This thesis, therefore, intends not only to contribute to the study of theological approaches but also to provide an example for future theological work as writers explore the self and determine the path that has led to their current convictions. As the general theological community reflects on its own biographies, in the manner that some feminist theologians often do as a matter of course, they will gain a sharpened perception of the influences in their lives that have stimulated the motifs they write about and agendas they pursue. These insights will result in theology more attuned to its own reason to exist, more open to future changes, more sensitive to the changes in society and more able to connect profoundly with readers as they gain insight and connection with the author. Indeed, biographies will increasingly become the context in which theology is both understood and written.

Karl Barth: His Life and Theology

THE THEOLOGY OF KARL Barth is most accurately observed in the context of the life changes he encountered and according to the significant influences that surrounded him at these key moments. There were three major periods of thought that Barth experienced that correspond with two major changes. These are identified in his shifts from student to pastor and then from pastor to professor.[1] Each new life situation brought new challenges requiring a shift in theological thought. It is evident that the surrounding influences impinging on Barth during these changes directed his path and include a combination of schools of thought, particular individuals, and significant religious writings. However, it is believed that one must also note Bruce McCormack's contention[2] that while significant changes occurred in Barth's theology, important consistencies are also to be found. Consequently one can speak of Barth's shifts in emphasis as a result of new influences, rather than new starting points, or turns in direction.

Most of the material written by Barth and about him does not cover his early years of childhood.[3] Yet it is known that Barth was raised in the Swiss Reformed tradition, and that this influence remained with him for the rest of his life. His father was a Reformed pastor and a teacher of some note. While Fritz Barth's conservatism was not shared by his son during Karl's university study, it is evident that he did embrace something of his father's conservatism later in his career. Karl Barth's theological training at the universities he attended was dominated by Protestant liberalism,

1. Forde has referred to these shifts as "two major crises in Barth's theological development." Forde, "Does The Gospel Have a Future? Barth's Romans Revised," 69.

2. McCormack, *Karl Barth's Critically Realistic Dialectical Theology*.

3. Bolich raises the need to look further into this important factor in Barth's life. Bolich, *Karl Barth and Evangelicalism*, 218.

its influence being evident in his early publications. However, the realities of pastoral work soon flung Barth into a world he felt ill equipped to deal with. Here began Barth's search for a new direction that resulted in a journey of discovery lasting the rest of his life.

Barth's prodigious theological output gives a clear outline of the changes to his theological thinking. This chapter will discuss these shifts in thought in some detail and discuss the influences that appear to have contributed to the subsequent pilgrimage. It must be said, however, that Barth did not shift theology from one direction to another, as if wiping the slate clean so as to start from a totally new beginning. There was a distinct logic and continuity to his theological development. His final agenda for a theology of the Word of God did not emerge ex nihilo, but is clearly seen to have derived from a long process of theological interaction and reflection. Central to this process was Barth's rejection of a subjectively based theology founded on philosophy, and a desire to replace it with an objectively based theology founded on the Word of God. To be sure, Barth's theology of the Word of God became one of the most recognizable features of his work throughout North America, resulting in both extensive criticism and widespread appreciation.

Karl Barth was born in Basel, Switzerland, on May 10, 1886 into what Robert Jenson describes as a "churchly and academic family."[4] His Father, Johann Friedrich ("Fritz") Barth, was a minister of the Swiss Reformed Church[5] and a teacher at the local Preachers' school,[6] the Evangelical School of Preachers in Basel.[7] He was later appointed Professor of Early and Medieval Church History (and New Testament)[8] at the University of Bern[9] before his death in 1912.[10] Fritz Barth's theology was mildly conservative[11] and highly influenced by pietism. During his university days the Swabian pietist, Johann Tobias Beck, had been a leading influence, resulting in Fritz Barth possessing a theology that valued experi-

---

4. Jenson, "Karl Barth," 24.

5. Mueller, *Karl Barth*, 14.

6. McCormack, *Karl Barth's Critically Realistic Dialectical Theology*, 36.

7. Mueller, *Karl Barth*.

8. Torrance, *Karl Barth*, 36.

9. McCormack, *Karl Barth's Critically Realistic Dialectical Theology*, 36.

10. Torrance, *Karl Barth*, 15.

11. Although Bolich refers to him as "a conservative Reformed pastor and theologian." Bolich, *Karl Barth and Evangelicalism*, 103.

ence over doctrine.[12] David Mueller noted that both of Karl's grandfathers were also Reformed ministers, and that it is noteworthy that his roots also lie deeply embedded in the Reformed or Calvinistic wing of the Swiss Reformation.[13]

Barth was raised in Basel until he was three years old. He returned in 1935 until his death in 1968.[14] His formative school years were spent in Bern, where he received his early religious training and formal education. Later in life he recalled that his interest in theology first began while undertaking instruction for confirmation at the age of sixteen.[15] It was at that time, Thomas Torrance noted, that Barth first became interested in systematic theology.[16]

Barth, at the age of eighteen, began his studies at the University of Bern. After spending four semesters there he transferred to the University of Berlin in Germany. It was there that the young Barth came under the tutelage of Adolf von Harnack (1851–1930), Julius Kaftan (1848–1926) and Herrmann Gunkel (1862–1932). During his first semester he read Immanuel Kant (1724–1804), Friedrich Schleiermacher (1768–1834) and, most importantly, Wilhelm Herrmann's *Ethics*. Bruce McCormack made the comment that "(f)rom his first reading of *Ethics* Barth knew himself to be a devoted disciple of Herrmann."[17] Wilhelm Herrmann (1846–1922) lectured on Dogmatics and Ethics at Marburg University, and so it was to Marburg that Barth knew he must go.[18]

At Marburg Barth enrolled in Herrmann's Dogmatics I (Prolegomena) and Ethics classes. He also attended the lectures of Adolf Jülicher, Wilhelm Hietmuller and Martin Rade. The latter was well known as an intellectual who made himself readily available to students. Barth spent many happy hours at Rade's open house for students and would later assist Rade to

12. McCormack, *Karl Barth's Critically Realistic Dialectical Theology*, 36.

13. Mueller, *Karl Barth*, 14.

14. Ibid., 14.

15. Ibid., 15.

16. "What was much more important . . . was that he learnt how fine and good a thing it would be not only to know and affirm the great statements of the Creed, but to understand them from within." Torrance, *Karl Barth*, 16. Bolich also notes that one should not forget that Barth's theological training up until 1906 was conducted under the conservative scholarship of his father. See Bolich, *Karl Barth and Evangelicalism*, 103.

17. McCormack, *Karl Barth's Critically Realistic Dialectical Theology*, 37.

18. It was quite usual in Germany at this time for a student to transfer between universities in the course of study.

edit *Die Christliche Welt*, perhaps the most influential theological journal in Germany at the time.[19] Important to this discussion on the theological influences upon Barth's early years is that Rade, as well as Herrmann, were both advocates for the dominant Ritschlian school.

Alister McGrath observed that Barth's disillusionment with Hegelian idealism left an ideological vacuum that Albrecht Ritschl was successfully able to fill at a critical phase of German intellectual history.[20] Bruce McCormack noted that "(t)he hallmark of this theological movement was its commitment to a churchly theology, oriented towards God's self-revelation in the historical person of Jesus Christ."[21] Significantly, Ritschl had been an historian of dogma before becoming a dogmatic theologian. This resulted in historical enquiry being at the heart of most Ritschlian theology. Ritschl also restored an emphasis upon ethics, which he believed to have been lost through Friedrich Schleiermacher's emphasis upon "feeling". Ritschl believed that an emphasis upon "feeling" led to introspection. As a consequence he urged the Christian to be concerned for ethical action. Supernaturalism was excluded in favor of a "tradition of Christ propagated in the church."[22] McGrath commented that "(t)his 'tradition' is essentially empirical and historical, referring to a general ethical and religious principle or idea first embodied in the historical Jesus."[23] However, by the end of the nineteenth century the Ritschlian School had undergone significant changes. By the turn of the twentieth-century Adolf von Harnack, who up until this time had been a prominent leader of liberal Protestantism, was regarded as belonging to an older more conservative faction within Ritschlianism.[24] Consequently, his influence diminished. McCormack observed that the source of this change in direction was "the explosive emergence in the mid-1890s of the *Religionsgeschichtliche Schule* ('history of religions school') led by Ernst Troeltsch."[25]

Troeltsch's new form of Ritschlianism challenged the assumption that held to the absoluteness or finality of Christianity, which was thought

---

19. McCormack, *Karl Barth's Critically Realistic Dialectical Theology*, 38.

20. McGrath, *Making of Modern German Christology*, 82.

21. McCormack, *Karl Barth's Critically Realistic Dialectical Theology*, 21.

22. McGrath, *Making of Modern German Christology*, 82–83.

23. Ibid., 84.

24. McCormack, *Karl Barth's Critically Realistic Dialectical Theology*, 39.

25. Ibid., 39.

to be "evidence of a residual commitment to a supernatural conception of revelation on the part of the Ritschlians—a thing which Troeltsch felt had been rendered impossible by the modern understanding of the historical-critical method."[26] Consequently, he ruled supernatural revelation out of court and regarded Christianity as, at best, only relatively superior to other forms of religion. By 1897 the "older" more ecclesially orientated Ritschlians and the "younger," scientifically orientated history of religions school, could no longer tolerate companionship.[27]

McCormack commented that by the first decade of the twentieth century Troeltsch's program had become the most important factor defining the theological situation in Germany. While the older Ritschlians attracted a fair following there was still one other alternative left to students, the theology of Wilhelm Herrmann. One such student who followed this road was Karl Barth. Barth had concluded that Troeltsch's theology had gone beyond the limit he could follow.[28] Mueller commented that "in this period Barth was not satisfied with a purely historical-critical understanding of the biblical text, which did not come to grips with its subject matter."[29]

While a student at Marburg, Barth embraced Herrmann's alternative with enthusiasm. In a lecture of 1932 Barth looked back to this period in his life and recalled: "The air of freedom blew through his lecture room. It was certainly not by chance that for decades, every semester a small party from Switzerland made the pilgrimage to Marburg and felt especially at home there. Our rebellious minds, repudiating all authority, there found satisfaction."[30] John Macquarrie described Herrmann's theology as one that illustrated the neo-Kantian character of Ritschlianism.[31] It stood for the repudiation of metaphysics, and the practical emphasis on moral

---

26. Ibid., 40.

27. The split took place in that year as the whole saga was documented by Gustav Ecke in his book, *Die Theologische Schule Albrecht Ritschl*, 41.

28. Herrmann's theology represented a form of Ritschilianism, however by the time Karl Barth studied with him Herrmann's relationship with Ritschlianism had almost completely dissolved. Ibid., 41.

29. Mueller, *Karl Barth*, 17.

30. Busch, *Karl Barth*, 45.

31. Conversely, McCormack has noted: "Herrmann is customarily described in histories of theology as a Ritschlian. But that is a distortion of the truth. During the years in which Barth studied under him, Herrmann had already broken free of the central tendencies of Ritschl's theology . . . Herrmann's theology is best described as a kind of Schleiermacherianism." McCormack, "The Unheard Message of Karl Barth," 60.

values.[32] In contrast to Troeltsch's thorough rationalism Barth found in Herrmann one who could show that "theology could have its own professional fervor, not merely as a parasite on the fourth faculty, but in its own right."[33] Barth was used to hearing about theology as an adjunct to history or philosophy. Yet there was a more compelling reason that attracted Barth to Herrmann at this time. It was an emphasis that would re-emerge in Barth's theology at a later time, yet in a radically different manner.

Barth was also attracted to what he described as Herrmann's "Christocentric Impulse."[34] Along with this approach Herrmann attached a reverential attachment to the person of Jesus. He contended that human beings had a need to gain an orientation for their lives in this world. Metaphysics, he believed, was not able to fill this need. Only religion, expressed in concrete faith, could respond to the need. The nature of Herrmann's faith was subjective and consisted in a self-authentication that was able to arise out of the power of Jesus' personality. Of most importance to Jesus' personality was his religious personality, specifically his "inner being", which was able to impact upon the heart of a believer. This sentiment was expressed in Herrmann's celebrated book, *The Communion of the Christian with God*, the first edition of which was written in 1886. It was this concentration on the inner life of Jesus that brought Herrmann's theology in conflict with Ritschl's, which placed a high value on the life and teaching of Jesus. For Ritschl and his followers, to ground theology historically meant to ground it by means of the discipline of historical enquiry. "Not so for Herrmann; for him 'historically grounded' meant grounded in the communion with God which only comes about in history."[35] According to Herrmann, the certainty of faith is able to arise out of the impression, which the Jesus of the Gospels is able to make upon the sensitive reader,[36] at his own place in history. From this perspective Herrmann's theology swung itself in the direction of the kind of subjective responsive reading of the gospels found in Schleiermacher. McCormack comments that it became a kind of existentialized Schleiermacherianism

32. Macquarrie, *Jesus Christ in Modern Thought*, 259.

33. Busch, *Karl Barth: His Life and Letters and Autobiographical Texts*, 45.

34. Ibid., 45.

35. McCormack, *Karl Barth's Critically Realistic Dialectical Theology*, 52.

36. McGrath, *Making of Modern German Christology*, 89.

belonging to no existing school.[37] Significant to our study is that it was this later Herrmann/Schleiermacherian theology to which Barth initially committed himself.

It was at Marburg, at the age of twenty-three, that Barth concluded his formal theological education. After completing the theological examinations set by the Church of Bern in 1909, he was ordained by his father in the cathedral in Bern[38] before returning to Marburg.[39] Not feeling experienced enough to take on a pastorate he took the position of assistant to Martin Rade, the editor of *Christliche Welt*, "an influential liberal periodical which concentrated upon the church's responsibility in the world."[40] This decision to put pastoral ministry on hold may well have been due to Herrmann's repeated emphasis that all true preaching must grow out of the experience of the preacher.

During this time Barth began producing his first published theological works in which he showed he was an enthusiastic follower of Wilhelm Herrmann.[41] The first of these was a work on modern theology entitled *Modern Theology and Work for the Kingdom of God*. In it Barth concluded that the essence of modern liberal theology lies in religious individualism. The starting point, he claimed, was ethics. However, Barth contested that no ethical norm may be imposed from without. Rather, such norms are generated by "the willing activity of the individual." In the case where such ethical demands are impossible to fulfill one might encounter a Power, yet "(t)he source of the revelation of this Power will vary." For some it may come from reflection upon the Christian tradition, or the life of the Church.[42] The second characteristic of modern theology, claimed Barth, was "historical relativism." Because modern theology accepted the tenet of the prevailing historiography that there were no absolutes in history, it maintained that there were no absolutes in the biblical witness.[43] These sentiments fitted well with Herrmann's theory of subjective response. Barth, in these early years, was quite clearly a product of Marburg. He

37. McCormack, *Karl Barth's Critically Realistic Dialectical Theology*, 54.

38. Mueller, *Karl Barth*, 17. In Torrance's opinion he was ordained in 1908. See Torrance, *Karl Barth: An Introduction to His Early Theology*, 16.

39. Busch, *Karl Barth: His Life and Letters and Autobiographical Texts*, 46.

40. Torrance, *Karl Barth: An Introduction to His Early Theology*.

41. McCormack, *Karl Barth's Critically Realistic Dialectical Theology*, 68.

42. Ibid., 69.

43. Mueller, *Karl Barth*, 18.

would later reflect on this time. "At the end of my student days I was second to none among my contemporaries in credulous approval of the 'modern' theology of the time. With the views that I have indicated, in 1909, I went into the pastorate."[44]

THE BEGINNING OF CHANGE: BARTH AT SAFENWIL

On the 16th of September 1909, Barth moved to Geneva where he took on a position of assistant pastor to Adolf Keller. In 1911, he accepted the call to become the pastor of the Reformed Church of Safenwil, in north central Switzerland. Mueller notes that "(h)e served as pastor of this village church until 1921."[45] It is clear that this appointment came to represent a significant time in Barth's theological development. Out of the cloistered environment of academic debate and into a new world of pastoral life, with all its shades and colors of human existence, Barth found himself in a new situation requiring a reorientation of thought. He later wrote: "It was during my time at Safenwil that I changed my mind decisively in a way which also affected the outward form of my future career."[46] The path leading to Barth's reorientation began with his renewed friendship with a former fellow student from Marburg, Eduard Thurneysen.[47]

Thurneysen was a significant influence on Barth's theological reorientation. Thurneysen was a pastor of a parish on the other side of the mountain from Barth at Leutwil.[48] Though they were not able to meet as often as they would have liked, the two corresponded regularly and frequently journeyed together to Bad Boll in Württemberg to hear the Lutheran Pietist, Christoph Blumhardt, teach of his passionate concern "to bring the message of the Kingdom and compassion of God to bear upon the daily life of man in all its redeeming power [. . .] (At Württemberg) they faced the fierce critical and indeed atheistic questions of modern man and sought their answers in the Word of God."[49] The teaching of

---

44. Busch, *Karl Barth: His Life and Letters and Autobiographical Texts*, 51.

45. Mueller, *Karl Barth*, 18.

46. Busch, *Karl Barth: His Life and Letters and Autobiographical Texts*, 46.

47. Mueller, *Karl Barth*, 19.

48. Ibid., 19.

49. Torrance, *Karl Barth: An Introduction to His Early Theology*, 17. Blumhardt's proclamation spoke of "the coming kingdom of God as a world transforming power." McCormack, *Karl Barth's Critically Realistic Dialectical Theology*, 123.

Blumhardt, reminiscent of his father's pietism, had a powerful influence on Barth, and opened up for him a fresh understanding of the kingdom of God as that which breaks through into human existence. A year after his first encounter with Blumhardt, Barth wrote that "Blumhardt always begins right away with God's presence, might, and purpose: he starts out from God; he does not begin by climbing upwards to Him by means of contemplation and deliberation. God is the end, and because we already know him as the beginning, we may await his consummating acts." This reflection is indicative of Barth's change of direction.[50]

Though residual elements would remain for some time, Barth's break with Marburg was now complete.[51] McCormack noted that during "the course of the following summer, concrete evidence emerged that Barth had now adopted a new *Ansatz* (a new starting-point) for theological reflection."[52] This was initially evident in a letter Barth wrote to Rade in answer to an article he had written in *Die Christliche Welt*. In his letter Barth wrote that "the *world,* understood as the totality of our life's conditions, is godless and that Jesus and His message stand over against it in relation of antithesis as a reality which is also complete in itself."[53] Along with theological issues Barth was also influenced by the group's politics. As Torrance noted, "(i)n the younger (Christopher) Blumhardt the eschatological character of the message of Jesus, realistically acknowledged, was related with corresponding realism to the rising socio-political movement, and he, together with Leonhard Ragaz and Herrmann Kutter became the fathers of the religious socialism in which Barth himself took part, yet not without strong reservations."[54] In time, these reservations led to a final break as Barth came to see that human effort had no place to play in bringing about the fulfillment of God's future.[55] Barth's primary arena for further theological reflection was within his role as pastor and preacher.

Involving himself in pastoral activity and exegetical work Barth, as he wrote in the preface of *The Epistle to the Romans*, "tumbled himself

50. Ibid., 122.
51. Ibid., 125.
52. Ibid., 123.
53. Ibid., 124.
54. Torrance, *Karl Barth*, 36–37.
55. Ibid., 40.

into a conflict, the inward and outward significance of which he could not foresee."[56] Mueller observed that in an address to a group of ministers in 1922, Barth provides us with an important statement concerning the context in which his theological reorientation took place. In this address he confessed:

> Once in the ministry, I found myself growing away from those theological habits of thought and being forced back at every point more and more upon the specific minister's problem, the sermon. I sought to find my way between the problem of human life on the one hand and the content of the Bible on the other.[57]

It is here that one finds the kernel of Barth's change of mind. His university training had not prepared him for the issues of pastoral life. His professors had stimulated his mind, but had not given him the tools that would enable him to take the message of Christianity to his parishioners in any way that spoke with meaning into their life situations. More and more Barth found, in the context of his ministry, that the subjective historicity of his academic training was unable to speak with significance into the lives of his parishioners. It was this realization that lead to the necessity for Barth to break through into a new realm of thinking.

John Webster noted that Barth's ten years spent as a pastor were a period of intensely concentrated development. A new outlook born out of his experiences as a pastor carried him beyond the traditions of the eighteenth and nineteenth centuries, in which he had been so thoroughly schooled. Webster further noted that Barth's "immersion in local social and political disputes, fed by the writings of Christian social thinkers such as Kutter and Ragaz [. . .] began to eat away at his confidence in the bourgeois religious ethos of his teachers." He also became disillusioned with the collusion of mainstream theology with the ideology of the Great War.[58] When, in August 1914, ninety-three German intellectuals came out in support of the war policy of the imperial German government, Barth believed that he needed new foundations for his theological system. In his response to this document Barth later wrote:

> I found to my horror the names of nearly all my theological teachers whom up to then I had religiously honored. Disillusioned by

56. Ibid., 17.

57. Mueller, *Karl Barth*, 19.

58. Webster, "Introducing Barth," 3.

their conduct, I perceived that I should not be able any longer to accept their ethics and dogmatics, their biblical exegesis, their interpretation of history, that at least for me the theology of the nineteenth century had no future.[59]

As a result Barth sought a new path. "Above all he immersed himself in an amazed rediscovery of the biblical writings, and especially of the Pauline corpus."[60]

During this period of searching Barth concerned himself with the task of preaching, and its significance to his congregation. He soon came to the conviction that preaching could not be anything else than an announcement of the Word of God that is grounded on a thorough exegesis of the Scriptures. Thus Barth grappled with the issue of how to expound the message of the Bible "as the message of Christ and the coming of his kingdom in such a way that the man of today can understand it, be moved by it and be changed through it." Therefore, at this point in his development, Barth had moved beyond his understanding of the church as a community concerned with its own religious experiences and meanings, as with Schleiermacher, to that which exists as a living community addressed by, and responding in life and act to, the Word of God.[61] Torrance commented that "(i)t was out of this sermon-preparation and the fundamental encounter between Word of God and modern theology into which he plunged, that the new direction and movement in theology associated with the name of Barth arose."[62] Barth came to the decision that he needed to break away from the subjectivism he had been previously influenced by; a mode of thinking he later came to describe as "a theology in the succession of Descartes." He saw it as a religion which expressed itself within the framework of "our modern outlook on the world,"[63] and therefore came to see this expression of the faith as "indistinguishable in its manifestation from the mind or life of the world around it—it was all

59. Torrance, *Karl Barth: An Introduction to His Early Theology*, 38. Note Bolich's comment: "When ninety-three German intellectuals, including many of Barth's former teachers, declared their support of the Kaiser's war policy, Barth made his final break with liberalism." Bolich, *Karl Barth and Evangelicalism*, 104.

60. Webster, *Introducing Barth*, 4.

61. Torrance, *Karl Barth: An Introduction to His Early Theology*, 41.

62. Ibid., 35.

63. Ibid., 33.

an expression of the same thing."[64] In contrast, "Barth was determined to hear the Word of God out of itself, as it came straight from above."[65] He came to understand that the Bible was not the expression of humanity's spiritual aspirations, nor was it a record of humanity's religious development through the centuries, or the embodiment of the best and highest thoughts of humanity about God. In Barth's assessment "(t)he Bible tells us not how we are to speak to God, but how God has spoken to us; not how we find a way to God, but how He has sought and found a way to us." Scripture is not humanity's cry to God, Barth concluded, but God's answer to that cry.[66] His many years of wrestling with these issues finally bore fruit in the publication of the first edition of *Der Römerbrief* in 1919.

ROMANS I

In the first edition of *Der Römerbrief* [67] Barth acknowledged the rightful place of the modern historical-critical method. However, he also affirmed that the traditional Protestant doctrine of inspiration had a greater depth, in so far as it sought to discover the true meaning of the text. Therefore, by the time of this first edition, Barth had well and truly broken with "the philological and historical study of the biblical text which characterized the commentaries of modern liberalism."[68] The result was him leaving behind the anthropocentric and cultural Christianity of Herrmann to seek an expression of faith that magnified the sovereignty of God. Yet Barth was ultimately dissatisfied with what he had written. As Mueller commented that "(i)t was Barth's dissatisfaction with what he had said which led to the radically revised second edition."[69]

Due to the circumstances surrounding his life and his reflections upon them, Barth came to the conviction that humanity, due to its essential nature, could not bring about the kingdom of God in any way. The cultural crises that followed the war dashed to pieces any concept of the advancement of human society, according to humanity's coopera-

---

64. Ibid., 34.

65. Ibid., 65.

66. Coates, "Barth's Conception of the Authority of the Bible," 596.

67. Barth, *Der Römerbrief, 1919.*

68. Mueller, *Karl Barth,* 22. Torrance, on the other hand, notes that the first edition marks the climax of his early philosophical period. Torrance, *Scotsman,* 4.

69. Ibid., 23.

tion with God, or Christian Socialistic ideals. As Christoph Schwöbel has observed, "the collapse of German social democracy by its support of the war had taken away the possibility of reorienting theology towards social tasks in the way the Religious Socialists had recommended."[70] In Barth's new understanding the "Kingdom of God is understood as that which brings about *the dissolution of all things, the cessation of all becoming, the passing away of this world's time.*"[71] Consequently, Barth abandoned the theology of Romans I for what Schwöbel referred to as the abandonment of an organic model for a radically dialectical "theology of crisis."[72]

In the first edition of *Der Römerbrief* McCormack believed that Barth developed his thesis on the basis of an organological model of eschatology. In this model, as Hans Frei noted, Barth talked of the "organic growth" of the kingdom.[73] This is probably what Mueller meant by Barth's idea of the possibility of continuity between God and man.[74] Therefore, as McCormack has contended, the most fundamental element of change between the two editions was this exchange of one model of eschatology for another.[75] In the second edition there was no room for an organic model of the kingdom. The kingdom will break in from beyond and will not seek human cooperation. He also noted that there are distinctive changes of tone and emphases between the two editions; he observed that the "rich battery of explosive images found in the second edition are largely lacking in the first, as is the widespread use of paradox."[76]

Barth's second edition of his commentary on Romans marked a significant period of his thought.

ROMANS II

In 1921, when Barth set out to write his second edition of his Romans commentary,[77] he began a new stage in his theological development.

---

70. Schwöbel, "Theology," 19.

71. McCormack, *Karl Barth's Critically Realistic Dialectical Theology*, 208.

72. Schwöbel, "Theology," 20.

73. Frei, *The Doctrine of Revelation in the Theology of Karl Barth, 1909–1922*, 156.

74. Mueller, *Karl Barth*, 24.

75. McCormack, *Karl Barth's Critically Realistic Dialectical Theology*, 208.

76. McCormack also makes the comment that the tone of the second edition is one of anger, which is absent from the first. Ibid., 139.

77. K. Barth, *Der Römerbrief, 1922.*

Against the subjectivism of his training he set out on a new course that held to the objective concept that God has made himself known to humanity from beyond. As Torrance noted, in Barth's new understanding, the Gospel is the mighty Word of God that falls upon humanity and questions it down to the bottom of its being, uprooting it from its securities and satisfactions, totally tearing asunder all that keeps humanity a prisoner in its own ideas in order to free humanity for God and his wonderful new work of grace in Jesus Christ. In this second edition the "emphasis was quite definitely upon what became known as 'diastasis,' the distance, the separation, between God's way and man's way, God's thoughts and man's thoughts, between Christianity and culture, between Gospel and humanism, between Word of God and word of man."[78] Torrance summarized this shift in thought well when he wrote that Barth

> set himself to show that the teaching of St Paul cannot be made to fit into our man-made syntheses, or coordinated with our philosophical or cultural presuppositions, or be interpreted in line with the striving of mankind for its own betterment. Rather does the Gospel as proclaimed by St. Paul cut against the grain of man's own vaunted needs and desires and against the so-called upward evolution of the human spirit; for the Gospel comes plumb down from above as a judgment cutting into man's life, setting it into crises, and it comes above all as grace setting man's existence on a wholly new basis . . .[79]

The second edition raised a storm in the theological and philosophical thought of both Germany and Switzerland. Barth cut across the thinking of his colleagues in his masterful handling of the task, which allowed Scripture to speak out as the very Word of God. "The main theme can be described as: Let God be God, and let man learn again to be man, instead of trying to be as God."[80]

A number of factors led to Barth's change of emphasis. Mueller believed that the most significant influence was Barth's deeper involvement with Paul and the Roman epistle. Second to this was the influence of Franz Overbeck (1837–1905) who had impressed Barth "with his polemic against the prevailing form of cultural Christianity characteristic of lib-

78. Torrance, *Karl Barth: An Introduction to His Early Theology*, 49.
79. Ibid., 49.
80. Mueller, *Karl Barth*, 24.

eral theology."[81] Overbeck had spoken repeatedly of the radical eschatological nature of Christianity, and Barth was one who heeded his words.
In addition to this, Thurneysen introduced Barth to the Russian novelist
Feodor Dostoevsky (1821–1881), through whom Barth was able to gain
a greater understanding of the predicament of humanity's sinfulness.
This period of transition was also highly influenced by Barth's reading
of Søren Kierkegaard (1813–1855), whose dialectical method pervaded
so much of the second edition.[82] Barth's frequent references to "paradox,"
"decision," "crisis," and "infinite qualitative distinction," to describe the
divine-human encounter, are reminiscent of Kierkegaard.[83]

The use of dialectics is so prominent in the second edition that many
have referred to Barth's thought as "dialectical theology" or a "theology of
crisis."[84] In Barth's understanding "the theme of the Bible is a *dialectical
relation;* the relation of a holy God to a fallen creature and the crisis which
results from such an encounter."[85] However, Barth's interest in dialectical
theology was not an isolated incident. Dialectical theology was a movement in Europe that reflected a general disillusionment surrounding the
events of the First World War, and has been seen as a "theological expression of Spengler's historical and cultural pessimism as he had set forth
in his 'Decline of the West'."[86] Yet what was Barth's particular emphasis?
Torrance understood Barth's dialectical thinking as indicating "the basic
reversal that takes place in our thinking as we are confronted by God: we
know God or *rather we are known by God.* It is God who speaks, man who
hears, and therefore man may only speak of God in obedience to what
he hears from God."[87] Humanity, therefore, must not derive its theology
from the centre of itself, but from the centre in God. Humanity remains as
humanity, but in that state in which God is met, listened to, answered, and
spoken of.[88] For a more detailed study the discussion now turns to Bruce

---

81. Ibid., 24.

82. Torrance, in his correspondence with *The Scotsman*, does not attribute the influence of Kierkegaard until the first volume of Dogmatics. Torrance, *The Scotsman*, 4.

83. Mueller, *Karl Barth*, 24.

84. Berkouwer, *The Triumph of Grace in the Theology of Karl Barth*, 23.

85. McCormack, *Karl Barth's Critically Realistic Dialectical Theology*, 271.

86. Berkouwer, *Triumph of Grace*, 23.

87. Torrance, *Karl Barth: An Introduction to His Early Theology*, 81.

88. Ibid., 83.

McCormack. In his treatment of Barth's dialectics there is a dividing of Barth's approach into a number of categories.

McCormack, in his *Karl Barth's Critically Realistic Dialectical Theology*, firstly discussed the nature of Barth's dialectical theology as that which consisted of dialectic between time and eternity. This amounts to "the judgment of God over every effort of man to find, in one manner or another, a way to God that shall begin with himself."[89] At this point, contended Barth, humanity must die in its judgment, "because it has pleased God to put an end to all human righteousness and—at that barrier—to reveal *His* righteousness." Therefore the intent of God's judgment, his divine No upon humanity, must not plunge us in to despair, because the "divine No proclaims that all our ways are futile, and thereby his way, the way of life, is opened to us."[90] It is therefore necessary, as Barth stated in *Der Römerbrief*, that humanity "becomes conscious of this situation, that he(or she) becomes aware of the crisis, that he (or she) acknowledges it as a divine crisis, and that in this crisis he (or she) chooses the fear of the Lord." The individual must hear and understand the No of God as a divine Yes, because it is God's No.[91] It was this second edition that, as Karl Adam put it, "fell like a bomb on the playground of the theologians." Nevertheless, Barth's emphasis was about to change again. Two years later Barth was called to be Professor of Reformed Theology in Göttingen.[92]

Barth was installed in Göttingen in October of 1921. His professorship ran until 1925, during which time he worked night and day on the history of dogmatic theology, ancient and modern. Following this appointment Barth was appointed Professor "Ordinarius" in Münster where he remained until 1930 when he moved to Bonn. During his five years there he saw the rise of Adolf Hitler and his own ejection from Germany. He found refuge in the city of his birth, occupying the ancient chair of Theology in Basel. Torrance noted that by this time he had fully developed his main position and had begun the publication of his monumental *Kirchliche Dogmatik*,[93] which, in Torrance's opinion, was the "most

---

89. Berkouwer, *Triumph of Grace*, 26.

90. Ibid., 27.

91. Ibid., 27–28.

92. Torrance, *Karl Barth: An Introduction to His Early Theology*, 17.

93. Ibid., 18.

formidable and massive work of theology since the *Summa Theologica* of Thomas Aquinas."[94]

TRANSITION TO DOGMATICS

Transition to Christian Dogmatics

As Mueller observed, Barth's transition from being a village pastor to theological professor was filled with misgivings. Yet in spite of the size of the challenge Barth worked assiduously on his lecture preparations. He found these to be difficult years, since he not only had to learn and teach continually, but also vindicate and protect himself in the form of lectures and public discussions.[95] John Webster noted that during this period "Barth also positioned himself more clearly vis-à-vis his liberal heritage, notably in a lecture cycle on Schleiermacher, but also in external lectures, some of which were found"[96] in the publication of a collection of essays in 1928 entitled *Theology and Church*.[97] Barth also "reacquainted himself with the classical and Reformed Christian tradition [. . .] He took his students through texts like the Heidelberg Catechism or Calvin's *Institutes,* as well as offering theological exegesis of a variety of New Testament books."[98] He eventually taught a full-scale cycle on dogmatics, which were published posthumously as the so-called *Göttingen Dogmatics*.[99]

During the winter semester 1923/4, "Barth announced his intention to lecture on 'Prolegomena to Dogmatics' in the spring."[100] Consequently, for the spring vacation of 1924 he set himself a programme of intensive reading in preparation for the course. He later reflected on this period as one of discovery and transition. "I sat in my study in Göttingen, confronted with the task of giving my first lectures in dogmatics. No one could have been more plagued than I was with the questions 'Can I do it?' and 'How shall I do it?'" As Barth undertook his own biblical and historical studies, he found himself increasingly alienated "from almost the whole of contemporary theology." As he sought for an alternative path he

94. Ibid., 18.

95. Webster, *Introducing Barth,* 4.

96. Ibid., 4.

97. Mueller, *Karl Barth.*

98. Webster, *Introducing Barth,* 4.

99. Ibid., 4.

100. McCormack, *Karl Barth's Critically Realistic Dialectical Theology,* 331.

came to the conviction, so important to his reception among a number of North American Evangelicals, that, firstly, "the Bible has to be the master in Protestant dogmatics," and, secondly that Protestants needed "to take up the Reformers again."[101]

It was during this period that Barth came across Heinrich Heppe's old textbook, *Reformed Dogmatics*. So significant was the discovery of this work that by the second semester Heppe became his foundational text.[102] Barth's attraction to this work would appear to be related to his emerging agenda for a biblical-Reformational theology; a theology defined by the Word of God and the Church's historical reflection upon it. Barth found in Heppe an orthodox theologian who had reflected deeply on those confessions which had provided the Church's response to the reformed theologies of Luther, Zwingli, and Calvin.[103] In Heppe's work Barth found a dogmatics "which had both form and substance, which was orientated on the central themes of the witnesses to the revelation given in the Bible, and which could also explore their individual details with an astonishing wealth of insights."[104] These insights are found in the *Göttingen Dogmatics*, where Barth constantly referred to the Reformers and argued strongly for the recognition of Scriptural authority. However, Barth was adverse to fundamentalist formulations regarding the nature of the Bible. Indeed, he had concluded that the Bible has authority in its ability to bear witness to the event of revelation as it has occurred. The actual revelation to which Scripture bears witness lies beyond in the revelation of God in Jesus Christ.[105]

Barth's theology of the Word of God, so important to his reception in North America, was that "God can make himself known only by God," and that this leads us to the "centre of the concept of revelation, to the fact of Jesus Christ." God has revealed himself in Jesus Christ, and Scripture bears witness, in human words, to the ultimate Word of God. Barth found that the consequence of this assertion was in understanding Scripture as a "mediation of God's own word, the *logos*," which comes to us through human words, in the written form of Scripture. Therefore Barth was able

---

101. Busch, "Karl Barth: His Life and Autobiographical Texts," 153.

102. McCormack, *Karl Barth's Critically Realistic Dialectical Theology*, 337.

103. Ibid., 336.

104. Busch, "Karl Barth: His Life and Autobiographical Texts," 154.

105. Barth, *The Göttingen Dogmatics*, 202.

to conclude that the "participation of human words in God's Word is the principle element in the scripture principle."[106] He further concluded that one couldn't escape the proposition that in Scripture, revelation meets us only indirectly.[107] In Barth's thinking there is a "beyond" in Scripture. There is the event of revelation as it occurred in time, and to which Scripture bears witness. Yet Scripture is the only witness, and it is for this reason that it can be said to be the channel through which God speaks and the means by which a person may hear God speak. Consequently Barth asserted that "the Bible is the first mediation and norm, the standard or principle of all communication."[108]

Barth moved to Munster in 1925 and stayed until 1930. "During these years [he] consolidated the theological positions forged in the early part of the decade. It was during this period that he published, in 1927, his *Die Christliche Dogmatik im Entwurf* (Christian Dogmatics in Outline)."[109] The work is divided into four chapters, which primarily concern themselves with Barth's three-fold form of the Word of God. It was this definition of the Word of God that became so influential in Barth's reception among North American evangelicals. Terry Coates made the observation that here Barth looked back to the threefold conception of the Word of God found in Luther: Christ, Scripture, and proclamation.[110] Barth had come to understand that in the matter of revelation the "Word of God is first of all that speaking of God which is identical with God; identical, because it is a speaking by God."[111]

The first chapter came under the heading of "The Actuality of the Word of God." In this introductory chapter Barth set forth the thesis that God meets humanity in his Word. As he meets with us he speaks, and asks for a response of faith and prayer and worship.[112] Within the parameters of this approach Torrance detected the influence of Overbeck's notion of *Urgeschichte* in modified form. "Urgeschichte means for Barth that the Revelation of God enters into our actual history and meets us within it,

---

106. Ibid., 212.

107. Ibid., 215.

108. Ibid., 216.

109. Webster, *Introducing Barth*, 30–32. Barth, *Die Christliche Dogmatik im Entwurf.*

110. Coates, *Barth's Conception of the Authority of the Bible*, 599.

111. McCormack, *Karl Barth's Critically Realistic Dialectical Theology*, 338.

112. Torrance, *Karl Barth: An Introduction to His Early Theology*, 108.

God speaking in person in concrete particular ways, but in such a way that Revelation is not tied to history or resolved into it, for that would mean that Revelation, like all else that is placed under history, only comes in order to perish."[113] In his conclusion Barth strongly asserted that the speaking of God in his Word is not found in a book, but in the Word made flesh. Consequently the Word does not depend on humanity. It is beyond our capacity to write it, even to be inspired to write it, for the Word is God and in God.[114]

Under the second heading of "The Revelation of God" Barth sustains the theme "that Revelation is God himself, and therefore belief in Revelation is precisely coincident with belief in God, and belief in God is exactly belief in God in his Revelation."[115] Barth unpacked this assertion by strongly contending with the objectivity of this Revelation. As Barth understood it, God reveals himself in his Lordship as one who confronts humanity in a divine address. Humanity has no authority over such a Word, but can only receive, listen and respond. In Barth's further development of his thesis he dealt with God as one who reveals himself as Trinity, and more particularly in Jesus Christ. "In him the Word of God is made flesh of our flesh, and the Truth of God is Actuality in our midst." Furthermore, this pure Word of God in Jesus Christ strikes us, meets us, encounters us and transforms us in our meeting with the Word, which, in Barth's reckoning, is Jesus Christ.[116] Having established this method of Revelation, Barth discussed "The Holy Scripture."

Under this third heading the consequences of Barth's Christological understanding of revelation became apparent. His understanding of Scripture amounted to seeing it as a human word regarding a divine Word. In Barth's concept the Bible is not itself God's revelation but serves as a channel to the revelation. As Barth stated: "What we have in the Bible is *witness* to the Word of God [. . .] a word concerning the Word and not the perfect divine Word itself."[117] For this reason he defined it as having

---

113. Ibid., 110.

114. Ibid., 111.

115. Ibid., 133.

116. Ibid., 115. In an earlier letter to *The Scotsman* (1952) Barth referred to this period as "a theology of analogy in which Christology plays a dominant role." Torrance, *The Scotsman*, 4.

117. Coates, *Barth's Conception of the Authority of the Bible*, 597–98.

the same transparency and fallibility as any human speaking and acting.[118] Yet this fallibility did not concern Barth, or diminish in any way his quest to establish a theology of the Word of God. As D. F. Ford has observed, Barth was more concerned with the sort of God portrayed in the Bible than with the verifiability of any detail in the narratives. More important still, in Barth's conceptualization of what the Bible represented, God's freedom is clearly such that if he chooses he may speak through the Bible despite any errors in it.[119] George Hunsinger referred to this aspect of Barth's theology as his motif of realism. Hunsinger contended that in this motif there is the admission of the incapacity of human language to refer to God.[120] According to this view Barth was not so much concerned with literal fact,[121] but a "good enough" witness to the living God the writers point towards.[122] Yet Barth was still able to attribute authority to Holy Scripture.[123] While it is a human word its object is God's Word. Therefore God speaks in it and so, while not being the Word, Scripture echoes the Word in the form of a testimony.[124] In Barth's opinion this is a Word to be heard in the context of the Church.

Barth consequently professed that Christians must receive the speaking of God in the Scriptures through the concrete authority of the

---

118. "For when God speaks His Word to the prophet, the prophet first of all speaks the Word to himself. It meets and strikes him, in his opposition, as the Word of Another and becomes broken like a ray of light in a prism . . . For it is not inerrancy, or any other human virtue, which makes witnesses for God, but the light of divine truth itself shining in the witness of erring and only partially good men." Coates, *Barth's Conception of the Authority of the Bible*, 598.

119. D. F. Ford, "Barth's Interpretation of the Bible," 70.

120. Hunsinger, *How to Read Karl Barth: The Shape of His Theology*, 43.

121. Hunsinger, "Beyond Literalism and Expressivism," 209.

122. Hunsinger, *How to Read Karl Barth*, 48.

123. Hunsinger, under the heading of "Particularism," notes that "Barth strove to take his teachings strictly from the particularities of the biblical witness, especially its narrative portions." Hunsinger, *How to Read Karl Barth*, 33.

124. Torrance sums up Barth's position with the comment: "The Word of God comes to us in the Bible through the speech of sinful, fallible men to whom God has spoken and who bear witness to his speaking. We do not have here a direct speaking of God from heaven, but a speaking through a transient and imperfect human medium. No doubt the human word we hear in the Scriptures is not always appropriate or adequate to the Word which its authors have heard and to which they bear testimony, but nevertheless it is a human word which God has freely chosen and decided to use as the form in which he speaks his Word to us." Torrance, *Karl Barth*, 120.

Church. In holding to this stance Barth revealed something of the historical component to his theological approach. He stated in his *Christian Dogmatics* that "in acknowledging the Bible to be the Word of God we are also acknowledging the authority of the Church, and are summoned to honor our fathers and mothers in the faith who handed it down to us."[125] However in Barth's perspective this is not a matter of mere institutional authority. What he wanted to assert was that the Word of God needs to be interpreted and applied within "the fellowship of others, within the sphere of reciprocal personal relationships."[126] Following his discussion on hearing the Word in the context of the church Barth moved on to cover the final topic of proclamation in his prolegomena to Christian Dogmatics.

Under the heading of "The Proclamation of the Church," Barth took up the final part of his inquiry. In this section Barth sought answers to the question of how far one can be said to communicate divine Revelation in the present.[127] To what extent is the proclaimed Word of God to be regarded as the Word of God itself spoken and heard to humanity? Trevor Hart interpreted Barth's theology as stating that preachers must not confuse their words with those of the apostles and prophets, which are the true source of preaching. However, in Hart's opinion, Barth still believed that preaching amounted to a proclamation of God's Word, albeit in the form of a witness to God's self-revelation in Jesus Christ.[128] According to Torrance, however, Barth recognized the impossibility of the task. In Barth's reckoning, Torrance stated, human speaking is not only fraught with weakness but also with error.[129] Yet, as McCormack noted, the complete inadequacy of the human language for revelation is not set-aside in the least.[130] Barth believed that the church must dare to seek the impossible, that is, "to speak God's eternal Word in its human words."[131] Indeed, his greatest concern became the necessity to let the Word of God speak for itself. Barth's theology had now unambiguously become a "Theology of the Word."

125. Ibid., 122.

126. Ibid., 123.

127. Macquarrie, *Jesus Christ in Modern Thought*, 281.

128. T. Hart, "The Word, the Words, and the Witness," 85.

129. Torrance, *Karl Barth*, 124.

130. McCormack, *Karl Barth's Critically Realistic Dialectical Theology*, 341.

131. Torrance, *Karl Barth*, 124.

Henceforth the concrete Word of God speaking to him out of the
Scriptures becomes the object of theological knowledge activity,
the way that that Word took in coming to man in the Incarnation
yields the way in which his theological knowledge of God, Father,
Son and Holy Spirit, is to take, and the form which that Word assumed in Jesus Christ yields the inner logic whereby that theological knowledge is to be articulated.[132]

As Barth wrestled with his new discoveries so emerged the third
great stage in his theological development in which, as Barth himself put
it, he emerged out of his eggshells.[133]

Transition to Church Dogmatics

In Torrance's opinion the really decisive transition in Barth's thinking
took place in about 1930.[134] It was in that year that Barth held his seminar
on Anselm's *Cur Deus Homo* in Bonn and published, with his brother
Heinrich, a book on the Holy Spirit, *Zur Lehre vom Heiligen Geist*. In
the following year he published a work on Anselm under the title *Fides
Quaerens Intellectum*.[135] Torrance noted that these works are of great significance since "they show us the transition from the *Christliche Dogmatik
im Entwurf* of 1927 to the *Kirchliche Dogmatik* of 1932."[136] Indeed,
Barth's reading of Anselm lead him "to a new starting point in thought; a
thought-form so new that he was forced to abandon his original project
in dogmatics as a *false start* and begin again at the beginning with a new
dogmatics, the *Church Dogmatics*."[137]

The *Christian Dogmatics* had brought Barth's second stage to a head.
It was designed to be a theology of the Word of God, in the tradition of
the prophetic-apostolic witness and developing out of exegesis. In it Barth
aimed to shun philosophic constructions and methods, and sought for
the Word of God to speak for itself. However, in the subsequent reviews
and debates that Barth was lead to engage in after its publication, it was
made only too clear to him that he was still "too entangled in the philo-

---

132. Ibid., 132.

133. Ibid., 132.

134. Ibid., 133.

135. Barth, *Anselm*.

136. Torrance, *Karl Barth: An Introduction to His Early Theology*, 133.

137. McCormack, *Karl Barth's Critically Realistic Dialectical Theology*, 421.

sophic presuppositions from which he had tried to emancipate himself."[138] Consequently Barth, after contending with the reviews, debates, and reading of Anselm, felt compelled to carry out a complete rewriting of his work, in the same manner in which he had set himself the task of rewriting his Romans commentary some twelve years earlier. In Torrance's assessment of this period "(t)he two chief questions he had to face and clear up, for they affected everything else, were the relation of theology and culture and the nature of theological method."[139] In regard to culture, Barth was clear in recognizing a need for the Church to be apart from it. Therefore he contended that the Church "must learn to interpret its life against the stream of the culture in which it swims. It must proclaim the divine No against all human attempts [. . .] to identify the Kingdom of God with the achievements of society and civilization."[140] Therefore Barth set himself the task of ridding himself of the last remnants of philosophical foundations in his work, and consequently endeavored to make his position unambiguously clear. The Church cannot address itself to culture on its own terms or on any laws embedded in its thinking.[141] It was a process that von Balthasar termed a "turn from dialectic to analogy."[142]

In Barth's new method of analogy "dialectic was seen as an attempt to ground theology philosophically by means of the categories provided by existentialism and phenomenology; analogy as an attempt to develop a pure theology, grounded in revelation alone."[143] However, Barth made the point of insisting that this analogy be understood as *analogia fidei*, an analogy of faith, which established the correlation between God and the world on the basis of divine revelation. Barth held that because of humanity's sinfulness the will, emotions, and reason, are in ruins and incapable of allowing anyone to discover God. Barth developed further his earlier conviction that while humans may be able to respond to God's self-disclosure they cannot possibly have a role in the self-disclosure.[144]

---

138. Torrance, *Karl Barth*, 134.

139. Ibid., 134.

140. Ibid., 134.

141. McCormack, *Karl Barth's Critically Realistic Dialectical Theology*, 421.

142. This was the position taken by the "Confessing Church" of Germany in "The Declaration of Barmen" in May, 1934, in its stand against the "German-Christians" and "National-Socialism". Torrance, *Karl Barth*, 136–37.

143. McCormack, *Karl Barth's Critically Realistic Dialectical Theology*.

144. Schnucker, "Karl Barth," 124.

Theology for Barth, therefore, could never be a matter of human enterprise[145]; it must be grounded on the proposition that "God speaks."[146] Theology for Barth could no longer arise out of subjective speculation based on human constructs of philosophy, but from the objective Word spoken to humanity.[147] As McGrath has summarized it, "(t)he analogy always leads from the creator to the creature, and never from the creature to the creator."[148] Never-the-less Barth did see the necessity of humanity to speak of God on the basis of what has been revealed. Indeed Hunsinger interpreted Barth's use of analogy in terms of "the incapacity of human language to refer to God [. . .] (while allowing) [. . .] for the occurrence of genuine and proper reference."[149]

Yet Barth's shift in thinking was not absolute. The fact that Barth's shift to a theology of analogy was a shift in emphasis, rather than a complete change, is seen in the continuing presence of dialectical thinking in this period. In the sovereign act of self-disclosure God takes up and speaks through the language of human weakness. "He (God) must reveal himself in and through the 'veil' of human language." As McCormack noted, "(t)he dialectic of 'veiling and unveiling' in revelation which was so characteristic of Barth's thought in the phase of *Romans II* was taken up into the doctrine of analogy and preserved in it . . . In truth, the *Realdialektik* (a dialectic in objectively real relations) of veiling and unveiling is the motor which drives Barth's doctrine of analogy and makes it possible."[150] Indeed, McCormack highlighted the consistencies within Barth's theology over the course of his life. McCormack agreed with Ingrid Spieckermann's assessment that Barth did not so much "turn" from one theological direction to another, but changed emphasis. Therefore, McCormack declared that "the 'shift' is a shift in emphasis, not a qualitative leap forward."[151] Yet,

---

145. These being derived from Cartesian and Kantian teaching, and belonging to the fundamentally subjectivist tradition of Protestant philosophy. Barth believed himself to have been misled by phenomenological and existentialist thinking. See Torrance, *Karl Barth*, 141.

146. Maquarrie, *Jesus Christ in Modern Thought*, 281.

147. Hunsinger, *How To Read Karl Barth*, 10.

148. McGrath, *Making of Modern German Christology*, 133.

149. Hunsinger, *How To Read Karl Barth*, 43.

150. Ibid., 17.

151. Ibid., 13. See Ingrid Spieckermann, "Gotteserkenntnis: Ein Beitrag zur Grundfrage der neuen Theologie Karl Barths.".

while McCormack seemed to make much of this continuance, it is true to say that Torrance, in his publication of 1962, also understood Barth's development as a *shift in emphasis*.

Torrance's conception of Barth's "shift to analogy" saw a change between humanity's qualitative differences to God, to one of humanity before God in his own self-disclosure. For Torrance dialectics continued, but in Barth one is now drawn deeper into the subject of God as he reveals himself in his Word. In biblical terms this shift demands a greater concern for biblical exegesis, and consequently a *theology of the Word of God*.[152] Torrance described Barth's theology of the Word as the exact antithesis of Kantian subjectivism, by describing Barth's assertions in wholly objective terms. As R. Preus so clearly stated, Barth now "speaks out against humanism for a living God and a God who has spoken."[153] Indeed, Torrance commented that in Barth's theology: "It is the assertion of the Lordship of the Word, of God in his freedom and grace, who gives himself to us to be known by us, but who does not resign himself to our control."[154] Yet as Torrance understood it, Barth, while benefiting from the contribution of orthodoxy, wanted to distinguish his position from the scholastics and orthodoxy.

While Barth may have applauded the objectivism of orthodoxy he did not concur with its approach. He was concerned that a rationalistic objectivism, which is concerned with objective sentences, is in danger of falling prey to converting the truths of God into rationalized objects. "In so far as the objective descriptions of the Truth are confounded with or confounded for the Truth, and do not fall under its questioning and judgment, they easily become assimilated to the prevailing intellectual trends and fall under the power of its patterns of thought and speech and their philosophical presuppositions."[155] Indeed, while Barth had deep sym-

---

152. Torrance, *Karl Barth*, 96.

153. Preus, "The Word of God in the Theology of Karl Barth," 105.

154. Torrance, *Karl Barth*, 99.

155. "Barth's studies in the history of Protestant theology convinced him that when it took over so much of the medieval intellectual apparatus with which to articulate doctrine in the sixteenth and seventeenth centuries it became overloaded with philosophical presuppositions, and so compromised itself with natural theology, and a supposedly enlightened understanding, that it easily fell in with the stream of philosophical development, at length assimilating into itself or becoming assimilated to Cartesian subjectivism, in which the objective truths of the Word of God were converted into psychological objects, to a much greater degree than many modern champions of seventeenth and eighteenth century orthodoxy would care to admit." Torrance, *Karl Barth*, 102.

pathy for Protestant orthodoxy, and had learnt much from the primary sources, such as Calvin and Heppe, he remained determined to stay on his guard against the ominous trap of rationalism in which one becomes entangled by submitting to its approach to doing theology. In Barth's understanding Protestant orthodoxy's attempt to secure the authority of Scripture in the high view of inerrancy failed "because it misconstrued the nature of the Bible and did not account for its humanity and there with its fallibility."[156] Barth saw its approach as a retrogression from the positions held by Luther and Calvin, since it had moved direction to such a place that venerated a "paper Pope."[157] Furthermore, in the subverting of Scripture's human character and elevation of its divine status, they had allowed docetism to creep into their thinking unnoticed, and consequently had, in a quite ironical turn of events, invented an objectified document devoid of miracle and reduced to a collection of propositional truths.[158] It was this aspect of Barth's approach that proved to be so appealing to North American evangelicals who sought to align themselves with a new kind of moderate orthodoxy, free from the constraints of fundamentalist rationalism.

In this matter Barth found considerable reinforcement in the teaching of Herrmann Kohlbrugge, who understood that the problem of nineteenth-century theology was in its confusion of the Word of God with "our faith and our formulations of it."[159] In Barth's understanding, derived from his "turn to analogy," the Word of God speaks for itself, indeed attacks our formulations and breaks through the net of the subjectivity we throw around it. For Barth, "(t)he Word of God retains his own objectivity, and therefore remains mystery, transcendent to us, exalted above us."[160] It was this conviction that led Barth further away from his earlier dialectical thinking and deeper into a theological approach of the Word of God, which was, in Barth's reckoning of it, Christological.[161]

Barth's Christological approach, began during the writing of his *Christian Dogmatics*, came to maturity in his *Church Dogmatics*. As has

---

156. Mueller, *Karl Barth*, 58.

157. Ibid., 58.

158. Hart, *The Word, the Words, and the Witness*, 90, 93.

159. Torrance, *Karl Barth*, 103.

160. Ibid., 103.

161. Preus, *The Word of God in the Theology of Karl Barth*, 107.

been noted, Barth came to comprehend that "God's Word is identical with Jesus Christ."[162] Torrance summed up the nature of Barth's fundamental shift in thinking by stating:

> (I)t had become perfectly clear to him that the dialectical rejection of mysticism and dogmatism was not enough—the theology of the Word required a positive doctrinal articulation adequate to the positive truth of the Word of God and yet appropriate to its nature as event and grace. The way forward must come from a concentration upon Christology, upon the Word made flesh, for therein there opened up the possibility of a dogmatics genuinely bound up with a form taken from the Word rather than from temporal philosophies . . . (Therefore), dialectical thinking had to fall away and positive Christological thinking had to take its place. [163]

Therefore Barth's shift to *Church Dogmatics* was a shift centered on Christology. Barth became a theologian of the Word of God, and this meant for him the Word of Jesus Christ. Furthermore, he came to the position that Jesus Christ *is* the Word of God, the one to whom the Scriptures bear witness.[164] The description of Scripture as a witness to God's revelation is a key emphasis in his thesis. It is clearly evident in his *Church Dogmatics,* in which Barth contended that Jesus Christ is God's Revelation.[165] He stated that "(t)he Word of God is God Himself in Holy Scripture," and that the Scripture, therefore, was "a witness to divine revelation."[166] In regard to Scripture being a witness Barth sought to differentiate between the authority of the written word and the event of revelation itself. Barth was clearly concerned with pointing to the event of revelation as being the Word of God, which as an event of revelation itself, "precedes both proclamation and Holy Scripture,"[167] both of which point beyond themselves. The significance of Holy Scripture, therefore, is that it is a witness to the event of revelation, as it occurred, "by means of the words of the prophets and apostles written in the Bible, in which they are still alive for us as the immediate and direct recipients of revelation, and by which

---

162. Torrance, *Karl Barth*, 103.

163. Ibid., 106–7.

164. Ibid., 143.

165. Barth, *Church Dogmatics, 1/1,* 1.

166. Barth, *Church Dogmatics, 1/2,* 457.

167. Ibid., 457.

they speak to us."[168] To this extent, the written word of Scripture is human in nature, yet its authority is in its capacity to bear witness to the event of revelation, since its authors were direct recipients of those events. Indeed, the human words of Scripture point away from themselves and "towards a fact."[169] Therefore, for Barth, Holy Scripture is a witness, "a human expression of God's revelation." However this does not weaken the role of Scripture. For Barth Scripture is more than a human expression, it is a witness to revelation, and through it we hear revelation, and so it is "the very Word of God."[170]

Barth's Christocentric theology is also profoundly evident in his doctrine of election. His approach to this doctrine has its origins at a congress he attended in 1936. In the June of that year he had traveled to Geneva in order to attend the "Congrès international de théologie calviniste," which was held as a celebration of Calvin's arrival in the city 400 years earlier. The conference took the theme of Calvin's doctrine of predestination. While attending the conference Barth was profoundly influenced by an address delivered by Pierre Maury entitled, "Election and Faith." Barth later reflected that Maury's main thesis, that humanity is elected in Christ, contributed decisively to his fundamental direction in constructing his own doctrine of election. [171] The outcome of Barth's new direction is reflected in his *Church Dogmatics* where he stated that the "doctrine of election is the sum of the Gospel,"[172] since it describes God's gracious covenant election in Jesus Christ, who "is indeed God in His movement towards man," in his covenant with the people represented in the one man Jesus of Nazareth.[173] Indeed, Jesus Christ is both the electing God and the elected man.[174] "He is the Lord and Head of all the elect, the revelation and reflection of their election, and the organ and instrument of all divine electing. For this reason His election is indeed the type of all election. For

---

168. Ibid., 463.

169. Ibid., 464.

170. Ibid., 473.

171. McCormack, *Karl Barth's Critically Realistic Dialectical Theology*, 457.

172. Barth, *Church Dogmatics: 2/2*, 3.

173. Ibid., 7.

174. Ibid., 3.

this reason we must now learn really to recognize in Him not only the electing God but also elected man."[175]

As humanity has been elected in Christ so is it to live in him. Barth's Christological orientation was also evident when he wrote that the sanctification of humanity "is actually accomplished in the one Jesus Christ."[176] Indeed, sanctification amounts to participation in Christ[177] and conformity with him.[178] It is a situation in which one is summoned by Christ, who discloses and reveals himself "in order to claim and sanctify" as his own.[179] It is seen by Barth to be integral to the Christian's relationship with Christ. As God calls and sanctifies he calls for obedience to his command and faithful discipleship, which "binds a man to the One who calls him."[180] Indeed, God "establishes His particular relationship [with Christians] by commanding them."[181] It was on the basis of the command of God in his Word that Barth formulated his ethical response to Hitlerism.

In the midst of the "new" Germany, under the Nazi dictatorship, and the compliant "German Christians," Barth's strongly held conviction was that God's command was the "foundation of ethics." When Hitler came to power he became determined to control the heart and mind of the entire nation, especially the German Church. Those who capitulated to his agenda were known as the German Christians. Those who resisted the "German Christians" founded the "Confessing Church." Its first synod, held in Barmen, on May 5, 1934, adopted "a Theological Declaration which was largely drafted by Barth." As Klaus Scholder pointed out, the confession affirmed the unity of the church of Jesus Christ, whether Lutheran or Reformed, and explicitly rejected the Aryanism of the German Christians. It sought to assert the need for a free church in a just state that rejects totalitarianism.[182] Furthermore, Barth refused to take an unconditional oath of loyalty to the Führer, which finally resulted in his dismissal as chair of systematic theology at Bonn University, in December of 1934. He was finally expelled from Germany in June of 1935. Resistance was

175. Ibid., 117.

176. Barth, *Church Dogmatics*, 4/2, 518.

177. Ibid., 530.

178. Ibid., 529.

179. Ibid., 534.

180. Ibid., 536.

181. Ibid., 535.

182. K. Scholder. *The Churches and the Third Reich: Vol. 1,* 581.

important to Barth's thinking. He later reflected that much worse than the German Christians was a "point-blank" lack of resistance to them.[183] The desperate shallowness of the anti-German Christians proved to be a great disappointment to him.[184]

Barth's work continued following a call to Basel. "From Basel he encouraged the Christians of Europe, offering theological arguments for political resistance to National Socialism."[185] He also traveled extensively. During 1937–38 he delivered the Gifford Lectures in Scotland. Following the war, in 1946, Barth taught in Basel and continued to write his *Church Dogmatics*. However, he did not just teach. "He also welcomed a large number of visitors to his Bonn home and dealt with an extensive correspondence." After returning to Basel his gracious hospitality continued. Through the 1950s Barth continued writing his *Dogmatics* and welcomed students from all over the world.[186]

On March 1, 1962 Barth gave his final lecture at the University of Basel.[187] However, his lecturing was not over. In April and May of 1962 Barth traveled to the United States and addressed overflow congregations at the University of Chicago and at Princeton Theological Seminary, where he delivered the Warfield Lectures. It was his only visit to the United States. These addresses, together with his final Basle lectures, were published under the title, *Evangelical Theology: An Introduction*.[188] In America Barth "had a great many conversations, with students, with businessmen, with Talmudic Jews, with actors, with Roman Catholic theologians, with a small group of real live communists, and with Mircrea Eliade, the historian of religion and with the evangelist Billy Graham."[189] From Chicago, Barth visited Dubuque Theological Seminary and the Union Theological Seminary at Richmond before visiting Los Angeles and San Francisco, "especially to the Theological School at San Anselmo, and finally a second visit to New York and to Union Theological Seminary."[190] His academic work continued until the autumn of 1965. He died in the early hours of

183. Ibid., 437.

184. Ibid., 535.

185. Jüngel, *Karl Barth, A Theological Legacy*, 26.

186. Busch, "Karl Barth: His Life and Autobiographical Texts," 338.

187. Ibid., 457.

188. Barth, "Evangelical Theology."

189. Ibid., 459.

190. Ibid., 460.

December 10, 1968. In the words of Thomas Torrance, he was "the great Church Father of Evangelical Christendom, the one genuine Doctor of the Evangelical Church the modern era has known."[191]

CONCLUSION

Through years of struggle and reflection, of starting and then starting again, Barth produced a theology of such magnitude and importance that one must place him among the greats of Christian thinking. It is clear that Barth's mature approach to theology was a theology of the Word of God that was particularly Christological in its nature. His conviction was that only God is the one who can speak of God and that humanity is the one who does not speak but listens. The Word of God is Jesus Christ, Scripture is the witness to this Jesus Christ and the Church is the proclaimer. The journey started with Barth's struggle to preach to his parish with meaning. A passionate study of the Word encouraged by Thurneysen and Blumhardt led him to write his famous commentary on the Book of Romans. This was the start, but it was not the finish. His appointment to teach led him to rethink his theology once more, and so began his period of dogmatics. Both new starts were stopped and started again as Barth continued to read and reflect. As a professor now preparing lectures, rather than sermons, his new mentors were theologians of the church, including the writings of the early church, Luther, Calvin, Heppe, and Anselm. Each new circumstance brought new challenges, and the need for guiding influences that led Barth to the fulfillment of his agenda for a theology of the Word of God.

Having surveyed Barth's life and work, it is appropriate now to study the history and nature of the evangelical North American environment. It was this group that primarily interacted with Barth's work and comprises the context of this thesis.

---

191. Statement by T. F. Torrance. In Barth, *Christian Dogmatics,* 4/4, vi.

2

North American Evangelicalism

CONSIDERING THAT THIS THESIS is primarily concerned with the positive reception of Karl Barth's theology in North America, and his influence in the construction of a new evangelical theology in that part of the world, it is necessary to provide an historical background that forms a context from which to address the issue of Barth in North America. This chapter identifies the development of three distinct groups, each one responding to Barth in distinct ways. Firstly, the chapter will study fundamentalists who represent a particular religious phenomenon. This will provide a constructive background for the understanding of the nature of Christian fundamentalism in North America. In general terms it is understood as a movement bearing many of the common marks found in the fundamentalism of the World Religions. More specifically it is defined as an orthodox movement within Protestant Christianity. It is in this context that the response of North American Christian fundamentalism to the theology of Karl Barth will be studied. This will be done by assessing the responses of two representative figures: Cornelius Van Til and Fred Klooster.

Following this discussion there will be an investigation into the characteristics of a second and subsequent group that emerged *out of* Christian fundamentalism. This group will be identified as the "conservative evangelicals." It will be demonstrated that the conservative evangelicals shared many of the characteristics common to the fundamentalists while also possessing some notable differences. The conservative evangelicals differed from fundamentalists by seeking to remain orthodox while constructively engaging with the wider church and society. This group, initially led by theologian Carl Henry, evangelist Billy Graham, and Fuller Seminary president, Harold Ockenga, appreciated some of the aspects of Barth's theology, but were essentially opposed to it. They communicated their ideas through the popular magazine, *Christianity Today*. The conservative evangelical group grew to be a significant force with a considerable amount of influence. However, a number within its ranks saw it as more of a neo-fundamentalist group than the thoroughgoing and sophisticated evangelicalism. Consequently, they developed a third movement. This thesis will refer to this group as the "new evangelicals."

The new evangelicals felt that the conservative evangelicals had retained too much fundamentalist "baggage" that needed to be discarded if they were going to engage the world with the riches of their own tradition in a thoroughgoing manner. It is a broad group existing alongside the still continuing influence of the fundamentalists and conservative evangelicals. Their response to Barth was considerably different. Though not uncritical at some points, the new evangelicals were highly appreciative of Barth's theology. They were far more assertive. Indeed, the new evangelicals positively engaged with the theology of Barth and saw it as a means of enabling evangelicalism to deal with the issues and thoughts of our time with depth and sophistication. Along with Barth they were concerned with fundamentalism's rationalistic objectivism which always stood in danger of converting the truths of God into rationalized objects. These new evangelicals were empowered by the efforts of Bernard Ramm who called for a post-fundamentalist expression of evangelical theology and Donald Bloesch, who called on the evangelical world to embrace a renaissance of its own tradition.

THE FUNDAMENTALIST PHENOMENON

Martin Marty and Scott Appleby have described fundamentalism as a global phenomenon covering all major world religions and possessing distinct and identifiable characteristics. According to Bruce Lawrence while fundamentalism looks to the past, it is to be defined as a movement of the modern era. He called it "a twentieth-century phenomenon with 'historical antecedents, but no ideological precursors.'"[1] This highlights the irony of this phenomenon, since it claims to uphold the orthodoxies of the past[2] which have, as they see it, been eroded by the compromises of modernism. Indeed, fundamentalists have often used "modernism" as

---

1. Quoted in Marty and Appleby, "Conclusion: An Interim Report on a Hypothetical Family," 814.

2. Shepard, "Fundamentalism Christian and Islamic," 363.

a code word for those forces perceived to be a threat and which have inspired action. "Modern cultures include at least three dimensions uncongenial to fundamentalists: a preference for secular rationality; the adoption of religious tolerance with accompanying tendencies toward relativism; and individualism."[3] Consequently, since fundamentalists look at the world from this reactionary perspective they have developed traditionalist forms of expression, particularly those not likely to flourish in a liberal or "modernist" environment. Marty and Appleby agreed that fundamentalism is reactionary. They believed that its purposes are achieved by possessing five "fighting" characteristics.

Firstly, fundamentalists can be characterized by their *fighting back*. Marty and Appleby believed that this group always start as traditionalists "who perceive some challenge or threat to their core identity, both social and personal." They come to asserted, however, that if they lose on the central issues, they lose everything. Consequently, in order to defend their most sacredly held "fundamentals," they react and "fight back with great innovative power."[4]

Secondly, fundamentalists *fight for*. They fight for a world view they have inherited or adopted and which they constantly reinforce. "They will fight for their conceptions of what ought to go on in matters of life and death."[5] They have particular theological, moral, and social causes that they consistently fight for against the changed attitudes of a new secularized world order.

Thirdly, fundamentalists *fight with*

> a particularly chosen repository of resources which one might think of as weapons. The movements . . . reached back to real or presumed pasts, to actual or imagined ideal original conditions and concepts, and selected what they regarded as fundamental . . . (F)undamentalists are selective. They may well consider that they are adopting the whole of the pure past, but their energies go into employing those features which will best reinforce their identity keep their movement together, build defenses around its boundaries, and keep others at some distance.[6]

3. Marty and Appleby, editors, "Introduction: the fundamentalist project: a user's guide," vii.

4. Ibid., ix.

5. Ibid., ix.

6. Ibid., ix–x.

Fourthly, fundamentalist *fight against*. There is always an enemy that must be identified, named, and considered an agent of assault on all that the fundamentalist holds dear. Those who pose the greatest threat are, more often than not, those considered dangerously close to the core values of the group. Such a person may agree on many matters and yet seek compromise, middle ground, or a civil agreement to disagree. Such a person may be called an "insider," who poses a serious threat because he or she is likely to negotiate with modernity and seek to bring change to the organization.

Fifthly, and lastly, fundamentalists *fight under* God. They believe that they are specially called by God to defend the fundamentals, which are actually seen as fundamental to God before they are fundamental to the group.[7] Other definitions have been given. Giles Kepel, for example, viewed fundamentalism in more minimalist terms. He saw it as a phenomenon emerging in the 1970s as a reaction against the inroads of modernism in the 1960s. To support his case he cited various fundamentalist victories during that period and across the religious spectrum. These include the election of Jimmy Carter to the United States Presidency, the rise of the Ayatollah in Iran, the election of Pope John Paul II, and the swing to the right in the 1977 Israeli election.[8] However, it is unlikely that fundamentalism simply emerged out of nowhere during a single decade as a reaction to the one before. Fundamentalism still exists and as discussed below it is possible to trace its development from at least the early years of the twentieth-century, if not before that time. Indeed, Martin Marty was probably more helpful in his discussion of the sociology of fundamentalism.

Marty defined fundamentalism as a social dynamic. He firstly observed that fundamentalism occurs on the soil of traditional cultures. This means that newly established cults do not qualify as fundamentalists. The second element is that of threat. People have a tendency, claimed Marty, of leaning towards fundamentalism when they fear losing a world they consider worth defending against "outside" influences.[9] Associated with this is a sense of uneasiness, discontent, fear of identity diffusion, and lack of focus. Amidst such heightened social unrest a leader must emerge who is able to identify the enemy and name it. Out of this comes a characteristic of aggression. As this is done battle lines are formed and leaders

7. Ibid., x.

8. Kepel, *The Revenge of God*, 2.

9. Marty, "Fundamentals of Fundamentalism," 21.

distinguish between "fundamentals" and "non-fundamentals."[10] The contradiction here is that often these chosen 'fundamentals' are not necessarily traditional, as is contended, but adequate enough to enable their group to stand out and be noticed as objecting. Therefore, fundamentalists seek authority. This can take many guises, whether it is a particular charismatic figure, religious text, or a classic event. The other common feature of fundamentalism be it doctrinal, practical, behavioral, or cultural, is that it seeks to offend. Fundamentalists make it their business to "cause scandal."[11] The desired outcome is a heightened sense of purpose and identity. Their black and white agenda identifies them as a select people chosen by God for a purpose. They culturally enhance their identity by wearing particular clothes, learning code words and phrases, or adopting social behaviors that help them recognize one another.[12] Therefore fundamentalism, according to Marty, is very much a social phenomenon that is evident in all world religions as a reaction to the modern world. It uses traditional social behavior and orthodoxy as its front and, in doing so; it forms distinct socio-religious groups that have common distinguishing features. While these characteristics can also be found in all world religions, Christian fundamentalism possesses its own particular profile.

CHRISTIAN FUNDAMENTALISM

Christian fundamentalism has a distinct history, with the origins of the actual term traced to the first part of the twentieth-century. In his *Sir Robert Madgwick Lecture* of 2001, Philip C. Almond described Christian fundamentalism as "the extreme end of that form of Protestantism known as Conservative Evangelicalism."[13] David Parker, in his landmark *Fundamentalism and Conservative Protestantism in Australia,* described Christian fundamentalism as a "conservative movement which opposes 'modernism' or the liberalization of Protestant doctrine."[14] He believed that the term can be used in either of two ways. The first of these is described as "classic fundamentalism," which "refers to the American movement of the 1920s which opposed the liberalization of the historic and doctrinal standards and beliefs of the main Protestant churches." Parker's

---

10. Ibid., 21.

11. Ibid., 22.

12. Ibid., 22.

13. Almond, *Fundamentalism, Christianity, and Religion,* 5.

14. Parker, *Fundamentalism and Conservative Protestantism in Australia,* 26.

second classification is termed "militant or separatist fundamentalism." This second type "refers to fundamentalism of a later period when it was characterized by the highly polemic defense of the faith [. . .] It is based upon belief in the Bible as the verbally inerrant (in historical and scientific as well as doctrinal terms) Word of God and its literal interpretation, and is characterized by heavy emphasis upon 'soul-winning' or revivalistic evangelism and missions, a rigid system of personal ethics, and premillennial eschatology."[15]

Fundamentalism is indeed an historical development. As Almond pointed out, the "term 'fundamentalist' was perhaps first used in 1920 by Curtis Lee Laws in the *Baptist Watchman-Examiner* to identify those who believed and actively defended the fundamentals of the faith."[16] Laws had previously called together 'fundamentalists' within the Northern Baptist Convention to a conference in Buffalo, New York. This group, popularly called the "fundamentalist fellowship," believed that modernists were surrendering the 'fundamentals' of the gospel.[17] Its beginnings, however, can be traced back much further. It is impossible to put a precise date to its start; however, significant early events can be cited. Garry Dorrien points to 1875 as a year of importance. It was during that year that "a group of hard-line conservatives" organized the founding of a convention that would later be known as the Niagara Bible Conference. "This summer resort meeting became the prototype for hundreds of Bible conferences at which evangelicals gathered for two weeks to preach and defend the fundamentals."[18]

The emerging fundamentalists deemed modernism to be synonymous with liberalism. They understood modernism as "the liberalizing process by which the Protestant teachings of the Bible and theology are reinterpreted in the light of modern learning."[19] North American Christian fundamentalism has been particularly defined by its doctrine

---

15. Ibid., 27. Parker later notes that "Premillennialism, including dispensationalism, gained its important place in fundamentalism because it was considered by its teachers to be not just an optional type of eschatology, but because it employed a literalist hermeneutic, the only view which they believed was consistent with the doctrine of the verbal inspiration of Scripture." Ibid., 506.

16. Almond, *Fundamentalism, Christianity, and Religion*, 6.

17. Shelley, *Church History in Plain Language*, 453.

18. Dorrien, *The Remaking of Evangelical Theology*, 15.

19. Parker, *Fundamentalism and Conservative Protestantism in Australia*, 28.

of Scripture. The classic rhetoric of American Protestant fundamentalism is in the assertion that the Bible is "inerrant". "For fundamentalists this claim means that the Bible is not only an infallible authority in matters of faith and practice, but it is also accurate in all its historical and scientific assertions."[20] On this basis, the "fundamentals of faith", including such themes as the virgin birth and the bodily resurrection of Christ, are strongly defended. The logic of the argument is straightforward: The Bible is infallible—it amounts to God's very words, and so its truth must be upheld and defended. The reinterpretations of "liberal teaching" are seen by fundamentalists to undermine what they believe to be key biblical teachings that should not be altered.[21] The list also includes a denial by liberal theologies of the supernatural birth of Christ, his miraculous powers, his atoning death, his bodily resurrection, and his imminent return.[22] What emerged, however, was a new form of Christianity with no historical precedents.

A New Historical Development

Its inner apologetic passion drove fundamentalism into a fortress mentality behind walls that were built to keep different views outside. They were erected to keep out any vestige of the changes occurring in North American theology. Consequently, while purporting to uphold the theology of the Reformation against the inroads of German higher criticism, and a variety of "isms," it produced a form of evangelicalism that the Reformers would find totally incomprehensible. The paradox of Christian fundamentalism is seen in that while it claims to be traditionalist and orthodox, it actually emphasizes theologies that cannot be found in traditional doctrine. What Christian fundamentalists have actually done is promote a series of teachings in reaction to changes in society. Consequently, their reaction to "modernism" has not created a revived orthodoxy, as they claim, but a distorted traditionalism that can be largely defined in sociological terms. They have done so by emphasizing certain doctrines, such as the inerrancy of Scripture, biblical prophecy, and the second coming of Christ.

20. Marsden, *The Fundamentalist Phenomenon*, 23.

21. Fundamentalists have particularly objected to liberalism's denial of "the unique inspiration and sufficient authority of scripture as a result of the use of higher criticism and evolutionary theories of the development of religion." Parker, *Fundamentalism and Conservative Protestantism in Australia*, 28.

22. Ibid., 28.

These have served to provide them with necessary distinguishing features that have (1) consolidated their sense of identity and (2) successfully set them apart from the "liberals." Almond added to this in his observation that

> neither Luther nor Calvin were fundamentalists in the modern sense. Quite the contrary; Luther saw the authority of the doctrine of Justification by Faith overriding the authority of Scripture, and would have been quite content to see the Epistle of James taken out of the Canon of Scripture. In contrast to the modern fundamentalist, the Reformers were able to distinguish between the Word of God and the words of God. For the Reformers, the Word of God lay behind the words of God; for fundamentalism, there is no distinction between Word and words.[23]

The Reformers would also be quite bemused by the dominant theme of millenarianism found within fundamentalism. Fundamentalists often insisted that belief in the pre-millennial return of Christ is a condition of orthodoxy, an emphasis the Reformers would have never considered. Clearly, then, its emphasis had nothing to do with orthodoxy. It is a feature which served to distinguish the fundamentalist from liberalism and reinforce their literal interpretation of the Bible. Fundamentalism can also be recognized according to the modernist philosophy it has employed.

Modernism Fighting Modernism

Fundamentalism can be characterized by the irony of being a modernist movement at war with modernism. Indeed, fundamentalists do not actually reject the ways of the modern era. Instead, they "exist in a type of symbiotic relationship with the modern, finding, for example, technology, mass media of communications, and other instruments of modernity congenial to their purposes."[24] The modernism of the fundamentalists includes a rationalist and scientific view of Scripture as the inerrant word, and detailed, indeed complex, theories of the return of Christ, which must be strictly assented to if one is to be called a true 'biblical' Christian. Donald Bloesch found this form of Christianity to have bowed the knee to rationalist philosophy in order to prove its point. To illustrate his view Bloesch cited Carl Henry, a leading evangelical (1913–2003), who called

23. Almond, *Fundamentalism, Christianity, and Religion*, 7.
24. Ibid., vii.

for a return to the rationalistic idealism of the early Enlightenment. Bloesch responded to Henry's charge with the contention that this approach arrives at truth by beginning with universal principles, before proceeding to deduce particular conclusions.[25] The result, claimed Bloesch, is a theology comprised of a simple set of rationalistic propositions. Indeed, he placed fundamentalism alongside liberalism as a movement dependent upon the rationalism of the Enlightenment. Almond supported this claim when he observed that truth for the fundamentalist Christian is propositional. According to Almond, fundamentalism contends that "(r)eligious truth is primarily truth that can be put into sentence form, for intellectual assent."[26] Almond further noted that the "claim that fundamentalist discourse is markedly empiricist and rationalist may come as something of a surprise to many, who are inclined to think of fundamentalism as archetypically irrational."[27] Indeed, Almond, like Bloesch, rightly found a rationalist relationship between fundamentalists and Deists.

Indeed, fundamentalists appear to have a preoccupation with scientifically verifying biblical events. To this extent fundamentalism, as a popularist movement seeking to enlist members from a modern culture is itself culture bound. Indeed, the rational ordering of fundamentalist conceptions of the second coming of Christ clearly originates out of eighteenth-century Enlightenment. The most striking example of this is the dispensationalist theology of Plymouth Brethren theologian J. N. Derby and the *Scofield* (and subsequent *New Scofield*) *Reference Bible*. The highly rationalistic nature of their thinking is seen in Almond's outline of their doctrine of the return of Christ.

> According to Scofield, the history of the world can be divided into seven distinct dispensations or ages, the first five taking us from Innocence to the death of Christ, the last two from the death of Christ to the Second Coming and personal reign of Christ. Crucially dispensationalists are pre-millenialists, who expect the eventual deterioration of the world will culminate in a seven-year period of tribulation, an outpouring of the divine wrath and judgment which will close with the second coming of Christ and then his reign on earth during the millennium. True believers will not suffer on earth during the time of tribulation, but will be raptured

25. Bloesch, *A Theology of Word and Spirit*, 253.

26. Ibid., 6.

27. Almond, *Fundamentalism, Christianity, and Religion*, 10.

from off the earth until they return with Christ to reign with him in the millennial period. In this sense then, this is a third coming. At the end of this period, the last Judgment occurs, and all are sent to their eternal destinations—heaven or hell.[28]

A Social Phenomenon

In his introduction to *Fundamentalism in Comparative Perspective*, Lawrence Kaplin defined fundamentalism as "a world view that highlights specific essential 'truths' of traditional faith and applies them with earnestness and fervor to twentieth-century realities."[29] Kaplin's view understood fundamentalism as a movement not only concerned with "traditional dogma," but more ardently with traditionalism's usefulness as a rhetorical tool against the perceived threats of the modern age. Therefore, fundamentalism is to be defined as both a religious and a social phenomenon in reaction to modernism. Similarly, George Marsden contended that while Christian fundamentalism in North America must be primarily viewed as a religious movement, it is true to say that it is also a social phenomenon. He believed that the cultural crises in North America, which followed in the aftermath of the First World War, "shaped and modified the movement in important ways."[30]

Indeed, "the post war crises helped to intensify feelings, increase militancy and harden resistance to change." Marsden's contention was that the peculiarities of the American environment to some extent determined the specific form that the fundamentalist controversies took in that place. America was a large and new country still in the process of being settled and, while experiencing major cultural changes, it had to somehow manage a massive array of diversities. The difference between the rural and urban communities accentuated this diversity, as did the country's remarkable ethnic diversity. "Social prejudices were reinforced by denominational differences, which often entailed different institutions [. . .] within ethnic and denominational groups there might also be wide regional diversities. Northerners, Southerners, Easterners, and Westerners might have their first real encounter with a new idea decades, or even

---

28. Ibid., 12.

29. Kaplin, *Fundamentalism in Comparative Perspective*, 5.

30. Marsden, *Fundamentalism and American Culture*, 201. Also see Sandeen, *The Roots of Fundamentalism*; Dollar, *A History of Fundamentalism in America*.

generations, apart."[31] Marsden's thesis is that these circumstances greatly increased the probability of religious conflict when these diverse groups came into contact following World War I, and through the growth of mass media. This new form of communication accelerated the contact of these previously diverse groups. "Suddenly national consciousness overrode local and parochial concerns. Individuals with wide differences in background and belief were forced by the war to work closely together." Marsden believed that one side effect was a national paranoia "and a chain reaction of crusades against various cultural enemies."[32] He concluded that these circumstances help explain the timing of the fundamentalist rise in popularity as well as its hallmark extremisms. In the fundamentalist's mind a need arose to protect one's own tradition. In this sense fundamentalism is a reactionary enclave within a wider group.

Nancy Ammerman also understood fundamentalism in America as having emerged in response to the changes experienced in American society. However, she traced its origins to a much earlier time. She saw the rise of fundamentalism to have emerged over time in response to changing conditions. In her view there developed a sub-group in society that had negatively felt the effects of the advance of science, technology and business after the *civil war*. These were seen as growing at the expense of previous pillars of society, which included tradition, prayer and faith. "At the same time, streams of European immigrants were arriving, bringing Catholic and Jewish traditions that began to introduce a more dynamic pluralism into American Religion."[33] These changes brought about a reactionary type of Christianity possessing certain characteristics.

Martin Riesebrodt believed that "in the fundamentalist interpretation, society is in severe crisis, for which there is but one solution: a return to the principles of the divine order once practiced in the original community, whose laws have been handed down in writing."[34] Emmanuel Sivan contended that behavior is paramount to the enclave mentality. "Behavior endows belief with a mimetic and affective dimension. A viable enclave wields efficient group constraints and should thus be able to have its individual members conform to homogeneous public norms. And

31. Ibid., 201.

32. Ibid., 202.

33. Ammerman, *Bible Believers: Fundamentalists in the Modern World*, 205.

34. Riesebrodt, *Pious Passion*, 47.

their most immediate product is a separate space." This is not a hidden agenda. During the Prophetic Bible Conference of 1914, A. C. Gabelein proclaimed that "God's greatest call is separation."[35]

Almond was right in characterizing this group as one with a self-perception of struggling for true Christianity against new forms of thought, such as liberalism, modernism, or secularism.[36] While having a degree of similarity with other forms of evangelicalism, fundamentalists see themselves as more faithful to the Bible, more vigilant in the face of moral evil, and less ready to cater to the social and intellectual respectability of other "more liberal" evangelicals.[37] From within this culture came the response to Karl Barth by Cornelius Van Til.

Cornelius Van Til and the New Modernism

Phillip Thorn was right when he asserted that Cornelius Van Til has been one of the most prolific, well read, and influential interpreters of Karl Barth in North America. "He held an important post at an influential institution during a crucial period of time, and exerted a significant influence."[38] Van Til joined the staff of Princeton Seminary to teach apologetics at the time when huge changes were taking place and just prior to major developments during 1929. At that time Van Til joined Gresham Machen, Oswald Allis, and Robert Dick Wilson in their decision to resign their posts at Princeton and found Westminster Theological Seminary. They believed that Princeton had become too influenced by modernism and sought to found a new institution more faithful to traditional Presbyterian doctrine.

At Westminster Van Til became both an advocate and significant proponent of North American fundamentalist Calvinism. Indeed, he contributed significantly to evangelical apologetics.[39] The fundamentalist nature of Van Til's apologetics is seen in his presuppositionalism, which

35. Sivan, "The Enclave Culture," 205.

36. Almond, *Fundamentalism, Christianity, and Religion*, 10.

37. "Evangelicals for their part would see fundamentalists in contrast to themselves as being more anti-intellectual, having a mechanical view of the inspiration of the Bible, having a literalistic approach to interpreting the Bible, rejecting involvement with Christians who do not share their views, and denying the social relevance of the Christian Gospel." Ibid., 5.

38. Thorne, "Evangelicalism and Karl Barth," 33.

39. Ibid., 33.

carried with it a highly rationalistic framework. His presupposition was that reality and experience can be characterized into a cohesive and ordered framework. Indeed, Philip Thorne summarized Van Til's thought with the observation that "(t)he essential insight of presuppositionalism is idealist; the manifold diversity of reality requires conceptual ordering to be meaningfully experienced, and the principles of order must logically precede the experience. This means that the 'facts' of experience are unintelligible apart from their relation to the interpretative framework."[40]

Van Til's earliest and most substantial apologetic work against Barth's theology is found in his 1946 publication *The New Modernism: An appraisal of the Theology of Barth and Brunner.*[41] Important to this thesis is Van Til's analysis of Barth's theology of the Word. As a fundamentalist Van Til was critical of any theology of the Word that did not define it as inerrant in its written form. As has been discussed, Barth did not hold to this view. Consequently, Van Til's critique of Barth accused him of compliance to philosophy. Van Til was clear in his contention that the "broadest and most general background [to Barth's theology of the Word] is the critical philosophy of Kant."[42] Van Til understandably found this in Barth's 1919 edition of *Romans.*[43]

However, it would seem that despite Barth's well-established turn from dialecticism to a theology of the Word of God, Van Til continued to view Barth's theology as patterned after Kant's critical philosophy.

Indeed, Van Til claimed that Barth's theology can only be truly discerned "through the spectacles of Kant's *Critique of Pure Reason*."[44] Furthermore, Van Til came to the astonishing conclusion that Barth, governed by his own critical, that is Kantian, principles, "did not (permit him to) presuppose a triune God who exists prior to and independent of man."[45] Van Til's summary was that "(m)odern dialectical philosophy may be said to be a child of Criticism," this being a product of Kant's philoso-

40. Ibid., 33.

41. Van Til, *The New Modernism*.

42. Ibid., xv.

43. See also Van Til discussion on the influence of Kierkegaard on Barth's theology. Van Til wrongly works on the assumption that there had been no substantial change. Ibid., 66.

44. Ibid., 366.

45. Ibid., xv.

phy.[46] The problem with this observation is that it placed Barth alongside the liberal schools he sought to challenge. However for Van Til this is the irony of Barth's theology. He should have dealt with the situation he faced by steadfastly refusing to deal with any part of Kantian philosophy and by decisively breaking "with the stem and the root from which these branches [that is, Schleiermacher and Ritschl] have sprung."[47] Indeed, Van Til contended that there was little change in Barth's thinking from his publication of *Romans*, other than a greater influence of existentialist philosophy.

Van Til asserted that the critical motif controls the construction of Barth's *Dogmatics* in the same way as it did in his *Romans*. What changed was not the abandonment of critical method, that is, a dialectical method having its roots with Kant, but a greater influence of Søren Kierkegaard (1813–1855)[48] and Martin Heidegger (1889–1976)[49] in its construction. Van Til claimed that these men are to be found guilty of applying a large dose of irrationalism into the minds of "convulsive patient, modern man."[50]

Furthermore, Van Til made the observation that in Barth's conception of the Bible the Word of God is in the spoken words of God. This means, however, that the Bible as we know it provides access to the Word without being the actual Word in and of itself. Furthermore Van Til believed that Barth conceived of the Bible as a "maze of the interrelations of ordinary space and time. It is the heavy layer of ashes that must be removed if we would get at the fire of the more basically phenomenal." Only by looking through it and at the back of it can one discover reality. However, this world of reality is wholly other than the world of appearance. The real is God's spoken word. That is, this active speaking of God must come through the medium of the Bible, the surface-phenomenal, if we are to hear it. "A veil must be taken away when revelation comes to men. But while it is taken away, the veil is also there."[51] From these observations

46. Ibid., 43.

47. Ibid., 366.

48. Kierkegaard was a Danish existentialist philosopher and theologian. Erickson, *Concise Dictionary of Christian Theology*, 92.

49. Heidegger was a German existentialist philosopher. Ibid., 72.

50. The result is termed by Van Til as the "surface-phenomenal." Van Til, *New Modernism*, 366.

51. Ibid., 143–44.

Van Til came to the startling conclusion that Barth differs from 'historic orthodox Christianity' since he viewed the historic events of the creation of Adam, the fall, the incarnation, redemption through Jesus Christ in his death, resurrection and ascension as being "left out as enemy aliens, or given their extradition papers. They represent what is to Barth the most objectionable form of the idea of a theology of consciousness, a theology which man possesses and can manipulate at will."[52] Van Til further concluded that Barth's theology presents a dim picture of God's revelation, since all that is available to humanity is a man made edifice. In this sense he not only stands against Scripture, but also the Reformers.

Indeed, Van Til, in his *Christianity and Barthianism*,[53] further described Barth's theology as not being a true theology after the manner of the Reformers. At the start of his fifth chapter, with the ominous title: *Against Orthodoxy*, Van Til protested strongly against Barth's claim "to have built his theology upon the Reformers." In contrast Van Til believed that Barth is "simply against" the Reformers.[54] Indeed, in his earlier *The New Modernism* Van Til claimed that "(n)othing could be more untrue to history than to say that the theology of Barth [. . .] is basically similar to that of Luther and Calvin."[55] Van Til advanced this interpretation of Barth's theology in the belief that Barth's disdain arose because the Reformer's (Luther and Calvin) "central teaching is destructive of the idea of Christ as the electing God and the elected man, that is, of Christ as divine-human *Geschichte*."[56] Van Til again added that Barth stood against the Reformers since he was far more influenced by Immanuel Kant. However, it is doubtful that Barth would have recognized the kind of theology Van Til ascribed to him. In contradistinction, Barth had a high regard for the theology of the Reformers. His *Church Dogmatics* are filled with positive references to them, even though he sought to develop those aspects of their theology he believed needed change in the light of new understanding. None of this, however, does anything to prevent Van Til's contention that Barth is a Kantian.

52. Ibid., 144.

53. Van Til, *Christianity and Barthianism*.

54. Ibid., 67.

55. Van Til, *New Modernism*, 366.

56. Ibid., 67.

In his fifteenth chapter of *The New Modernism* Van Til asked: "Will Barth side with the Reformers as over against Kant? Will he challenge the basic presuppositions of Kant? No, he will not. He will seek to go *beyond* Kant. He will seek to go beyond Kant further, *much further* beyond Kant than any other theologian has done since Kant."[57] Van Til further connected Barth's theology with Kantian philosophy with the claim that "Barth recognizes the validity of Kant's method as he builds up the world of human experience in terms of abstract form and purely contingent matter as these are based upon the assumption of human autonomy."[58] Van Til believed that part of Barth's flaw was that he pinned his hopes on the fact that Kant limits the autonomous interpretation of humanity to science and philosophy.[59] Consequently Van Til claimed that Barth abandoned the Reformers in the interest of meeting the demands of pure reason. Therefore Barth was not a theologian of the Word, as he claimed to be, but a philosopher caught in the trap of Kantian dialecticism and clearly "on the road to Rome."[60] Furthermore, Van Til dismissed Barth's claim of constructing a "theology from above," since it is actually a "projection of the human consciousness in its vaunted independence."[61] These are weighty criticisms of Barth's theological edifice, but as will now be pointed out, there are serious flaws in Van Til's argument.

Thomas Torrance, in his *Karl Barth: An Introduction to His Early Theology*[62] made the point clearly that Barth, in the now famous second edition of his commentary on the Book of Romans, "determined to renounce the use of all idealistic and neo-Kantian conceptions of exegesis."[63] Furthermore, in answer to Van Til's claim that Barth's theology was "a projection of human consciousness," it must be noted that Torrance observed that in the second edition "Barth expressed his deep dissatisfaction with the insidious subjectivism of Protestant theology which confounded man

57. Ibid., 408.

58. Ibid.

59. Ibid.

60. Ibid., 411.

61. Van Til further states: "For the God of this practical reason is a mere projection into the unknown on the part of the supposedly independent theoretical reason of man." Ibid.

62. Torrance, *Karl Barth*.

63. Ibid., 50.

with God and put man in the place of God."[64] Indeed, Torrance made the observation that the theme of Barth's second edition to his *Romans* can be described as: "Let God be God, and let man learn again to be man, instead of trying to be as God."[65] Torrance successfully argued that the transition away from a subjective theology, derived from Cartesian and Kantian teaching, to an objective theology of the Word of God, became a central theme in the development of Barth's theology from 1930 onwards.[66]

Fred Klooster's critical analysis

Another early fundamentalist critic of Barth's theology is found in Fred Klooster, who was Professor of Systematic Theology at Calvin Seminary. Thorne pointed out that "(b)etween 1957 and 1962 Klooster published three articles and one book on Barth, and spent an academic year on sabbatical in Basel (1959–1960). In 1985 he penned an important critical review of Bernard Ramm's *After Fundamentalism*."[67] In this chapter two of Klooster's articles and his book will be studied. These best summarize his response to Barth.[68]

In 1959 Fred Klooster wrote an article for the *Bulletin of the Evangelical Theological Society* entitled: *Aspects of the Soteriology of Karl Barth*. It was written in response to the growing interest in Barth's *Church Dogmatics*. It appears that Klooster was alarmed that some evangelicals, such as Arthur Cochrane, were suggesting that Barth's latest contribution in the English language, IV/2, should be read with "the keenest interest" among his readers in America.[69] Indeed, it was believed to have made an "exciting" contribution to the topic of soteriology. This was puzzling to Klooster since he wondered if it was in fact possible to speak of Barth's soteriology. Klooster was amazed that "(t)here is no section of Barth's *Dogmatics* which bears the heading 'Soteriology.'"[70]

---

64. Ibid.

65. Ibid., 52.

66. Ibid., 141.

67. Thorne, *Evangelicalism and Karl Barth*, 43.

68. The third article, not covered here, deals with Barth's doctrine of reconciliation. Klooster, "Karl Barth's Doctrine of Reconciliation," 170–84. Klooster repeats this theme in his book, "The Significance of Karl Barth's Theology."

69. Klooster, "Aspects of the Soteriology of Karl Barth," 6.

70. Ibid., 6.

Klooster further doubted the reliability of Barth's *Dogmatics* because it did not compare well with the dogmatic procedure used by Charles Hodge(1797–1878), an Old Princeton Calvinist, in the writing of his *Systematic Theology*. Hodge clearly "does it as it should be done" as he "brings together on one major *locus* entitled "Soteriology" all of these significantly related matters: the plan of salvation (predestination), the covenant of grace, the person and work of Christ, the *order salutis* (vocation, regeneration, faith, justification, sanctification), a section on ethics (exposition of the Law), and concludes with the means of grace (the Word, sacraments, and prayer)."[71] Klooster consequently believed that Barth failed because he did not follow the classic Reformed pattern of approaching theology.

These observations can only lead one to the conclusion that Klooster could only conceive of theology as being done in the manner of the North American Calvinist School. The fact that Klooster's fundamentalism seriously clouded his reading of Barth is seen in the rationalist proposition that soteriology can only be discussed under the proper heading, "Soteriology," and the necessary sub-headings. However, this "intriguing" reflection on Barth's theology can only lead to a total misreading and utter misunderstanding of his theology. It is this approach that is retained in Klooster's analysis of Barth's doctrine of the resurrection.

In another article written for *The Westminster Theological Journal* in 1962, Klooster provided an analysis of Barth's theology of Christ's resurrection. He discussed at length Barth's differentiation between *Geschichte* and *Historie*. As Klooster saw it, Barth accepted the historicity of the resurrection of Christ, but believed that Barth's explanation of what this entails is uncertain and dubious. Klooster contended that on the surface Barth appeared to espouse the orthodox belief that Christ really rose from the dead. However, as one moves beyond Barth's popular works and investigates his more academic publication, such as his *Romans* and *Church Dogmatics*, one finds a complex web of beliefs that leads one to doubt Barth's true convictions. Klooster asserted that Barth actually seeks to return "to the theology of the eighteenth and nineteenth century evangelical theologians."[72] That is, Barth was just another existentialist. Indeed, while Barth apparently "wants to accept Paul's assertions regarding the

71. Ibid., 7.

72. Klooster, "Karl Barth's Doctrine of the Resurrection," 140.

central, gospel importance of the resurrection of Christ [...] (i)t would be irresponsible [...] to conclude [...] that Barth simply affirms the historicity of the resurrection in the way that orthodox Christianity has done throughout the centuries."[73]

The evidence Klooster assembled for his bold claim is to be found in Barth's use of two significant terms to describe the death and resurrection of Christ. Klooster noted that whenever Barth refers to the historicity of the resurrection he always used the term *Geschichte*. Klooster's problem is that although Barth "affirms that the resurrection is historical in the sense of *Geschichte*, he always denies that it is historical in the sense of *Historie*." Unfortunately, claimed Klooster, "Barth does not give a full and clear discussion as to the precise distinction between these terms."[74] Klooster's conclusion is that while Barth affirmed the historicity (*Historie*) of the crucifixion and the empty tomb, he failed to use this important defining word for the resurrection. For the resurrection Barth used *Geschichte*, which is a term used to describe history as "saga" or "legend." At the same time, asserted the baffled Klooster, Barth believed in the resurrection as a real event.[75]

Klooster contended that Barth must be brought to account for using the "nebulous concept of *Geschichte*" instead of the clear and easy to understand *Historie*. Indeed, in spite of Barth's assurances that the resurrection really happened, his refusal to change his terminology lead Klooster to the conclusion that Barth is simply introducing "another type of historical relativism."

> Barth's rejection of the resurrection as an event of *Historie* is simply consistent with his total rejection of a direct, given revelation of God in history . . . In all of this one also recognizes that Barth has been unwilling to see the whole of the world and its history under the direct providence of God. His view actually involves the removal of all ordinary history from the all-controlling hand of God. The acts of God are then regarded as somehow breaking into this ordinary world without actually becoming part of world history.[76]

73. Ibid., 141.
74. Ibid.
75. Ibid., 156.
76. Ibid., 168.

Klooster found that Barth presented a dubious theology that clearly put him outside the realm of orthodoxy. Accordingly Barth's entire theology must be put into question,[77] since he obviously did not trust Scripture[78] and has a theology that "does not involve a genuine incarnation with a personal union of the divine and human natures."[79] Indeed, Klooster concluded that Barth saw no need for a resurrection.[80] Klooster's rationalistic reading of Barth can also be found in his 1961 study, *The Significance of Karl Barth's Theology*.

In this work Klooster had no difficulty in stating that Barth was a significant theologian. At the same time he had no reservations in declaring Barth's theology to be fundamentally wrong. Barth cannot be called a Reformed theologian since he clearly departed from this tradition. Also, Barth cannot be termed a theologian of the Word of God since he did not adhere to the view that Scripture is the infallible revelation of God. In a chapter dealing with Barth's doctrine of election Klooster believed that Barth is wrong since he departed from Calvin's theology. Klooster's contention was that "Calvin's exposition and defense of the doctrine of double predestination was due to his unyielding obedience to Holy Scripture. Repeatedly Calvin asserts that he teaches and defends this doctrine simply because God teaches it in his authoritative Word."[81] The result was that Barth's theology, while claiming to be Reformed and being a theology of the Word, bore no resemblance to "the orthodox Reformed tradition [. . .] because [. . .] it [. . .] stands in contrast to the view of Calvin."[82] Furthermore, Barth could not be trusted to hold to a Scriptural theology since he believed that Scripture "is not the inspired and infallible revelation of God."[83]

The inadequacies in Klooster's analysis of Barth's theology are numerous. It is sufficient here to conclude, however, that Klooster's fundamental flaw, out of which his many misunderstandings and incorrect statements flow, is a complete misunderstanding of the term *Geschichte*.

77. Ibid., 169.
78. Ibid.
79. Ibid., 170.
80. Ibid., 171.
81. Klooster, *Significance of Karl Barth's Theology*, 40.
82. Ibid., 47.
83. Ibid., 44.

On the premise of this substantial failure Klooster totally misread Barth. Is it any wonder that Barth saw the need to inform Arthur Cochrane that he was one of the few North American theologians who understood his theology?[84]

The terms *Geschichte* and *Historie* are two German terms which can both be translated as "history." While *Historie* refers to events that take place in history, *Geschichte* refers to "events which transform personal experience or *make* history."[85] The term was popularized by Martin Kahler in his important 1892 publication: *Der sogennante historische Jesus und der geschichtliche, biblische Christus.* (The So-Called Historical Jesus and the Historic, Biblical Christ.) Kahler was alarmed by the subjectivism of his contemporaries, such as Schleiermacher, von Hoffmann, Ritschl, and Herrmann, and attempted to rectify this. He challenged the Christology of the Enlightenment and liberal school "on the grounds of its implicit [. . .] dogmatic presuppositions."[86] According to Alister McGrath he rightly saw that their dispassionate and provisional Jesus "cannot become the object of faith."[87] Consequently, he employed the term *Geschichte* to emphasize Jesus as the object of faith and not a mere historical figure. *Geschichte* looks beyond the facts of history to describe the impact of an event upon a person. Kahler's terminology is exactly the basis on which Barth stood and used the term. He came to share Kahler's disagreement with Schleiermacher's subjective existentialism and sought to uphold an objective understanding of revelation which saw the Christian apprehending God's self-revelation as an event in which God works upon them.[88] Here one comes to acknowledge and affirm the reality of the resurrection of Christ as an act of faith. While Klooster gave reference to Barth's belief that only faith gives rise to understanding, he obviously never fully grasped what Barth really meant by it. Klooster was clearly caught within the framework of fundamentalist rationalism. It therefore follows, now that Klooster's most basic assumptions have been successfully challenged, that the rest of what he has to say about Barth's theology was flawed.

84. Bloesch, pers. comm., September 12, 2002, 1.

85 McGrath, *The Making of Modern German Christology: 1750–1990*, 227–28.

86. Ibid., 112.

87. Ibid., 111.

88. Thorne, *Evangelicalism and Karl Barth*, 20.

TRANSITION FROM FUNDAMENTALISM
TO CONSERVATIVE EVANGELICALISM

While Christian fundamentalism remains a distinct religious sub-group, a second group emerged out of it. Thorne believed that following the Second World War "America witnessed the emergence of a new phase of fundamentalist history."[89] This new movement was characterized by a greater and more comprehensive engagement with society. It was also marked by its own leaders and institutions. Billy Graham provided the movement with respectability, while the launching of *Christianity Today* (1956), under the leadership of Carl Henry, "created a forum for informed theological discussion and public communication."[90]

Carl Henry, who died December 7, 2003, at the age of ninety, was the first editor of *Christianity Today* from 1956 to 1968. James Packer, the current editor, believed that Henry "pioneered the renewing of the evangelical mind [. . .] and ended his life as the Grand Old Man of our theology, apologetics, and mission thinking."[91] In his 1947 publication, *Uneasy Conscience of Modern Fundamentalism,* Henry challenged "the withdrawal of fundamentalists from society." He sought engagement with society and intellectual credibility. In the same year evangelical leaders approached him about starting a new seminary on the West Coast. "In the fall of 1947, Henry arrived at Pasadena to become Fuller Seminary's first acting dean."[92]

The founding of Fuller Seminary (1947) and the formation of the Evangelical Theological Society (1949) "introduced new intellectual centers for evangelical reflection."[93] Fuller Theological Seminary was the corner stone of this movement. Its founders

> took for granted the existence of an extensive fundamentalist subculture, but they refused to accept their movement's sub-cultural status. They sought to create a new kind of fundamentalism that would engage the dominant culture and make conservative Protestantism worthy of respect. They saw themselves as

89. Ibid., 20.

90. Spring, "Carl F. H. Henry dies at 90," 20.

91. Ibid., 20.

92. Ibid., 20.

93. Ibid., 20.

reformers of what had become a strangely distorted and uprooted Protestant orthodoxy.[94]

George Marsden has described this group as "softened fundamentalists who wanted to preserve the essentials of the tradition but not its extremes. They retained the basic fundamentalist biblicism and opposition to liberal theologies, but they did not demand separatism; and they de-emphasized some of the strictest prohibitions of the fundamentalist moral code."[95] However, Thorne rightly observed that this new form of "evangelicalism" closely resembled its fundamentalist roots. Furthermore, it possessed little in the way of new thought. It represented more "a renewal of a broader, more culturally engaging conservatism that affirmed evangelical cooperation without theological compromise."[96] Positively, what this movement symbolized was a new direction away from a conservative reactionary impulse to a new impulse of engagement. Carl Henry, who is highly representative of this movement, reads Karl Barth in such a manner as to place this movement in a transitionary between rejection and appropriation of Barth's evangelicalism.

In an article written for *Christianity Today* in 1963 Henry praised Barth as one who "has made an epochal contribution to theology."[97] While Henry contended that many of Barth's emphases are but repetitions of the views of Augustine and Calvin, he believed that Barth's merit is best seen in his religious and ecclesiastical contributions. Henry asserted that by his detailed arguments Barth "has forced multitudes of liberals to realize that modernism, the pantheistic immanentism and the idealistic philosophy of the Schleiermacher-Ritschl-Herrmann line, leads logically to realistic atheism."[98] Alternatively Henry claimed that Barth, by stressing man's dependence on God, gave new vitality to the Reformation formula of *soli Deo gloria*. However, while being somewhat appreciative Henry essentially remained a Reformed critic of Barth.

Henry lamented that "in opposition to the Reformation principle of *sola Scriptura* Barth's view on the function of Scripture as a witness to God's revelation in Jesus Christ, together with his concept of saga, was

94. Dorrien, *Remaking of Evangelical Theology*, 17.

95. Marsden, "Fundamentalism," 30.

96. Thorne, *Evangelicalism and Karl Barth*, 21.

97. Henry, "The Dilemma Facing Karl Barth," 27.

98. Ibid., 27.

derived from non-biblical presuppositions."[99] Indeed, Henry was clearly critical of Barth's belief that the Bible is to be distinguished from revelation and that consequently the reader need not take everything in the Bible as true *in globo*. Quoting Gordon Clark, Henry contended that the only type of principle Barth required to interpret the Bible lay "in the use of some non-scriptural principle. Bible norms are impossible."[100] Therefore, Henry represented a new engagement with Barth beyond the fundamentalist's total rejection. It was an engagement characterized by an acceptance of many of Barth's emphases, yet highly critical of his doctrine of revelation. However, the situation was soon to change again. As Thorne observed, Protestant history did not stabilize at this point. A greater cultural respectability resulted in a more public and powerful evangelicalism, yet one that was more internally diverse.[101] Consequently, as this diversity unfolded it created increasing problems for the unity of the movement. As time unfolded a third evangelical movement became necessary, the "new evangelicals."

TRANSITION FROM CONSERVATIVE EVANGELICALISM TO NEW EVANGELICALISM

The *Henry-Graham-Christianity Today* form of evangelicalism had become well established and was known by its leaders and publications. However, many evangelicals felt the need to make further adjustments. This group sought "to throw off the peculiar forms of modernism that evangelical teaching acquired during its fundamentalist phase."[102] They represented a more moderate evangelicalism whose purpose was "to re-establish classical evangelical teaching and practices in ways that more faithfully reflect the heritage of catholic orthodoxy."[103]

New evangelicalism's objection to the Carl Henry type of evangelicalism was that it still, like its fundamentalist parentage, reduced "the gospel faith to the logic of a modernist philosophical method." It had imported themes into evangelicalism's reformational heritage and promoted em-

---

99. In his discussion Henry refers to the complaints of Klaas Runia and Gordon H. Clark. Ibid., 28.

100. Henry, "Barth's Turnabout From the Biblical Norm," 28.

101. Thorne, *Evangelicalism and Karl Barth*, 1.

102. Dorrien, *Remaking of Evangelical Theology*, 189.

103. Ibid.

phases such as the inerrancy of Scripture and the importance of eschatology that the reformers would have found inconsistent with their own primary convictions. Furthermore, in the fundamentalist and conservative systems, lamented Donald Bloesch, revelation is reduced to logical axioms, designed to be understood by believers as well as unbelievers. The problem with this is that it separates revelation from encounter and the agency of the Holy Spirit who alone is sent to illuminate the Word. To be sure: "The Word of God becomes a rational formula wholly in control of the theologian, and theology becomes a systematic harmonizing of rational truths."[104]

Stanley Grenz and Clark Pinnock have both sought to deal with the modernist debate by advocating a new evangelical theology. Grenz, in his *Renewing the Center*, took issue with theology that is too influenced by a rationalist agenda. He referred to David Well's observation that as "evangelicalism grew numerically and in stature in society [. . .] its fundamental ethos shifted from antagonism toward culture to adaptation of culture."[105] Grenz found that the root of the problem lay in modernist thinking impacting upon philosophical assumptions and subsequently creating a theological system he termed foundationalism. Two distinct theologies were constructed on the foundationalist platform: liberalism and fundamentalism.[106] Grenz believed that for evangelicals one of the pressing issues to be faced concerned theological approach in the postmodern era. Post-modernism, claimed Grenz, led to the demise of foundationalism. He asked: "How can evangelical theologians engage in the task of reconstructing evangelical theology by appropriating critically the insights of non-foundationalist or post-foundationalist epistemology?"[107]

Grenz's alternative approach began with learning from the insights of philosophers Alvin Platinga and Nicholas Wolterstorff, who "question strong foundationalism while not rejecting the basic foundationalist insight." These philosophers grappled with the issue of establishing basic unequivocal truth within a framework that argued that reason is "person specific" and "situation specific." This led Grenz to ask how evangelicals can assert objective truth within a subjective mind-set. Being an evan-

104. Ibid.
105. Grenz, *Renewing the Center*, 12–13.
106. Ibid., 189.
107. Ibid., 199.

gelical, Grenz placed his approach firmly in the traditional mould of Scripture, since the Bible is at "the heart of evangelical theology." While this assertion is nothing new, Grenz proposed a new reading of the Bible. In the rationalism of the foundationalist's schema "the Bible was all too readily transformed from a living text into the object of the scholar's exegetical and systematizing prowess."[108] The alternative, demanded by the new post-modernist situation, was envisaged by Grenz as being along the lines of Wolfhart Pannenberg's approach.

Grenz described Pannenberg's approach as rejecting the idea that "truth is found in the constant and unchanging essences—or the eternal presence—lying behind the flow of time." In Pannenberg's alternative concept, which according to Grenz is the biblical view, "(t)ruth is what shows itself throughout the movement of time, climaxing in the end event. This end, he added, is anticipated in the present, a point Pannenberg finds evident in general human life, for we continually modify our understandings in the light of subsequent experience [. . .] Consequently, all truth comes together in God, who is the ground of the unity of truth."[109] On the basis of this appreciation for Pannenberg's thesis, Grenz advocated a reading of Scripture that sets aside the quest for reasoned propositions to advocate a Spirit guided approach in which the "the Spirit orients our present on the basis of the past and in accordance with a vision of the future [. . .] The task of theology, in turn, is to assist the people of God in hearing the Spirit's voice speaking through the text, so that we can live as God's people, as inhabitants of God's eschatological world—in the present."[110]

The goal to which this approach pointed, was the fashioning of a community "that lives the paradigmatic biblical narrative in the contemporary context."[111] For Grenz, reading within community also meant considering the faith community that spans the ages. This amounted to including tradition in theological structures, since the "luminaries of the past have an ongoing role in the contemporary theological conversation."[112] On the basis of this grounding comes Grenz's thesis that *community* is theology's integrative motif. He maintained that community is "the central, organiz-

---

108. Ibid., 206.

109. Ibid., 196–97.

110. Ibid., 207.

111. Ibid., 208.

112. Ibid.

ing concept of theological construction." It is the theme around which systematic theology may be structured, since it "provides the integrative thematic perspective in light of which the various theological foci can be understood and significant theological issues explored."[113]

As the different theologies of this thesis are observed it will be seen how structures have changed and developed with the addition of new sources that have arisen out of new influences in the course of life experiences. In contradistinction to theology structured on the basis of a set list of fixed propositions, this thesis will contend that theology is a developing thought concept that emerges out of the experiences of theologians, as these were encountered over time, and within a specific theological context. Furthermore, it will be demonstrated that the new evangelicals who sought to be influenced by Barth did so after rejecting liberalism and fundamentalism as constructions of rationalism and its propositional objectivism. Indeed, they sought to be informed by the insights of Barth, who sought to avoid the pitfalls that reactionary movements, described by Grenz as foundationalism, produced.

Clark Pinnock has also made a significant contribution to the discussion on approaches to theology. Pinnock described theologians as cooks, who "utilize ingredients in a certain manner [. . .] follow procedures, appeal to sources, place them in order [. . .] and weigh their importance."[114] According to Pinnock, theology, as described in this way, underlines what theologians do and affect what they say. He was right when he stated that the manner in which theologians construct their writings holds the key to the theological system, or school of thought, that the theologian seeks to represent. Pinnock also explained why such approaches need to be explored. He claimed that evangelical theologians "have been provoked to explain their approaches by the willingness of other sciences to explain theirs. They are shamed when the often naïve way they do theology is compared to the sophisticated ways science is done."[115] Central to this naivety is an adherence to a theology that simply articulates "what the Bible says," without really acknowledging the role played by tradition or reason, even though they would be unable to deny that either is fundamental to their thought. In the era in which we now live the articulation of truth, as

113. Ibid., 215.

114. Pinnock, *New Dimensions in Theological Method*, 197.

115. Ibid., 198.

it is proclaimed as a series of logically ordered propositions that appeal to laws of rationalism, will not suffice. We live in a new post-modernist, era that is not content with mere pronouncements.

The contemporary mind now seeks to get beneath what is said and study the mind of the thinker and the manner in which their thoughts are constructed. This does not, however, spell the end of certainty for the evangelical. What it does amount to is a new way of talking about knowledge and certitude. Objective reality still stands in the new era, but it is to be conceived within the framework of a subjective observations. In the past evangelicals would have found this approach to be unacceptable, since it would only serve to undermine all of their strongly held beliefs. However, in our current era knowledge cannot be conceived in any other way. Indeed, the contemporary mind is quite accustomed to asserting reality in this way. What this leads to, claimed Pinnock, is a change and a growth in understanding of the "many and varied ways in which God speaks in Scripture and in the way theology listens. Many are awakening to the fact that more is involved in grounding their work in the Bible than in appealing to a flat rule."[116]

Indeed, Pinnock believed it would be true to say that evangelicals have tended not to realize that "(b)eyond the Bible are other factors that come into play when we assess meaning."[117] Evangelicals have tended to "give the impression that they have a one-source method, but in reality they have always used several sources."[118] Yet Pinnock saw positive signs of change as he read the works of evangelicals who have moved beyond the rationalistic or philosophical biblicism of the fundamentalists. Pinnock's contention was that evangelicals are learning to work more self-consciously with a fuller pattern of sources as they approach their theology. The result of a fuller approach is the enrichment of theology. Indeed, Pinnock correctly stated that it "makes theology more catholic and less parochial, more comprehensive and less strident, more timely and less irrelevant."[119]

It is to be noted that there is a common thread running through the significant contributions of Grenz and Pinnock. They both recognized the

116. Ibid., 203.
117. Ibid., 204–5.
118. Ibid., 205.
119. Ibid., 206.

need for change and assess, in the light of changes in society, the directions in which these changes should head. Important to this thesis is that they have understood their world as now operating in a post-modernist era; one in which unquestioned, and unanalyzed, rational propositions are no longer adequate to define knowledge. This thesis rests on the observation that the post-modernist mind seeks the investigation of truth and an understanding of the components that constitute the making of the whole presentation. It is a picture that is yet to be completed. Indeed, Grenz referred to Pannenberg's thesis, which implied that we currently have access to truth that will culminate at the end of history. Furthermore, Pinnock believed that a post-modernist theology will seek to come to terms with reality and understand theology as a human search to explain a divine reality. Given these observations, it would appear to be highly pertinent to study theological structures in the manner outlined in this thesis. To be sure, theology is the subjective task in the search for objective truth. It is a study of theological development over time, within the life of a theologian, as he or she exists within the movement of history, and within the experiences of a theological community. Furthermore, the study of theological approaches is necessary to develop the self-consciousness that is required for one to understand post-foundationalist theology.

The contention of this thesis is that it was Donald Bloesch, in his call for an evangelical renaissance, and Bernard Ramm, in his design for a post-fundamentalist evangelical theology, which formed the theological impetus for an evangelical response influenced by Karl Barth. They found that the neo-orthodoxy of Karl Barth provided a means for them to remain evangelical, discard the distortions that the fundamentalists and conservatives had imported into the Reformational heritage of evangelicalism, and engage thoroughly and with sophistication with the wider Christian community. Unlike those groups which appeared to be subject to rationalist constructs, they sought to engage constructively with the modern world. Indeed, James Barr believed that this form of neo-orthodoxy was bound to be of interest to some evangelicals because of its sharp opposition to liberalism *and* fundamentalism.[120] Indeed, many of the new evangelicals saw Barth as ideally suited to their cause; being, as he was, located between these two extremes. Barr was right in his belief that the neo-orthodoxy of Barth "performed the very important service of a

120. Barr, *Fundamentalism*, 214.

bridge by which people of very conservative tendencies were able to cross over into the main stream of Protestant Christianity."[121]

Donald Bloesch's Evangelical Renaissance

In his 1972 critique of evangelicalism, *The Evangelical Renaissance*, Bloesch outlined his vision for a new evangelicalism influenced by Karl Barth. In his introduction he set the tone for what he had in mind by advocating an evangelicalism that is flexible and open to various forces. He believed that evangelicals should let themselves be corrected by their Catholic and Orthodox brethren and be willing to learn from liberal Protestants, "who have not been entirely off the mark in some of their protests and concerns." Indeed, Bloesch contended that evangelicals have much to learn from liberal scholarship's concern for the historical and cultural background of Scripture. Indeed, "(t)he denial of the principle of historical criticism can be just as mindless as the acceptance of the rationalistic philosophy of some of the higher critics."[122]

Bloesch's view clearly represented a significant shift away from the worldviews of the fundamentalists and conservative evangelicals, who, as has been seen, are characterized by a fortress mentality antagonistic to other views, which, they believed, would erode their most cherished convictions. Bloesch, in contrast, advocated a broader and more engaging evangelicalism. He did so with a critique of fundamentalism, which he saw as rationalistic and accommodating to culture. Fundamentalists, claimed Bloesch, are rationalistic Biblicists whose "appeal is made to the axioms of formal logic or the evidences of the senses to buttress the claims of biblical faith. A few conservative scholars today even go so far as to hold that the resurrection of Christ can be rationally proved to the natural man."[123] Furthermore, Bloesch warned that when "an absolute identification is made between the words of the biblical text and the truth of revelation, the doorway is opened to rationalism." The consequence for fundamentalists, claimed Bloesch, is the potentially naïve and embarrassing trap of putting a greater emphasis on Jonah's edibility than on what God is actually seeking to proclaim in his Word.[124] This approach

121. Ibid., 221.

122. Bloesch, *Evangelical Renaissance*, 8.

123. Ibid., 21.

124. Ibid., 28.

only serves to reduce God's Word to the accessibility of human reason.[125] In contradistinction Bloesch contended that it is possible to hold to the divine inspiration of Scripture "without reducing its truth to a datum available to human perception."[126] To support his argument and demonstrate that he was seeking to promote a true and vibrant evangelicalism free of modernistic compromise, Bloesch turned to Martin Luther who asserted that "(f)aith directs itself towards the things that are invisible. Indeed, only when that which is believed on is hidden, can it be proved an opportunity for faith."[127]

Bloesch's other contention with fundamentalism was that its rationalistic approach usually goes hand in hand with an anti-theology bias. Indeed, Bloesch observed that with fundamentalists the doctrinal exposition of Scripture is often regarded with mistrust. This betrayed, believed Bloesch, "a markedly cultural orientation in which the authority of reason is substituted for that of revelation."[128] Ghettoism is also seen by Bloesch to be a problem with fundamentalists. He contended that such groups put themselves in danger of falling victim to the legalism of taboos "in which visible marks of separation are drawn between Christians and their worldly neighbors." Sadly these communities identify themselves as holy and separate by emphasizing abstinence from such social practices as dancing, cosmetics, drinking, and card playing, but say very little about the sins of racial injustice, the exploitation of the poor and unscrupulous business practices.[129] In response to these callous legalisms Bloesch referred to Count von Zinzendorf who believed that discipleship of Christ should not be a "legalistic duty" but "our life" and "our joy."[130] What Bloesch advocated as a remedy to this dilemma is the formation of a new evangelicalism.

The new evangelicalism that Bloesch described is not only markedly different from fundamentalism but also wider and deeper than the initial reforming surge of evangelicalism, "which was limited mainly to those who were seeking to eschew the excesses of fundamentalism but

125. Ibid., 21.
126. Ibid.
127. Ibid.
128. Ibid.
129. Ibid., 22.
130. Ibid.

at the same time remain solidly biblical."[131] Indeed, new evangelicalism "acknowledges that the Bible is the word of man as well as the Word of God and that the divine Word is made known through a human word that bears the marks of cultural conditioning."[132] New evangelicalism has also contended that the Bible is infallible, however this does not mean the text itself, but the message contained in the text, which is available through the working of the Holy Spirit. The new evangelicals sought to stress the message of the messenger rather than the written witness of the messenger. Bloesch further reflected the influence of Karl Barth when he stated that the "new evangelicals are adamant in their contention [. . .] that the revealed Word of God, Jesus Christ, must not be set against the written Word."[133]

While Bloesch admitted that Barth has not been well received by "evangelicals" in the Anglo-Saxon countries he asserted that "Barth must be taken with the utmost seriousness by any theologian of evangelical or Reformed persuasion."[134] Indeed, Bloesch believed that Barth must be called an evangelical theologian, since his book, *Evangelical Theology,* contained a forthright call for Scriptural authority. Also, his monumental *Church Dogmatics* "is anchored in a deep study of the Scriptures and is replete with Scriptural references."[135] To be sure, Barth called Christians to pursue a theology of revelation "based upon the Word of God in Scripture and not upon human wisdom and imagination."[136]

Bernard Ramm's Idea of Evangelicalism after Fundamentalism

Clark Pinnock has described Bernard Ramm as "a quintessential postfundamentalist (evangelical) theologian of the post-war period in America."[137] According to Pinnock, Ramm's agenda was to create and promote a conservative Protestant faith "theologically profound and intellectually

---

131. Ibid., 30.

132. Ibid., 33–34.

133. Ibid., 34.

134. Ibid., 80–81.

135. Ibid., 81.

136. Ibid.

137. Pinnock, "Bernard Ramm: Postfundamentalist Coming to Terms with Modernity," 15.

respectable."[138] However, Ramm's task was not an easy one. As Pinnock stated, Ramm would have been aware that fundamentalism presented many difficulties with their appeals to an infallible Bible and claims for a miraculous history. However he was also aware that liberal theologians had, over the years, developed a world of scientific rationality which limited the miraculous sharply. Consequently Ramm's task "has been to try to explain how one can be intellectually responsible without making concessions to scientific rationalism on the one hand or resorting to blind faith on the other."[139]

Ramm's theological vision was spelled out in his significant *After Fundamentalism: The Future of Evangelical Theology*. It was a clarion call to the formation of a new evangelicalism free of the constraints and impossibilities associated with fundamentalism and its conservative offspring. In the preface to this work Ramm made his point strikingly clear. The Enlightenment had proved to be a shattering experience out of which orthodoxy had never recovered. Ramm's belief was that "(n)either religious liberalism nor orthodoxy had the right strategy for interacting with the Enlightenment with reference to the continuing task of Christian theology."[140] Indeed, Ramm later complained that the "fundamentalists" solution is simply to ignore the Enlightenment and to continue their work as if it never occurred. "This route commits them to the strategy of obscurantism."[141] What is the way forward for evangelicals? Ramm believed that "(o)f all the efforts of theologians to come to terms with the Enlightenment, Karl Barth's theology has been the most thorough [...] He thereby offers to evangelical theology a paradigm of how best to come to terms with the Enlightenment."[142]

CONCLUSION

The reception of Karl Barth in North America is reflected in the development of Protestantism in North America. The fundamentalists were opposed to Barth because he did not comply with their tightly defined agenda and compilation of rationalist propositions. However, many of their pro-

138. Ibid.
139. Ibid., 19.
140. Ramm, *After Fundamentalism*, vii.
141. Ibid., 43.
142. Ibid., vii.

tests were ill-founded. Cornelius Van Til erroneously protested that Barth was a captive of Kant and his existentialist successors. Furthermore, Van Til believed that Barth's theology of the Word was so flawed that his whole theological system should be brought into doubt. According to Van Til, Barth's inability to affirm Biblical inerrancy resulted in him not only being a child of Kant, but also an enemy of the Reformers. Fred Klooster, another North American fundamentalist, was opposed to Barth's use of *Geschichte*, which he mistakenly thought affirmed that the Bible is a work of myth. In addition, Klooster's rationalist mindset contended that it is difficult to speak of Barth's soteriology since his systematics did not contain a section bearing that title. Barth received a slightly modified reception with the emergence of the conservative evangelicals.

The conservative evangelicals, while seeking to move beyond many of the constraints of fundamentalism, appreciated Barth's contribution—indeed, saw him as an important theologian—yet were in fundamental disagreement. Carl Henry, their primary theological spokesperson, praised Barth as making an "epochal contribution to theology."[143] In contrast to Van Til and Klooster, Henry believed that many of Barth's emphases were repetitions of the views of Augustine and Calvin. Furthermore, Henry praised Barth for his religious and ecclesiastical contributions. Indeed, Henry, again in contrast to Van Til, asserted that by his detailed arguments Barth "has forced multitudes of liberals to realize that modernism, the pantheistic immanentalism and the idealistic philosophy of the Schleiermacher-Ritschl-Herrmann line, leads logically to realistic atheism."[144] Indeed, Henry claimed that Barth, by stressing man's dependence on God, has given new vitality to the Reformation formula of *soli Deo gloria*. However, while being somewhat appreciative Henry essentially remained a Reformed critic of Barth. Henry, in a similar vein to the fundamentalists, lamented that in opposition to the Reformation principle of *sola Scriptura* Barth's view on the function of Scripture as a witness to God's revelation in Jesus Christ, together with his concept of saga, are derived from non-biblical presuppositions. Henry was clearly critical of the Swiss theologian's belief that the Bible is to be distinguished from revelation. While the conservative evangelicals had reservations, the new evangelicals saw in Barth a model for their cause.

143. Ibid.; C. Henry, "The Dilemma Facing Karl Barth," 27.
144. Ibid., 27.

Indeed, the new evangelicals appreciated Barth's theology and saw it as a means of creating, as Ramm put it, a post-fundamentalism that represented a renewed evangelicalism in full dialogue with modernism. This is in contrast to the fortress mentality of the fundamentalists, who were trapped in an accommodation to modernist thinking that resulted in a theology distorted by its rationalism, narrow agenda, and specific emphases. Furthermore, it appeared to the new evangelicals that the fundamentalists and conservatives did not adequately reflect the evangelical tradition and only bore a slim likeness to the theology of the Reformers. Donald Bloesch claimed that fundamentalists were rationalistic Biblicists, who appealed to the axioms of formal logic or the evidences of the senses. Bloesch sought Barth's help to engage with the vibrancy of the Reformers to create a moderate orthodoxy, freed from the constraints of rationalism, and engaging thoughtfully with contemporary issues and debates. The new evangelicals found Barth to be their model and guide for creating a new evangelical theology in America.

The following chapters comprise the second and most substantial section to this thesis. These are the thinkers who found Barth to be a significant source in the construction of their theological motifs, and in the pursuit of their agendas. Bernard Ramm will be the first theologian studied. He represented, in his own theological development, the transition to new evangelicalism that is so much at the core of this thesis. Importantly, Ramm put out a call to construct an evangelicalism with Barth as the guiding light.

3

Bernard Ramm

Bernard Ramm was one of the earliest new evangelical advocates of Karl Barth's theology. In this chapter it will be shown that Barth became an important source for Ramm as he came to a major turning point in his life. After encountering Barth's writings Ramm saw in him ideas that would assist in constructing a post-fundamentalist orthodoxy. He was drawn Barth after a crisis experience which led him to set aside his fundamentalist background. The likely reason for Ramm's crisis, and change in direction, resulted from a failure on his part to synthesize his scientific and theological knowledge. His understanding of scientific enquiry and logic could not accommodate, or satisfactorily resolve, the tensions that had become apparent between these and his fundamentalist beliefs. Ultimately Ramm's scientific knowledge caused him to abandon his fundamentalist theology. It was in this situation that Barth's work presented itself as a solid edifice to enable Ramm to construct a new and moderate evangelicalism that maintained its orthodox identity while also being ready to employ the tools of modern scholarship.

The influence of Barth in Ramm's theology was enhanced by both literary and personal encounters. The full effect of these encounters came to maturity with the publication of Ramm's landmark study, *After Fundamentalism: The Future of Evangelical Theology.* In this work Ramm set forth a proposal for a new theological approach after the pattern of Barth. He proposed that Barth was a worthy influence whose theology was capable of being a valuable source in the pursuit of his new agenda. The application of his proposal was most evident in the later publication of his Christology: *An Evangelical Christology: Ecumenic and Historic.* The discussion begins with a survey of Ramm's life which will outline the influences that led to the theological position of his maturity.

A BACKGROUND IN FUNDAMENTALISM

Bernard Ramm was born in Butte, Montana, on August 1, 1916. He made a personal commitment to the religion of his upbringing through the influence of his brother John, during the summer before his freshman year at the University of Washington.[1] Subsequently, Ramm gained a BA from the University of Washington in 1938, before attending Eastern Baptist Theological Seminary in Philadelphia. He had initially planned to major in physical sciences, but when he decided to enter into Christian ministry he changed his major to speech and his minor to philosophy.[2] However, his interest in science continued. He obtained his MA in philosophy at the University of Southern California in 1947, and in 1950 he received his PhD from the same institution with a dissertation entitled *An Investigation of Some Recent Efforts to Justify Metaphysical Statements from Science with Special Reference to Physics.*[3]

For much of the 1940s Ramm was both student and teacher. Between 1944 and 1945 he served as professor of biblical languages at the Los Angeles Baptist Theological Seminary before becoming head of the Department of Philosophy and Apologetics at the Bible Institute of Los Angeles between 1945 and 1951. Both of these institutions were "dispensational schools within the orbit of Northern Fundamentalist Evangelicalism." From there he moved to the conservative institution of Bethel Baptist College and Seminary (1950–1954).[4] "In 1948 he was the mid-year lecturer at Western Baptist Theological Seminary, where he delivered the talks that eventually became his first published work, *Problems in Christian Apologetics* (1949)."[5] He taught at a number of training institutions for pastors, including Biola University, Bethel College, California Baptist Theological Seminary, Eastern Baptist Theological Seminary, Baylor University and then finally the American Baptist Seminary of the

---

1. Vanhoozer, "Bernard Ramm," 290. Miller, *The Theological System of Bernard L. Ramm*, 3.

2. David Miller is right in his observation that "the question of how to put his Christian faith together with science remained a burning issue with him." Ibid., 4.

3. As a boy Ramm had been introduced to atomic theory, relativity, and chemistry by a Russian engineer who was the father of a friend. Vanhoozer, "Bernard Ramm," 290.

4. Thorne, *Evangelicalism and Karl Barth*, 123.

5. Vanhoozer, "Bernard Ramm," 290.

West, where he retired as Pearl Rawlings Hamilton Professor of Christian Theology on December 31, 1986.[6]

During the 1950s, the years of his early academic career, Ramm published numerous books, articles and essays. Phillip Thorne commented that during these years Ramm produced four books, "which established his reputation as a leading scholar within the emerging evangelical movement: *Protestant Biblical Interpretation, Protestant Christian Evidences, Types of Apologetic Systems* and *The Christian View of Science and Scripture*."[7] It can be noted from these works that Ramm's early publications established him as a leader in fundamentalist scholarship. Fundamentalism formed the foundations of Ramm's early years of faith. Indeed in an interview with Ramm in 1981 David Miller learnt that "(f)or the first four years of (Ramm's) Christian life he was strongly influenced by friends from Dallas Theological Seminary. (Consequently Ramm) thought of himself as a fundamentalist-premillennial dispensationalist."[8] Therefore, like other fundamentalist works of that period Ramm's writings were apologetic in focus and had a fundamentalist self-understanding. He concerned himself with defending conservative Protestantism and the historic Christian faith which he saw as reflected in the creeds of the ancient church, the writings of the Reformers, and nineteenth century conservatives such as Benjamin Warfield and James Orr.[9] However, signs of change began to emerge.

In *A Christian View of Science and Scripture* Ramm contended that Scripture contains "prescientific" language that can only be described as theological in nature.[10] This view was distinct from the fundamentalist assertion that the language of Scripture is scientifically accurate. Therefore in this publication one can detect early signs of how Ramm's conception of science would come to impact upon and shape his theology. Indeed, this work stimulated many years of thought and reflection. His studying at Eastern Baptist Theological Seminary, where he had begun to develop reservations about the dispensational schools, assisted this process. It is evident that the influence of this seminary significantly contributed to

6. Brown, "Bernard L. Ramm," 9–10.

7. Thorne, *Evangelicalism and Karl Barth*, 6.

8. Miller, *Theological System of Bernard L. Ramm*, 4.

9 Thorne, *Evangelicalism and Karl Barth*, 124.

10. Ibid., 125.

Ramm's shift in thinking since it did not provide a culture that encouraged fundamentalism, but a more moderate environment that was able to assist Ramm in pursuing his agenda of relating science to theology. Furthermore it is clear that during his post-graduate study Ramm became aware of the cultural climate of his day. Indeed, further influences came about as he began increasingly to appreciate the impact of modernist rationalism upon American society. He subsequently saw it as a society borne out of the influences of Kantianism—so much an influence on Enlightenment thought—which had produced a dominance of skepticism, reason, and analysis.[11] In reference to these early works it is evident that Kevin Vanhoozer was correct when he made the observation that while Ramm was converted into American fundamentalism, which taught him to build walls in order to keep out modernism, he did in fact, due in part to the influences just outlined, begin to do the very opposite. Indeed, "(i)n his teaching and writing he strove to bring evangelical theology into the sphere of free and open discourse with the modern world."[12] However, Ramm's shift in thinking would change rapidly as his knowledge of science and fundamentalist theology seriously collided.

It is contended here that Ramm's conception of the rules of science, together with his modernist world-view along side a belief in fundamentalist theology, created a tension that was only to be resolved by a dismantling of many of his theological assumptions. The beginning of change occurred after Ramm had come to understand theology as a science.[13] Indeed, he came to speak of a need for theology and other sciences to be "wedded together in a single organism of knowledge. (As a result Ramm came to contend that science) needs the light of revelation and revelation needs the perspectives of science."[14] However, Ramm found himself in a situation of possessing a theology that was gradually being crushed by his scientific convictions. If, as Ramm believed, both secular and sacred sciences were to interact with each other in order to gain a true composition of knowledge[15], then rapid changes needed to be made in his theological system to avoid a crisis experience arising from the weight of

11. Miller, *Theological System of Bernard L. Ramm*, 17.
12. Vanhoozer, *Bernard Ramm*, 291.
13. Miller, *Theological System of Bernard L. Ramm*, 26.
14. Ibid., 27.
15. Miller, *Theological System of Bernard L. Ramm*.

such tensions. None-the-less, a crisis arose. Significantly, while seeking to find a way of accommodating both fundamentalism and science in a single theological structure he discovered, in the 1950s, the works of two prominent twentieth-century theologians: the Dutch Calvinist Abraham Kuyper and the Swiss neo-orthodox theologian Karl Barth. It was Barth's theology, however, that would form the basis of Ramm's soon to be new theological direction.

RAMM'S CRISIS EXPERIENCE

In his highly influential, *After Fundamentalism: The Future of Evangelical Theology*,[16] Ramm remembered the time that led him to search for a new direction. He recalled that he had just finished a lecture on his own version of American evangelicalism, when a shrewd listener asked him to define American evangelical theology more precisely. Ramm remembered that this question created within him an experience of inward panic. He commented: "Like a drowning man[17] who sees parts of his life pass before him at great speed [an experience I have had], so my theology passed before my eyes. I saw my theology as a series of doctrines picked up here and there, like a rag-bag collection." The experience caused Ramm to reflect. He came to the realization that theologically he was the product of the orthodox-liberal debate that had been going on among evangelicals in America for a century; a debate that had warped the foundations of evangelical theology. Consequently he came to the conclusion that he was unable to answer the important question that had been put to him since he did not possess a theology whose "methodology was scientifically ascertained, nor doctrines scientifically related nor properly defended." Ramm concluded that he needed a new beginning in theology with new foundations leading to a new direction in theological thought and orientation. Ramm had come to see his fundamentalist theology as captive to rationalism. What he subsequently sought was an orthodoxy that was free of the constraints of rationalism and open to critical scholarship. As he sought to reorientate his theology he looked around for a new option. This lead him to the theology of Karl Barth, the one theologian Ramm believed had the most to offer.[18]

16. Ramm, *After Fundamentalism*.

17. Ibid., 1–2.

18. Pinnock, "Bernard Ramm," 17.

THE INFLUENCE OF BARTH

As Ramm sought a new way forward he chose to be influenced by Karl Barth, the one he believed could best resolve the various tensions raging within his mind. Barth championed a new orthodoxy that read Scripture through the Reformers, yet was not uncritical in its approach. This was a far cry from the fundamentalist approach which somehow opposed the advances of the Enlightenment while at the same time being defined and constrained by it. Clark Pinnock wrote that Ramm was also attracted to Barth's depth and thoroughness. He commented that the North American Baptist found in Barth a "learned and believing scholar who waded in the deep waters of biblical and historical study."[19] However it was the relationships that Barth was able to establish between seemingly conflicting world-views that most attracted Ramm to Barth. This thesis is supported by a speech Ramm delivered in his retirement. He revealed that he regarded Barth as "a genius with imagination, who was able to see relationships obscure to others."[20] Ramm's encounters with Barth came in two stages and resulted in helping him establish the character of his new theological orientation. It is evident that these stages were significant influences that came to inspire Ramm's agenda for a new post-fundamentalist theology. He described the first stage as a literary encounter, whilst the second arose from his personal encounter with Barth while in Basel.[21]

Literary Encounter with Barth

Ramm's literary encounter with Barth began during his seminary education. This introduction was, in Ramm's own view, unsatisfactory and unfair.[22] However a more satisfactory and in depth literary encounter occurred while Ramm was professor of philosophy at Bethel College and Seminary in St. Paul (1951–1954) and director of graduate studies in religion at Baylor University (1954–1959). During this time he undertook daily readings of Barth's *Church Dogmatics*, and some other

19. Ibid., 16.

20. Ibid., 17.

21. Ramm, "Helps From Karl Barth," 121.

22. Mohler observes that Ramm later found the first volume to Barth's *Church Dogmatics* at the Los Angeles public library. Mohler, "Bernard Ramm: Karl Barth and the Future of American Evangelicalism," 31.

of Barth's writings, according to a set schedule. Ramm's conclusion was that of all the contemporary theologians "Barth was doing the best job of relating historic Reformed theology to modern biblical criticism,"[23] and consequently was "the one who was doing the best job of relating historic Reformed theology to the Enlightenment."[24] Indeed, Ramm found that the strength of Barth's neo-orthodoxy was in its ability to keep faith with the historical church while wishing "to preserve the advances of the Enlightenment and not be stuck with some of the impossible positions of classical Protestant orthodoxy."[25] The more Ramm read Barth's work the more he became influenced by his approach. Indeed, Ramm found that he was unable to support many of the typical superficial generalizations and caricatures commonly imputed by American evangelicals to a theologian who, in his belief, most profoundly defended "the ancient Christology of the church fathers as well as their doctrine of the trinity."[26] In contrast to the dismissiveness of most evangelical reviewers Ramm found in Barth an ally of orthodoxy who produced statements on the authority of Scripture,[27] together with sound defenses of the virgin birth,[28] the bodily resurrection and the cosmic, visible return of Christ.[29] However, while Ramm believed that fundamentalism had become subject to rationalism, he also contended that liberalism had succumbed to the same fate. Indeed, he contended that in the face of Enlightenment challenges, both liberalism and fundamentalism had failed. As a consequence Ramm's new agenda held to the belief that the best way forward was in an alternative that represented a true evangelicalism characterized by Barth's historic Christianity dependant upon the Reformers, his theology of the Word of God, and his openness to critical study. Indeed, Ramm conceived of this as a third way supported by neo-orthodoxy and in particular that part of the movement

23. Vanhoozer, *Bernard Ramm*, 291.

24. Ramm, *After Fundamentalism*, 10.

25. Ramm, *Evangelical Heritage*, 103.

26. Ramm, *After Fundamentalism*, 11.

27. Barth asserted that as the authority of Scripture is seen in its presentation of Jesus Christ, therefore, "in the servant form of a human word it speaks the Word of God." Barth, *Church Dogmatics: 1/2*, 538.

28. Barth refers to the mystery of Christmas. "This miracle is the conception of Jesus Christ by the Holy Ghost or His birth of the Virgin Mary." Indeed, Barth points to the two childhood narratives the virgin birth is "expressly indicated." Ibid., 173, 175.

29. Ibid., 16.

represented by Karl Barth. The influence of Barth provided Ramm with the approach he needed to pursue his agenda of resolving the problems he believed had come to beset evangelicalism. Consequently it is clear that Ramm's subsequent engagement with neo-orthodoxy and with Karl Barth in particular, chartered a new direction in his theological development and shaped his mature conception of evangelical identity.[30]

Personal Encounter with Barth

Ramm was able to follow up his reading of Barth with a series of personal dialogues in a sabbatical year (1957–1958) spent in Basel, Switzerland, "where he faithfully attended the Saturday-afternoon English-language seminars held in Barth's home."[31] As a result of these personal encounters Ramm experienced three significant challenges to his theological thinking which, together with his previous literary encounters, helped set him on an entirely new direction.[32] It was a period of intense and sustained influence in which Ramm sought to expand his knowledge of Barth's approach by direct conversation with the author. Ramm describes these as material changes.

The first material change stemmed from Barth's exhortation to be fearless in theology. It was a call for open dialogue and discussion with the modern world based on the Word of God. Ramm was present during one of Barth's discussions during which he stipulated that if one "truly believed that we had the truth of God in Holy Scripture we should be fearless in opening any door or any window in the pursuit of our theological craft."[33] It is clear that this first material change was instrumental in giving Ramm the impetus he was seeking to walk out of the fundamentalist fortress he had been encamped in and engage in a thoughtful dialogue with the modern critical tools of biblical scholarship. It is evident that Ramm saw in Barth a theologian who presented the most satisfactory approach that enabled Ramm's knowledge of science and faith to not only

---

30. Ibid., 31.

31. Vanhoozer, *Bernard Ramm*, 291.

32. It is important to note Ramm's thinking changed in time, through stages, as a result of thorough investigation and reflection. Pinnock has observed that Ramm was a theologian who was willing to change. He was "(d)ynamic and flexible in his thinking, he embodied the maxim: To live is to change, and to be perfect is to change often." Pinnock, *Bernard Ramm*, 17.

33. Ramm, *Helps From Karl Barth*, 121.

co-exist, but constructively contribute to each other. Indeed, Vanhoozer noted: "In a flash of insight, Ramm took this exhortation to heart and grasped its implications. It helped liberate him from the fortress mentality of fundamentalism, which continued doggedly to resist the siege of modern learning."[34]

Indeed, Ramm described the fundamentalist form of Christianity as "very defensive, suspicious, and protective." It was not the kind of theology accustomed to opening doors or windows. Quite the contrary, it constructed small forts with "very high walls."[35] Consequently, Ramm's new way required a reconstruction of his foundations and the establishment of a viable approach that served his new agenda. Referring to his work prior to 1957 as "futile and intellectually bankrupt," Ramm's study into approaches to theology became a major effort in his next stage of theological writing. Here one must speak of what must be termed a significant turn in Ramm's theological development, occurring some time after 1957.

The second material change in Ramm's understanding resulted from Barth's great respect for historical theology. "Ramm contrasted this with his earlier pietistic attitude (another holdover from fundamentalism), which tended to rely on the individual's present experience of the Holy Spirit rather than the Spirit's guidance of saints past."[36] Clearly, this orientation was a significant element in Ramm's initial attraction to Barth's theology.[37] It is contended here that Ramm sought the influence of Barth's high regard for historical theology because it provided him with sources that would, firstly, enable his approach to theology to be free of the naivety of fundamentalism, and, secondly, was representative of his desire to be identified with the biblical and historical sources used by the Reformers. Clearly, as Ramm continued to identify closely with Luther and Calvin he was able to maintain his identity as an evangelical.

The third material change in Ramm's thinking resulted from Barth's Christologically orientated theology of biblical inspiration and authority.[38] Clearly, since Christ was the revealed Word of God and Scripture an authoritative witness to him, then the historical teachings of the Church

34. Vanhoozer, *Bernard Ramm*, 291.

35. Ramm, *Helps From Karl Barth*.

36. Vanhoozer, *Bernard Ramm*, 292.

37. Mohler, *Bernard Ramm*, 31.

38. Vanhoozer, *Bernard Ramm*, 304.

could be opened up to a critical approach to Scripture. It is contended here that neo-orthodoxy was appealing to Ramm for this important reason.[39] Further, it is asserted that the Enlightenment had become for Ramm the central challenge that evangelicalism had to face. He believed that if evangelicalism was not to remain bound to obscurantism it had to form an intelligent dialogue with the issues arising from modernity.[40] Therefore, one must contend that Ramm believed Barth to have provided a paradigm by which orthodox theology might be written in a modernist world; the very task that Barth had undertaken. The fruit of Ramm's endeavor was the publication of his landmark *After Fundamentalism*.

AFTER FUNDAMENTALISM

As Philip Thorne has stated, the reception of Karl Barth by the American evangelical community received unprecedented attention following Ramm's publication of *After Fundamentalism* in 1983. Thorne commented that "(a)lthough it merely brought to the surface a process that had been occurring for some time, the proposal of Barth as a primary paradigm for the future of Evangelical Theology had never received such programmatic articulation."[41] Mohler observed that during this period of constructive and thoughtful dialogue with Barth "Ramm emerged as an important interpreter of Barth to the evangelical community [. . .] Barth, he suggested, was the great destroyer of the house of liberalism (whose) avalanche destroyed the notion that liberalism and static fundamentalism were the only two theological alternatives [. . .] Barth, Ramm argued, was a model of the greatest of theology."[42] Indeed, Ramm saw in Barth a constructive theologian who represented a true orthodoxy that had the possibility of steering clear of both the dangers of liberalism and the perils of rigid conservatism, which he believed had proved more dangerous than the older tradition.[43]

---

39. He found it to result in the necessary combination of the historic faith of the church and the advancement of the Enlightenment. Mohler, *Bernard Ramm*, 32.

40. Ibid., 36.

41. Thorne, *Evangelicalism and Karl Barth*, 123.

42 Mohler, *Bernard Ramm*, 34.

43. Ibid., 35.

By the time Ramm had published a number of articles evaluating Barth's possible contribution to evangelicalism's future directions,[44] he was no longer a leader among fundamentalists. Ramm's change in direction, and alternative agenda for evangelicalism, had taken him on a path that had left fundamentalism behind. This new path created tensions with the institutions that represented the very theology Ramm sought to abandon. Pinnock observed that as a consequence of this turn in direction "Ramm was forced to leave the Simpson College campus in Modesto, California, in the mid-seventies because of pressures from biblical inerrantists. [Furthermore] Trinity Evangelical Divinity School declined to hire him when they had the opportunity."[45] Positively, through these exclusions, Ramm was spared the fate of others, such as Bela Vassady and Edward Carnell, who had both suffered personally from fundamentalist criticism and rejection. In order to avoid these dilemmas Ramm wisely chose to work with relative ease in the more pluralistic context of the American Baptist Convention.[46]

Preaching and Method

In *After Fundamentalism*, Ramm began with Barth's theology of preaching. He believed he needed to do this for two reasons. The first arose out of Barth's own experience as a preacher which led him to a crisis realization that his theology needed to take a new direction. The second was that Barth's theology of preaching was easier to understand, and therefore a natural place to begin.[47] Indeed, Barth's approach to sermon preparation provided a valuable introduction to the basis of his overall theological approach. In starting with Barth's preaching Ramm presented the Basel theologian as a true evangelical, since he stood clearly in the tradition of the Reformers, but also a theologian concerned with how theology is done.[48] Ramm's agenda challenged how evangelicals approached their theology. He had come to the conclusion that when evangelicals consider

44. Including "An appraisal of Karl Barth," 36–38; "Europe God and Karl Barth," 10; "An Evaluation of Karl Barth," 8–11; "Karl Barth: The Theological Avalanche," 4–5, 48. "The Major Theses of Neo-orthodoxy," 18–19, 33.

45. Pinnock, *Bernard Ramm*, 16.

46. Ibid.

47. Ramm, *After Fundamentalism*, 50.

48. Thurneysen is used as a guide by Ramm to describe Barth's method of sermon preparation. Ibid., 52.

the means by which theology is approached a greater interest would develop in the new direction he had taken. Ramm sought to convince evangelicals of the benefits of his new approach by presenting to them, in a positive light, the theological approach of Karl Barth. Instructive was how Ramm assessed Barth's sermon preparation. During his preparation he would lay out before him on his desk the commentaries of the Reformers, the Biblicists of the following century, and modern critical commentaries. In this endeavor Ramm recalled Barth's "passion was to find the Word of God in the text before him, for that Word is the necessary basis of the sermon." Indeed, Ramm reminded the reader of Barth's contention that "preaching was itself a form of the Word of God."[49] This manner of sermon preparation obviously had an appeal to Ramm and it would have recommended itself to the evangelical readers he sought to engage and challenge. However, it was Barth's approach to Scripture that became central to Ramm's new evangelicalism.

The Nature of the Word of God

In his discussion of Barth's theology of the Word of God, Ramm specifically spoke to the concerns of fundamentalist evangelicals, since his first area of discussion concerned the inerrancy debate. It is evident that Ramm sought to inform this audience of his own theological maturation since this was one of the issues, arising from his background, that he was personally led to grapple with. In 1950 Ramm reflected a fundamentalist perspective when he wrote that infallibility and inerrancy were synonymous, meaning that the Bible could not teach any "sort of error."[50] However, in Ramm's later theology he rejected any definition of infallibility that made it synonymous with inerrancy (incapable of any sort of mistake). His mature understanding of infallibility was defined as the "absolute reliability in the intention of the person or document."[51] Here one clearly sees the influence of Barth on Ramm's later thinking. Indeed, Ramm observed that Barth pushed.the infallible point of reference back

49. Ibid. Following Luther, Barth contended that "if human language claims to be proclamation that can only mean that it claims to serve the Word of God, to point to its having previously been spoken through God Himself. That it is God's Word, that God sanctifies the human pointer to bear witness to Himself." Barth, *Church Dogmatics: 1/1*, 57.

50. Miller, *Theological System of Bernard L. Ramm*, 52.

51. Ibid., 53.

one stage to God himself. Ramm clearly saw this to be a preferable option as he concurred with Barth that the "primal meaning of the Word of
God is God in his self-disclosure; God in his act of revelation, which is
(as it originates in God) infallible, inerrant, and indefectible."[52] This new
assumption led Ramm to understand the written Word of Scripture in a
totally new way.

The contention that the words of the Bible constitute the very words
of God to the reader was challenged by Ramm on a number of fronts.
His agenda is clearly evident as he recalled Barth's assertion that the fundamentalist's view of Scripture is one that had arisen in reaction to the
Enlightenment, rather than anything inherent in Scripture itself. In his
1959 publication, *The Witness of The Spirit*, Ramm lamented the developments within "Protestant scholasticism" which he believed had become
enslaved to narrow dogmatism and formalization, leaving "the Church
saddled with a dead book whose truth is frozen in ancient thought categories which must be callously imposed upon modern man."[53] Undoubtedly
Ramm saw this as an unnecessary restriction imposed by a philosophy of
rationalistic propositionalism designed to counter the Enlightenment, but
ironically being a product of it. Ramm noted that Barth also contended
that evangelical theory often reduced the Word of God to a book, which
anyone can carry around in his or her pocket.[54]

In an article entitled *The Continual Divide in Contemporary Theology*,
Ramm was clearly influenced by Barth when he stated, quite unequivocally, that he believed revelation to be a dynamic event and existential,
rather than static and intellectual. Scripture is "God's personal presence,
not a piece of writing; holy history, not holy writings."[55] Referring directly
to Barth, Ramm concluded that the dry, flat rationalistic and intellectualist
view of revelation has resulted in the Word losing its spiritual dimension.[56]
This very much gets to the heart of what he believed to be the purpose
of Scripture. For example, he claimed that the Gospels "are not scientific,

52. Ibid., 90. Barth consistently claimed that "Jesus Christ is God's revelation." Indeed,
Barth proclaimed that the "answer of the New Testament to our question about the reality of God's revelation is to be found in the constant reiteration in all its pages of the
name Jesus Christ." Barth, *CD I/2*, 1, 10.

53. Ramm, *Witness of the Spirit*, 129.

54. Ibid., 129.

55. Ramm, "The Continental Divide in Contemporary Theology," 15.

56. Ibid., 15.

notarial lives of Christ; they are witnessing, kerygmatic documents whose purpose is not to satisfy exacting canons of modern scientific historiography but to summon to faith in Jesus Christ."[57] The influence of Barth is very evident here. Indeed, Barth, in his *Church Dogmatics*, pointed out that the authority of Scripture is in fact derived from the triune God, "who in His revelation is the object and as such the source of Holy Scripture."[58] Furthermore, Barth's theology of The Word of God taught that a form of the Word of God preceded both proclamation and written Scripture. Barth stated: "It is because God has revealed Himself that there is a Word of God, and therefore Holy Scripture and proclamation as the Word of God [...] For the Bible is a sign [...] which does at least point to a superior authority."[59] However the fundamentalist is concerned with the inerrancy of the *written* Word, and this has to be, in light of Barth's reflections, totally untenable.

The Humanity of the Word

In response to fundamentalism's concern for the inerrant written Word, Ramm discussed the nature of language. In this argument one observes the influence of science, and subsequent concern for the issues of modernity interacting with Ramm's orthodox convictions. In *After Fundamentalism* he began his debate by asserting that no human language can be a perfect mirror reflecting the Word of God. The Bible is a human book and as such it carries with it the specific peculiarities of the ancient Hebrew and Greek languages.[60] Indeed Barth, in his *Church Dogmatics*, discussed the limitation of the written word of Scripture. The Bible, claimed Barth, is a witness to the revelation of God and therefore is not itself the revelation. Indeed, Barth concluded: "(W)hen we have to do with the Bible, with the witness which as such is not itself revelation, but only—and this is the limitation—the witness to it."[61]

Ramm further drew from Barth as a source for his argument when he asserted that to state that there is such a thing as a perfect language is to fall into the trap of Hegelian philosophy. It is evident that Ramm's

57. Ramm, "Biblical faith and History," 524.

58. Barth, *CD I/2*, 539.

59. Ibid., 457.

60. Ramm, *After Fundamentalism*, 102.

61. Barth, *CD I/2*, 463.

resolution of his theological and scientific knowledge is well expressed in his claim that it was Barth who noted that "the Hegelians presumed there was a pure conceptual language that would be the language of truth."[62] Ramm also observed with amazement that this is exactly what many evangelicals did when they advanced the case for propositional revelation. Consequently, he proposed that this was nothing else than an alternate version of "the Hegelian theory of pure conceptual language."[63] Ramm's conclusion was that Barth surely had the linguists on his side when he argued that no such perfection in language can possibly be achieved, and is certainly justified in his criticisms of biblical orthodoxy's inability to come to terms with an adequate understanding of language. Indeed, Ramm believed that fundamentalist views on inspiration "run contrary to the science of linguistics."[64] As he wrote in his earlier work, *The Pattern of Authority* the voice of humanity cannot be substituted for the voice of God. Indeed, humanity cannot speak for God.[65] Therefore in regard to the humanity of the Word of God Ramm was in agreement with Barth that "Holy Scripture is totally a human book."[66] Indeed, the true and actual revelation of God is not trapped within the pages of a book, but can only be found in "the Triune God in self-revelation."[67] Therefore, Scripture is a human historical record and is to be described as only a witness.[68] To support his thesis Ramm referred to Barth's discussion of the creation account as being "of the earth" and therefore having all the marks of the earth. "It is a letter, a document, like all other letters, and does not have some magical property making it different from others."[69] Consequently, as a human letter, it is a letter with errors.

In his *Handbook of Contemporary Theology*, Ramm dealt with the topic of error in Scripture under the heading of the "Brokenness of Revelation." He presented his argument in open dialogue with Barth in

---

62. Ramm, *After Fundamentalism*, 90.

63. Ibid., 90.

64. Ibid., 102.

65. Ramm, *Pattern of Religious Authority*, 25.

66. Ramm, *After Fundamentalism*, 102.

67. Ramm, *Pattern of Authority*, 21.

68. Barth, *CD* I/2, 541.

69. Later, in dealing with the error one finds in Scripture Ramm recalls Barth's reference to the poor grammar found in the Book of Revelation. Ramm, *After Fundamentalism*, 102.

his declaration that the brokenness of revelation means that revelation can never be received in any kind of pure form, since the human element in Scripture is always present. Ramm recalled that "Barth speaks of the light of revelation striking man as light strikes a prism. No matter how deeply or profoundly or existentially man receives the Word of God he receives it in human act."[70] The consequence for Ramm was that the reception of the Word of God is always fallible. While the thought of an error may alarm the fundamentalist evangelical, since it supposedly negates the authority of God, Ramm had no such concern. Indeed, he alluded to Barth as his source, who asked why God would be ashamed of errors in the Scriptures. Why would he be? Is not the humanity of Scripture significantly related to the humanity of Christ? Indeed, Barth encouraged a thorough consideration of the virtues of the humanity of Scripture since the humanity of Christ is thoroughly studied without any difficulty. In his *Church Dogmatics* Barth asserted that one "must study it, for it is here or nowhere that we shall find its divinity."[71] Similarly, Ramm contended along with Barth that "(o)ne must affirm that the Son of God took actual sinful humanity in the incarnation and also that the Scriptures are vulnerable to error."[72]

Ramm also dealt with the critics of Barth who asked how, given these assertions, the truth can be discerned from error. Barth's answer to this, claimed Ramm, was in the interpreter's task of thoroughly exegeting the text. "When the interpreter has done a thorough, exacting task of examining the text, consulting all the commentaries and other specialized books, the text will stand before him or her exactly for what it is."[73] Ramm therefore asked the evangelical why he or she, while admitting to the humanity of Scripture, as one must do, did not go to the bottom of the argument as Barth clearly did. Ramm claimed that at least Barth wished "to make no half-hearted affirmation of the humanity of Scripture that is undermined by an overpowering affirmation of its divinity."[74]

Given that Scripture is a human document Ramm also agreed with Barth that there therefore exists a diastasis, or interval, between revelation

70. Ramm, *A Handbook of Contemporary Theology*, 109.

71. Barth, *CD I/2*, 463.

72. Ramm, *After Fundamentalism*, 104.

73. Ibid., 105.

74. Ibid., 103.

and The Bible. Barth seriously considered the implications of the humanity of the text which must be taken into account when interpretation of the biblical material takes place. Ramm restated Barth's warning that to bypass this observation may result in a misunderstanding of the text. The humanity of any biblical text implies that the author's culture, and corresponding world-view, is to be found in what has been written.[75] Barth, therefore, warned the interpreter to be careful lest he or she "convert something of passing culture into the very Word of God itself."[76] The Swiss theologian contended that with a thorough examination of the text by every means possible- philological and historical criticism, contextual relationships, and every device of conjectural imagination, the meaning of the text can be sought. Indeed, claimed Ramm, evangelicals have distorted the meaning of a number of texts by avoiding this necessary precaution. He referred to Ephesians 2:2 as being a good example. In this verse Satan is called "the prince of the power of the air." In Jewish thought the air or atmosphere was thought to be that space that intervenes between the earth and God's throne. Yet in Ramm's observation fundamentalists, in their unimaginative literalism, have used this verse to criticize radio and television since they broadcast over "the airwaves."[77] However, despite the need intelligently to bridge the interval, Ramm reminded us of Barth's assertion that the texts of Holy Scripture have authority.

The Divinity and Authority of the Word

In order to diffuse any unwarranted criticism, Ramm was keen to restate Barth's contention that language, while possessing these limitations, is none the less adequate for the purpose of revelation in so far as it contains those qualities that make it possible for Scripture to be a witness to revelation. Scripture does not contain magical language out of which God speaks.[78] However it does have authority for the very reason that it provides an authoritative account of the revelation that has already taken place. Furthermore, Ramm contended that as a witness to revelation

75. "For example, the Scriptures use ancient measuring systems—for dry measurement, liquid measurement, distances, and weight. The marriages and burial customs were customs of the times. The relationships within the families were those of the prevailing cultures." Ibid., 102.

76. Ibid., 92.

77. Ramm, *After Fundamentalism*, 91.

78. Ibid., 124.

Holy Scripture has always been authoritative, in that it has always been adequate in its function "to bring people to a saving knowledge of Jesus Christ."[79] Therefore, according to Ramm, Barth did not have a low view of Scripture, as some evangelicals alleged, since he understood a witness to be one among "the most select of all human beings,"[80] and therefore authoritative. According to Ramm, Barth attested to an authoritative Scripture that carries with it the "divine authority of God in this world and in the church."[81]

Indeed, Barth in his *Church Dogmatics* believed that the Scriptures are to be singled out and "appointed to a role and dignity peculiar to themselves alone."[82] They were penned by prophets and apostles who stood in close proximity (pseudo-presence) to the revelation itself.[83] Furthermore Scripture is a spiritual Word that is to be heard and appropriated by spiritual means, by the work of the Holy Spirit and therefore in faith as an encounter or event. Ramm pointed out that some evangelicals misunderstood Barth's theology to be a novel and subjective view of Scripture. Ramm responded by defending Barth who resolutely stood within the traditions of Luther and Calvin. Indeed, Barth's notion of the Word of God very much stood in the tradition of Luther's theology of the "spiritual clarity of the Word" and Calvin's "witness of the Spirit."[84] It was Ramm's contention, therefore, that as Barth promulgated his theology of the Word of God he was in fact reviving something of the theology of the Reformation. Along with this view of the role of the written word in revelation, Ramm agreed with Barth that the written word has an objective authority.[85]

In Ramm's Barthian theology of the Word, the written word of Scripture is objective in that it leads the reader to God's revelation because it bears witness to it. Furthermore Ramm found, in a personal interview with Barth (July 11, 1958), that the Basel theologian did in fact hold that the revelation of God was still to be found in the written Word.

79. Ibid., 91.
80. Ibid., 95.
81. Ibid., 96.
82. Barth, *CD I/2*, 495.
83. Ramm, *After Fundamentalism*.
84. Ibid., 96.
85. Ibid., 118.

As Ramm compared this comment with the *Church Dogmatics* he came to the conclusion that it is wrong to persist in affirming "that Barth's doctrine of inspiration is totally subjective and that he denies propositional revelation."[86] Indeed, Barth's theology of the Word testified that God is one who reveals himself to humanity. Scripture bears witness to a Word that comes from above and so is an authority free from subjectivism. As Ramm expressed it in *The Pattern of Religious Authority*, "the final authority in religion is God Himself . . . There is only one authority—God; and only one truth—divine revelation."[87] Clearly, therefore, Ramm did not challenge the evangelical doctrine of inspiration, but rather evangelicalism's approach that confined God's revelation to a book.

Certainly, Ramm chided the fundamentalist for creating a theology of verbal inspiration and inerrancy that has only arisen to serve their fanatic bid for religious certainty. Alternatively, Ramm establish a doctrine of revelation based on a passion for truth.[88] Indeed, he praised Barth for his renewal of that aspect of Reformational theology that sought to promote the spirituality of the Word of God as that which is encountered in faith, trust, obedience, prayer, and meditation. Therefore, Scripture is not a legal document but the living Word of God that comes alive in the believing heart[89] and is received by faith[90] through the work of the Holy Spirit.[91] Ramm was careful to point out that this view of Scripture is not new. It is found in Augustine's doctrine of illumination,[92] and from Calvin, who taught that "obedience is the beginning of all true knowledge of God. The Word of God is known as the Word of God only in obedience, not in apologetics."[93] In relation to the authority of God's revelation

86. Ibid., 119.

87. Ramm, *Pattern of Authority*, 21.

88. Ramm, *Continental Divide*, 15.

89. Ramm, *After Fundamentalism*, 120.

90. Ramm, *Pattern of Authority*, 20.

91. Taken from Ramm's comment: "Barth, speaking of the credibility of the creation account where of course no observers of creation were, says that this witness of creation 'is received and accepted through the power of the Holy Spirit' (Church Dogmatics 3/1, 82)" Ramm, *Biblical faith and History*, 534. Indeed, Barth clearly relates the authority of Scripture with the work of the Holy Spirit when he declares: "According to Holy Scripture God's revelation occurs in our enlightenment by the Holy Spirit of God to a knowledge of His Word." Barth *CD I/2*, 203.

92. See also Ramm, *Pattern of Authority*, 20.

93. Ramm, *After Fundamentalism*, 121.

the conclusion must be that God's authority is not restricted to the written Word.[94] This lead Ramm carefully to consider Barth's proposal that God has ultimately revealed himself in Jesus Christ.

REVELATION AND CHRISTOLOGY

George Hunsinger, in his *How to Read Karl Barth*, referred to what he described as the root metaphor of Barth's *Church Dogmatics*. Hunsinger stated that it is "a metaphor which is constantly employed to bring out the centrality of Jesus Christ," who is understood to be the central content of the Scriptural witness. "The one thing said in the midst of everything, the centre which organizes the whole, is 'Just this: the name of Jesus Christ' (*CD I/2,*720)."[95] According to Hunsinger this meant for Barth the necessity to read the Bible Christocentrically,[96] since Christ is the one alive at the centre of the Scriptural witness.[97] Basic to Barth's theological approach, therefore, was the assertion that the object of theological reflection must never be the self, but the Jesus Christ of Scripture who lies beyond and independent of personal experience and who, as the essence and existence of the loving kindness of God toward sinful humanity, saves those who are lost (*CD I/2* 443).[98] Indeed, in his early publication *The Pattern of Authority*, Ramm demonstrated that God's self-revelation is not restricted to words but does in fact generally precede words.[99] This Barthian perspective is reflected in Ramm's "chain of authority." The beginning of this chain is the authority of Christ.[100]

94. Ramm, *Pattern of Authority*, 24.

95. Hunsinger, *How to Read Karl Barth*, 59. In this section of the Dogmatics Barth further relates Christology to revelation as he states that the "Bible becomes clear when it is clear that it says this one thing: that it proclaims the name Jesus Christ and therefore proclaims God." Barth, *CD I/2,* 720.

96. Ibid., 107.

97. Ibid., 108.

98. Ibid., 122.

99. To illustrate this point Ramm alludes to the understanding of a period in sacred history during which there was no written authority—from Adam to Moses. Furthermore, there was a period in the early years of the Church when "Christianity existed only as the remembered Word and Person in the minds of the Apostles." Ramm, *Pattern of Authority*, 24.

100. Following the authority of Christ Ramm refers to the authority of the Spirit, who was delegated by God to speak about Christ to the Apostles, who in turn wrote Scripture. Following the Spirit's work comes the ministry of the apostles, and from the apostles

To further this claim, Ramm pointed out that there are many examples in sacred history when no written authority existed- from Adam to Moses, in the days of Abraham and in the period of the Apostles. Indeed, "(o)ur Lord taught with authority before a Word of His was written."[101] Consequently Ramm believed that he could assert with Barth that God's ultimate revelation, to which the written Word bears witness, is found in Jesus Christ. While not being an idea that originated with Barth, Ramm's assertion was that it is Barth who applied this thesis with ruthless consistency.[102] Therefore Ramm, having been influenced by Barth, asserted in his own theological writing that "Christ is the supreme object of the witness of the Spirit, and Christ is the supreme content of the Scriptures [...] The supreme revelation of God is Jesus Christ."[103]

RAMM'S HISTORIC CHRISTOLOGY AFTER THE PATTERN OF KARL BARTH

As well as an appreciation for Barth's Christology Ramm also saw the importance of Barth's historical approach. Bruce McCormack observed that this was a point taken up by some of Barth's critics. His reviewers noticed the prominence given to the medieval scholasticism of Anselm of Canterbury and the role played by seventeenth-century Reformed scholasticism.[104] Indeed, Barth came to consider the importance of the Church's confessions to the construction of an authoritative theology. McCormack has observed that in an address to the World Alliance of Reformed Churches in Emden on September 17, 1923, Barth took his first tentative step "beyond commitment to the Scripture-principle to the thought that the confessions too can bear an appropriate authority."

Scripture. "Scripture is the delegated authority used by the Spirit as a witness to Christ throughout the history of the church." Finally, Ramm refers to the authority of the history of theology. Ramm's point here is that "the Reformers' respect for the history of theology saved them from becoming sectarian and it preserved a sense of continuity between the generations of the church." Miller, *The Theological System of Bernard L. Ramm*, 65–66.

101. Ramm, *Pattern of Authority*.

102. Ramm alludes to earlier examples in Augustine, Luther, and Calvin. Ramm, *After Fundamentalism*, 127.

103. Ibid, 37. Also mentioned by Ramm in *Witness of the Spirit*, 130.

104. "The Perception was widespread among liberals that Barth was a theological reactionary who wanted to overthrow the fruits of scientific theology acquired since the 1780s . . . in order to return to the theology of a former age." McCormack, *Karl Barth's Critically Realistic Dialectical Theology*, 25.

Despite assertions that the confessions were human and subjective, and did not contain the same kind of authority on which the Church was grounded, that is Scripture, Barth acknowledged that the confessions possessed a relative authority.[105]

Undoubtedly Barth's high respect for church confessions came out of his historical approach to theology. Thomas Torrance commented that Barth had a consuming interest in history. Indeed, in Torrance's opinion, the "context of Barth's thought and the influence upon him can be measured only by measuring the whole history of Christian theology."[106] The Scottish theologian supported this thesis by pointing to Barth's *Church Dogmatics*, which carries on a discussion with, and embodies comprehensively, the whole history of dogma.[107] These two important elements of Barth's approach, of Christology and historicity, are evident in Ramm's two final theological works.

In 1985, after writing his manifesto regarding the possibilities of an evangelical theology after the pattern of Barth, Bernard Ramm published two other books: *Offense to Reason: The Theology of Sin* and *An Evangelical Christology: Ecumenic and Historic*. Clearly these works represent Ramm's mature position that arose after the impact of Barth had fully developed in his thinking.[108] In *An Evangelical Christology* Ramm appeared to construct his work on the basis of Barth's approach as guided by history and Christology, which he described as historic Christology. The first indication of this is seen in the introduction where he begins by stating that historic (or ecumenic) Christology is the true Christology of the church as believed by the Greek, Latin, and evangelical Protestant churches.[109] From this statement Ramm goes on to quote eleven historic confessions of faith, starting with the Apostles Creed and ending with an excerpt from the documents of Vatican II.[110] Ramm sought to present an approach to theology that is reformational in character, and distinct from the arid Biblicism present in fundamentalism. He did so by advocating an evangelicalism that remembers its roots in the historical approach of

---

105. Ibid., 318.

106. Torrance, *Karl Barth*, 29.

107. Ibid., 30.

108. Thorne, *Evangelicalism and Karl Barth*, 132.

109. Ramm, *An Evangelical Christology* 9.

110. Ibid., 9–14.

the Reformers. Ramm saw this in contrast to the fundamentalist's belief that the main tenants of Protestant Orthodoxy are self evident in a plain reading of the text.

Ramm's Christocentric approach, based on historic Christianity, is found in the first chapter of *An Evangelical Christology*, with the instructive title, *Christology at the Center*. Initially, the influence of Barth in the detail of Ramm's theological structure is seen in Ramm's echo of Barth's criticism of Schleiermacher. Ramm was clearly influenced by Barth in his view that Schleiermacher posed a serious threat to historic Christology. Ramm then followed Barth in promoting a Christian theology founded on and centralized in Christology, since to alter Christology resulted in the alteration of all other theologies.[111] To assist him in his argument Ramm employed the help of one of Barth's theological allies, Dietrich Bonhoeffer, who stated that to abandon historic Christology is to abandon the historic doctrine of the church. Indeed, Ramm held Barth in such high esteem that not only is his approach applauded, but also his whole contribution to theology as a great figure within the history of the church. In Ramm's discussion Barth is depicted as standing in the great tradition of Luther, Bonhoeffer, and Thielicke.[112] Certainly, in Ramm's reflections on the incarnation, Barth is seen as the one who best summarized the argument.[113] Ramm's conclusion, in the light of Barth's opinion, was that "after the incarnation the only real, significant, and saving knowledge of God is in Jesus Christ as God the Son incarnate."[114] Indeed, while an historical approach was seen as essential, Christology clearly dominated Ramm's mature theology.

In Ramm's theology Barth also appeared to lead the discussion connecting the theology of the incarnation with the virgin birth.[115] In a positive appraisal of Barth's theology, Ramm restated Barth's explanation of

111. Ibid., 16.

112. While it is true to say that these three theologians were Lutheran and Barth was Reformed, it is correct to assert that Barth's significance and stature as a theologian of significance is to be compared with them.

113. Barth, *Church Dogmatics: III/3*, 504f.

114. Ibid., 54.

115. Barth stated that it is God "who makes His Son hers, and in that way shares with humanity in her person nothing less than His own existence. He gives to her what she could not procure for herself and no other creature could procure for her. This is the miracle of the Virgin Birth as it indicates the mystery of the incarnation." Barth, *Church Dogmatics: IV/1*, 207.

the paradoxical status of the virgin birth. Barth asked why it was that the virgin birth, given such slight attention in the New Testament, came to occupy the attention of so many theologians throughout the history of the church. Barth's answer, claimed Ramm, was that "the church saw in such a small window an unexpected great witness to the incarnation."[116] Consequently, on the basis of an historical approach, Ramm echoed Barth's assertion that the virgin birth be connected theologically with the incarnation.[117] Ramm also followed Barth's thesis that "the virgin birth of Christ is a word about divine grace and human helplessness. The exclusion of the Father in the virgin birth is a sign of the exclusion of all human effort in salvation."[118] Barth's influence in Ramm's theology is seen as he expanded this argument with the support of the Barthian theologian Otto Weber. According to Ramm Weber also "centers the meaning of the virgin birth in the doctrine of the incarnation." Without doubt, Weber appeared to concur with Barth that the birth narrative exists as a profound theological witness.[119] The influence of Barth in Ramm's Christology is also seen in his coverage of Christ's bodily resurrection.

Ramm dealt with the doctrine of Christ's bodily resurrection by comparing two theologies. He firstly, and briefly, discussed the conservative evangelical opinion before making a direct comparison with a lengthier discussion of Barth's theology. Barth's agenda is clearly preferred to the conservative opinion which is described as simplistic and shallow. Indeed, Ramm depicted it as rationalist, "hard line," and unable to seriously engage with "sophisticated interpretations of the resurrection."[120] It was orthodoxy warped and distorted by the rationalism of the Enlightenment. Ramm compared this with the much-preferred second group, which "focuses on the uniqueness of the resurrection."[121] This alternate opinion viewed the

---

116. Ibid., 68.

117. Ramm adds: "To sustain this position Barth works out a theory of bracketing. Unless the life of Christ is bracketed at the beginning and at the end we would never be sure of the incarnation . . . The bracket at the beginning of the life of Christ is the virgin birth; and at the end of the life of Christ there is the bracket of the resurrection." Ibid., 69.

118. Ibid., 69.

119. Ibid., 69. Ramm also agrees with Barth that both the "anhypostatic" and "enhypostatic" concepts of the union of the two natures of Christ should be retained. See Miller, *Theological System of Bernard L. Ramm*, 78.

120. Ramm, *An Evangelical Christology*, 96.

121. Ibid., 96.

resurrection as so unique that it escapes ordinary historical reporting and therefore "cannot be set out as if it were an event like any other event in history."[122] Ramm stated that it was a unique event, unlike the facts associated with an ordinary historical event, in which the eschatological has "dipped into the ordinary course of history."[123] This second opinion, therefore, was distinct from the conservative evangelical view which was seen by Ramm, in the light of this argument, as thoroughly temporal, ordinary and quite unintentionally imprisoned within the limits of its own rationalist approach. It is contended here that this "second group" arose out of the theology of Karl Barth. It is believed that Ramm, in his *Beyond Fundamentalism*, quite clearly made it his objective to be guided by Barth toward a new kind of evangelical theology that is established in historical confessionalism, yet engaged with modernity. Here in *An Evangelical Christology* one finds the fruits of that quest.

In relation to this obviously preferred "second group" of thinkers Ramm declared that "Barth has been (its) most sustained defender." As was the case in *After Fundamentalism*, Ramm again dismantled misinformation regarding Barth's theology. In this instance it is a caricature of Barth in which he is depicted as believing that there "was a special space and time in which theological miracles take place." However, Ramm pointed out, in reference to Barth's own dealings with the topic, that there was "no such theological arena." Quoting a pamphlet of Barth's from 1945, Ramm outlined a theology that refuted any suggestion that Christ's resurrection was a myth, and clearly supported the belief in a resurrection that was an historical event. Indeed, the "resurrection is about an empty tomb and about the person of Jesus who was bodily (*leiblich*), visibly (*sichtbar*), audibly (*hörbar*), and tactily (*bestastbar*) manifested to his disciples."[124] Barth's point, claimed Ramm, was that God can never be a character in any book of history. According to its own criteria scientific historiography cannot read of the resurrection of Christ and understand it factually. Therefore, the resurrection cannot be ascribed to pure history. Barth would have us call it a saga. He claimed that the "resurrection is a saga in the sense that it actually, literally, and bodily took place; but because it took place by the initiative of God, historians cannot report it as

122. Ibid.

123. Ibid.

124. Ibid.

an historical event."[125] In comparing the two, Ramm clearly favored Barth on the basis of his superior approach. Ramm consequently asserted that "(h)istoric Christology can go with either view, although we think Barth's case is the best of the options because he has most thoroughly understood the nature of the historical issue."[126] In regard to the critical reading of Scripture Barth is also seen to have influenced Ramm's theology.

BARTH'S CRITICAL REALISM

Clearly Ramm was concerned to move beyond the impossibilities of fundamentalist hermeneutics and embrace a reading of Scripture that upheld historic Christianity and engaged with the critical issues emerging from modernity. Under the heading of *Christianity and Criticism*, Ramm discussed the reading of Scripture as a believing theologian. In doing so, the influence of Barth on his thinking is seen as he clearly upheld Barth's theory of critical realism.

Bruce McCormack argued that Barth developed an understanding of theology based on a theory of critical realism. In contrast to the subjectively based theologies associated with his theological education, during a major turning point while at Safenwil, Barth began to regard God as a Reality "which is complete and whole in itself apart from and prior to the knowing activity of human individuals."[127] This critical distinction between God and the world found expression during a lecture given in Basel, Switzerland, on the fifteenth of November 1915, in which he stated: "World remains world. But God is God."[128] However, while being realistic, Barth's new theology was also critical. He did not want to lose sight of the need to engage with modernity.[129] With Barth as his guide Ramm thoughtfully engaged with the issues of critical scholarship, while uphold-

125. Ibid.

126. Ibid. Barth's belief in the resurrection of Christ is evident in his comment that the "function of the empty tomb . . . is to show that he the Jesus who died and was buried was delivered from death, and therefore from the grave, by the power of God; that He, the Living, is not to be sought among he dead." Barth, *Church Dogmatics: III/2*, 453.

127. McCormack, *Karl Barth's Realistic Dialectical Theology*, 129.

128. McCormack observes that it is clear from this statement that Barth is now engaged in a self-conscious effort to distance himself from idealistic theology and religion. Ibid.

129. "In no way did Barth's realism represent a return to naive, metaphysically grounded, realism of classical medieval and post-Reformational theology," ibid., 130.

ing the authoritative vitality of Scripture as the Word of God. He initially did this by reviewing Barth's dialogue with Adolph von Harnack in the pages of the German journal, *Christliche Welt (The Christian World)*. In describing the nature of Barth's dialogue, Ramm outlined his own theological assertions. Von Harnack believed that there "was no limit to the application of scientific interpretation to Scripture."[130] However, while Barth had no quarrel with a critical reading of Scripture he strenuously maintained that as a theologian studies Scripture there will at some point "be a confrontation with the Word of God in Scripture."[131] Ramm echoed the sentiments of Barth, who "could not imagine any serious view of the Word of God in which the interpreter would ultimately remain a critic of the Scripture."[132] Ramm also recalled Barth's agreement with Bultmann's proposition that Scripture should be interpreted like any other book from classical antiquity, believing in a reading of the New Testament that was both scientific and critical.[133] However Barth insisted, as he had in response to von Harnack,[134] that as one interpreted Scripture in this kind of ordinary way one would encounter the extraordinary Word of God. Ramm's conclusion was that Barth, writing in the tradition of Luther and Calvin, upheld the belief that Jesus Christ meets with humanity in the garments of the Gospel. Any critical approach to Scripture must be seen in this light.[135]

CONCLUSION

While the early religious influence upon Bernard Ramm came from evangelical fundamentalism, it would seem that the accompanying influence of science created a tension within Ramm's thinking that he needed to resolve. It has been shown that the consequence of this tension, and subsequent agenda for resolution, resulted in a decisive break with his early theological formation. Clearly, Ramm felt compelled to do this in order to place his theology on the foundations of a new and clear agenda. Its aim was to provide a satisfactory means of resolving the tensions between

130. Ramm, *An Evangelical Christology*, 132.

131. Ibid., 132.

132. Ibid.

133. Ibid., 161.

134. Barth saw this debate as a return of his famous debate with Harnack. Ibid.

135. Ibid., 133.

the basics of Christian orthodoxy and the rules of science. To achieve his goal Ramm found guidance in the theology of Karl Barth. The renowned Swiss theologian provided the grounds for Ramm to establish his agenda to construct a new evangelicalism, freed from the constraints of fundamentalism and the ideology of liberalism. In all of this we note the earlier influences of orthodoxy, the influence of science and the later, and formative, influence of Karl Barth who became a significant source in Ramm's work. The result was a new evangelicalism embracing both orthodoxy and the Enlightenment and expressing itself with historical and Christological motifs after the pattern of Barth. Therefore, it is true to say that in Bernard Ramm's approach one finds a reconstructed evangelical who sought to construct a new evangelical theology.

Another early contributor to the emergence of this new evangelical theology is found in the writings of Geoffrey Bromiley, who provided the essential tools of translation and commentary that gave many North American theologians greater access to Barth's theology. Bromiley also advocated Barth's Christological understanding of revelation, shared Ramm's pursuit of an approach guided by Christocentrism and historical theology, and sought for an alternative theology to fundamentalism and liberalism. To him we now turn.

4

Geoffrey Bromiley

GEOFFREY BROMILEY WAS A significant contributor to the formation of a North American approach to theology after the pattern of Karl Barth. Born and educated in England, his contribution to North American theology resulted from his appointment to Fuller Theological Seminary, in 1958, as Professor of Church History and Historical Theology. At the time of his appointment he had already established himself with a reputation as an expert on Barth, having already translated two volumes of the *Church Dogmatics*. Indeed, Bromiley's major contribution to Christian theology came about as a result of his abilities in translation and theology.

The significance of Bromiley's role lies predominantly in his ability to translate Barth's work into English, as well as promote the Basel theologian as a scholar who had a significant amount to contribute to evangelical theology. Indeed, Bromiley provided the tools and inspiration that have lead to the establishment of a distinct Barthian theology within the context of North American evangelicalism. He clearly believed that Barth was able to be a mentor to a generation of evangelicals who sought an alternative to the two main streams of thought at the time, fundamentalism and liberalism. He strongly contended that the former was bound by the limitations inherent in its propositional rationalism and the latter to be guided by subjective anthropomorphic speculation. Barth, so Bromiley thought, provided a means by which one might remain within the orbit of orthodoxy while engaging thoughtfully with the issues associated with tools of German higher criticism. This agenda was brought about by translating Barth's work, carefully explaining the content of Barth's theology, succinctly summarizing its main points and positively presenting its approach to theology as a means for further theological work.

While it might be said that Bernard Ramm, in his *After Funda-mentalism*,[1] projected the vision of a theology after the pattern of Barth, Bromiley provided the tools of translation, interpretation, and analysis, which enabled this endeavor to be diligently undertaken in the English speaking world. The foundation of this "alternative" consisted of a theological motif based on Barth's theology of the Word of God. It is a motif arising out of an exposition of Scripture which it sees as a document giving witness to the actual event of revelation in the person and work of Jesus Christ. Since the contention of this thesis is that theology is to be understood within the context of a theologian's experience, an account of Bromiley's life will now be studied.

Geoffrey W. Bromiley was born into an evangelical Anglican home in Bromley Cross, Lancashire, England, where he was baptized, raised in the faith, and confirmed.[2] The Inter-Varsity Christian Union (CICU) nurtured his background in the Christian faith at Cambridge University. It was at Cambridge, in 1936, that he received first-class honors in French and German from Emmanuel College.[3] His commitment to his faith is particularly seen in his decision to train for ordination in the Anglican Church. Consequently, after completing theological studies at Tyndale Hall, he was ordained to the priesthood in 1938 and served in a number of parishes. His academic interests lead him to gain a PhD degree from the University of Edinburgh in 1943 with a dissertation concerned with German intellectual trends from Herder to Schleiermacher. Bromiley's "relationship with the University of Edinburgh is reflected in his years of lecturing at New College (1956–1958), where he built on his earlier ministry as Lecturer and Vice-Principal of Tyndale Hall, the Anglican theological college at Bristol (from 1946–1951)."[4] He brought this rich and diverse background to Fuller Seminary as Professor of Church History and Historical Theology in 1958, the first Anglican member of faculty.[5]

Clearly the richness of Bromiley's background derived from his scholarly interest in languages, theology, history, ministry and teaching.

---

1. Ramm, *After Fundamentalism*.

2. Hubbard, "Geoffrey W. Bromiley," xi–xii.

3. Ibid., xxi.

4. The university honored Bromiley with two further doctorates—a DLitt, in 1948 for his work entitled "Baptism and the Anglican Reformers," and a DD in 1961 for his overall ministry in theological teaching, translation, and scholarship. Ibid., xii.

5. Ibid., xii.

The result was an impressive production of numerous translations, edited works, theological volumes, and reference tools. He is best known for his contribution to translating major theological works from German and French into English. Indeed, in *Geoffrey W. Bromiley: An Appreciation*, David Hubbard made the important observation that Bromiley "is best known to scholars and ministers in the Christian church as a prolific and sensitive translator of major theological works."[6] However, it is with the works of Gerhard Kittel(1888–1948) and Karl Barth that Bromiley's name is most associated with,[7] and it is to the influence of Barth to which the discussion now turns.

THE INFLUENCE OF KARL BARTH

Bromiley recalled that it was while he was a student at Cambridge in 1937 that the work of Barth first came to his attention. He recollected that the demands of the curriculum prevented him from following up any in depth any study of Barth until final examinations and ordination were out of the way. Consequently, with an abundance of free time he had available before taking up his parish ministry, the new Anglican clergyman embarked on an independent study of the Swiss theologian. The influence of Barth initially came about as Bromiley read a number of secondary works before "plunging headlong into the German *Römerbrief*, and finally working through some of the other earlier writings."[8] After reading and reflecting upon these works Bromiley came to the conclusion that "Barth was obviously one of the greatest theologians of the century, and indeed of the whole modern epoch."[9] Out of this initial influence Bromiley recalled that three lasting consequences remained with him. Firstly, he gained a new sense of the priorities of biblical investigation. He recollected how Barth "opened the door to theological exegesis and to biblical theology."[10] For Bromiley this meant reading the Bible on its own terms, as distinct from those of the investigator. He came to find that this approach of studying the Bible "will not try to get behind the works in order to reconstruct something else" but endeavor, by way of

6. Ibid., xi.

7. Bradley and Muller, *Church, Word, and Spirit*, viii.

8. Bromiley, "The Karl Barth Experience" 65.

9. Bromiley, "The Karl Barth Centenary," 7.

10. Ibid., 65.

authentic exposition, to discover what the writings purport to be and do.[11] Secondly, Barth evoked in Bromiley "a heightened awareness of the relevance of historical theology."[12] He recalled that while historical theology was a component of his curriculum, his experience proved to be more one of tedium than inspiration or instruction. Conversely, he discovered in Barth one who had the gift of "breathing new life into these past figures, of lightening up their greatness, of bringing out their relevance to the various modern issues."[13] Thirdly, Barth won Bromiley over to an appreciation of dogmatics. In contrast to his previous encounters he found Barth's approach "had the obvious merits 1) of pursuing real theology, straightforward and unashamed, 2) of giving life and fire to the subject, 3) of achieving the devotional quality of prayer and praise that marks all the greater dogmaticians, and 4) of relating dogmatics not only to the intellectual questions of the era but also to the preaching ministry and all the church's work and witness."[14]

As Bromiley entered into parish life he immersed himself into the more developed Barth of the *Church Dogmatics*. Bromiley recalled that at first, due to the constraints on his time, he found this to be a difficult task. However, as he pursued doctoral studies at Edinburgh University he found that exploring the intricacies of German thought from the Enlightenment, from Herder to the Berlin Romantics, gave him a more adequate background for an informed study of Barth.[15] Indeed, a greater appreciation of the Swiss theologian's dogmatics soon eventuated when Bromiley received his first assignment as a member of the *Church Dogmatics* translation team then being assembled by Thomas Torrance.[16] It was at this time that the critics began to launch attacks against the whole enterprise.

As Bromiley increasingly immersed himself in an intensive study of Barth's work he became convinced that many of the critics "had not read much of Barth, or not read him carefully and scientifically enough to understand what they were reading." Indeed, on reflecting upon this co-

11. Ibid., 66.

12. Ibid.

13. Ibid.

14. Ibid., 67.

15. Ibid.

16. Bromiley finally translated IV/1(1956); II/2(1957); IV/2(1958); III/2(1960); III/3(1960); IV/3-1(1961); IV/3-2(1962); IV/4(1969); I/1(1975). All of these were published by T. & T. Clark, Edinburgh.

nundrum Bromiley referred to Barth's observation at the time "that some of his readers were either failing to grasp his concerns or (intentionally) misrepresenting them."[17] Later, on the occasion of the centenary of Barth's birth (1986) Bromiley repeated his earlier observation by declaring that comment in the evangelical world about Barth reflected "no great range of knowledge or depth of understanding."[18] It is contended here that these observations seem to explain why the bulk of Bromiley's contribution was taken up with the agenda of translating, summarizing, and consequently promoting, Barth as a truly evangelical theologian. It is believed here that as Bromiley set himself the task of translating the *Church Dogmatics* the influence of Barth continued to impact upon him.

The experience of translating Barth's work brought some "detailed rewards in addition to the deepening and strengthening of the original impression made by his work."[19] However, one must ask why Bromiley was so interested in his theology.

A THEOLOGY AFTER THE PATTERN OF KARL BARTH

Bromiley's commentary on Barth revealed his indebtedness to a theologian who enabled him to find a way out of "the incapacitating impasse of the controversy between liberals and conservatives."[20] It is uncertain why Bromiley was led to take this path. He never revealed the nature of events that accompanied his journey. Neither did he reveal that he had any particular problem with the dominant theology of his college or denomination. There are no narratives of crisis moments, as with Bernard Ramm, that would have led to Barth occupying a central place of an importance in Bromiley's life. It is contended here that Bromiley was at one point, early in his study, drawn to Barth's theology in such a manner that he felt compelled to look deeper into his work and be influenced by him. It would also seem probable that his detailed study of Barth's *Church Dogmatics*, for the purposes of translation, led to a deepening interest and appreciation. As fundamentalism became an increasingly influential force within evangelicalism, Bromiley, as an evangelical, needed to respond in some way. Just as he had sought to respond to the critics by promoting

17. Bromiley, "The Karl Barth Centenary," 68.

18. Ibid., 70.

19. Ibid.

20. Ibid.

Barth as a true evangelical, so he looked to Barth to define his own theo-logical approach. Indeed, faced with the decision of whether to embrace fundamentalism or liberalism, he chose neither. Karl Barth, so it seems, provided his only satisfactory way forward.

It is evident that the Swiss theologian was doing at the time what Bromiley also sought to do; to find an alternate path. Indeed, one must recall that Barth himself had broken away from the liberal subjectivism of the "Marburg School" yet he had not embraced, as an alternative, the doctrines of inerrancy that dominate fundamentalism. In order to find a constructive way forward Barth carved out an alternative third path. Clearly Bromiley, as he carefully sifted through Barth's work for trans-lation, became inspired by this fresh approach. Barth had upheld the essentially objective nature of Scripture, yet in a manner that left room for a thoughtful engagement with the issues arising out of the advent of modernism. Indeed, Bromiley found in Barth's approach an openness to historical-critical work that was not at that time available within evangeli-calism. Indeed, Bromiley would appear to have appreciated Barth "setting the Bible in a comprehensive doctrine of God's Word and focusing on the unique authority of Scripture within this context instead of worrying so much about its detailed authorship and inerrancy."[21] On the other hand there was caution at liberalism's emphasis on the historical-critical meth-od. Barth had, in contrast, stressed a careful exposition of the text that allowed God's Word to be heard through the biblical words.[22] Bromiley also appreciated Barth's theology of the Word that stressed the ongoing and dynamic work of the Spirit as the one who, "having given the biblical witness, does not abandon it, but comes in living power, so that its voice is in very truth the voice of God."[23] The result of this approach would produce quite different results, believed Bromiley, from those produced by the fundamentalists.

21. Ibid., 71.

22. Bromiley believed Barth to have rescued the Bible from both pontificating church leaders on the one side and authoritarian scholars on the other. Ibid.

23. Ibid. Barth argued that "God's revelation occurs in our enlightenment by the Holy Spirit of God to a knowledge of His Word." Barth, *Church Dogmatics: 1/2*, 203.

An Alternative to Fundamentalism

Bromiley's agenda to promote Barth as an evangelical in response to fundamentalist criticisms of his theology is highlighted by Bromiley's rigorous repudiation of their views. He first expressed his agenda of opposition to fundamentalism in an article he wrote for *Christianity Today* in 1957. He began his discussion with the observation that fundamentalist Christianity rests its case on what it believes to be the biblical argument. However he raised doubt as to whether fundamentalists "are really quite so biblical as they protest."[24] He maintained that fundamentalism is in fact influenced by those very same assumptions that underlie liberalism, "though biblical texts or tags may be found for the detailed outworking."[25] Indeed, Bromiley perceived the irony that fundamentalist emotionalism reflected the influence of Schleiermacher's subjectivism. He further stated that fundamentalism often, and quite unconsciously, displayed "an elementary failure to be biblical" in its action and approach to theology.[26] In many instances this has led to fundamentalists rebutting liberal arguments on modernist terms. The result, noted Bromiley, often lead to a criticism of modernist arguments on the one hand with an acceptance of modernist assumptions on the other.[27] The problem, he contested, is in the influence or "considerable infusion" of rationalism into Protestant Orthodoxy. The result is believed to be a dogmatics which, "while biblical in its materials, is very far from biblical in its basis, structure and method."[28] This is reflected in the understanding of the nature of Scriptural inspiration.

Bromiley pointed to Barth's concern that the fundamentalist doctrine of Scriptural revelation has resulted in "rigid and sometimes docetic views of inspiration."[29] He conveyed that Barth understood this as a result of the fundamentalist agenda to prove that, rationally speaking, Scripture had integrity. Furthermore, he did so as a reaction to liberalism. However, Barth would have us follow the "better way" of the Reformers, who

24. Bromiley, "Fundamentalism-Modernism," 4.

25. Ibid., 4.

26. Ibid.

27. Further, Bromiley adds that "the historico-critical work of fundamentalists, however conservative, is often conducted on non-biblical assumptions." Ibid., 5.

28. Ibid.

29. Bromiley, "Barth's Doctrine of the Bible," 15.

emphasized "the dynamic operation of the Holy Spirit."[30] Consequently, the point of inspiration, claimed Barth, is not the rationality of the Word as a document, but the "present action of the Holy Spirit giving life and actuality to the apostolic and prophetic word as it is heard and read."[31] As a result Barth did not define inspiration in terms of an attribute or state of Scripture, but as an event that takes place between God and the individual person.[32] Indeed, in his *Dogmatics* Barth made the pronouncement that by "the outpouring of the Holy Spirit it is possible for God's revelation to reach man in his freedom, because in it the Word of God is brought to his hearing."[33] Bromiley believed that the solution to the problem was for the fundamentalist to return to the Bible and allow it to correct what has so obviously gone astray. An example of how this alternative approach alters the nature of theology is seen in Bromiley's 1961 article for *Christianity Today*, "The Decrees of God."[34]

In this contribution Bromiley was chiefly concerned with the motif of the decree of God concerning the predestination of the elect for salvation. He reminded the reader that fundamentalist Calvinism[35] held to the view that God has decided who will be saved, and as is the case in some Calvinist systems, who will be damned. The primary source material for their argument, apart from Scripture, was the major Reformed confessions and articles, together with writings of Calvin and those who have stood in the Calvinist tradition. The influence of Barth is seen in Bromiley's complaint that this form of Calvinism[36] distorted a proper theology of the character of God. Bromiley stated: "In itself it emphasizes sheer power instead of holy, wise and loving power. It suggests harsh enforcement rather than beneficial overruling. It implies that which is fixed and static, so that man is an automaton and God himself, having made his

---

30. Ibid.

31. Ibid.

32. In such an event the past acts of God are recalled and his future acts are anticipated with hope. Inspiration, however, is concerned with the present act of this recollection and expectation. Ibid.

33. Barth, *CD I/2*, 246.

34. Bromiley, "The Decrees of God."

35. In this article Bromiley is contending with Calvinism.

36. Bromiley also notes that "Arminian statements only limit the range of the divine decree." Ibid., 18.

decree, is unemployed and uninterested."[37] Again, Bromiley made the link between fundamentalism and liberalism. Indeed, the Anglican professor believed that this brand of Calvinism is not dissimilar to the deism of Unitarianism in which God sets the world in motion and leaves it alone to take its course.[38] Bromiley, as a Reformed theologian, herewith challenged fundamentalist theology and its assumptions. He did this by thoroughly reviewing the sources that fundamentalism relied upon and then provided an alternative interpretation along the lines of Barth's analysis of these same sources. The result was an alternative interpretation that was at odds with classic Calvinism, one that alternatively followed Karl Barth's hermeneutical approach. In this article Bromiley also challenged fundamentalist conclusions by supporting Barth's theology of predestination, which perceived all to have been elected in Christ.

Bromiley began his thesis with reference to the *Westminster Confession*, which maintained that

> God from all eternity did, by the most wise and holy council of his own will, freely and unchangeably ordain whatsoever comes to pass; yet so as thereby neither is God the author of sin, nor is violence offered to the will of the creatures, nor is the liberty or contingency taken away, but rather established. (chap. III)[39]

In his reflection on this passage Bromiley pointed out that many interpretations have declared that God's determinism is asserted and his decree is seen as his "effective resolve or purpose" that is grounded in his free wisdom.[40] In this interpretation God, not humanity, has determined the way things will be. Further, since God is the one who "controls his creation" it is he alone who has decided the fate of the saved and the damned. Indeed, so determinative is God's action in this system that preceding his decree of election was his decree of the fall. Ultimately there is no choice. God has determined what will come to pass.[41] Bromiley was clearly not convinced by this argument, understanding it to be an error of infral-

---

37. Ibid., 18.

38. Ibid., 18–19.

39. Bromiley also finds Westminster's theology in such documents as the *Belgic Confession* (1561, Art. 16), and the *Thirty-Nine Articles* (1563, Art. 17), ibid.

40. Ibid.

41. He then notes that the confession, in the same way that Calvin had done it in his *Institutes*, moves from the general decree of God to discuss the special decree of election. Ibid.

apsarianism.[42] Later in the article he likened this brand of determinism to the kind of fatalism one might find, for example, in Islam. Indeed, he referred to Lutherans who detected an "Islamic impulse in Reformed teaching."[43] As a consequence Bromiley challenged fundamentalist assumptions by dealing with the use of the word "decree." Bromiley clearly had some reservations as to the appropriateness of the term "decree." He certainly agreed that if the word is used it must be safeguarded against misunderstanding. Historical theological documents consistently used the term and therefore it would seem that he was resigned to the fact that it is a word that cannot be avoided. However, since the Bible uses "decree" to describe the arbitrary, inflexible and often vexatious orders of despotic rulers, Bromiley advocated for its sparing use. This is why, it would appear, he concluded this part of his argument with the assertion that Barth had good reason to have "no enthusiasm for the word," and yet acknowledged that it does have its uses.[44] However, it would seem clear that Bromiley believed that fundamentalism had taken the word "decree" out of its Biblical context and out of proportion, in order to pursue its agenda of theological determinism. Yet how did he construct an alternative theology? He turned to Barth to enable him to construct an alternative reading of these historic church documents and confessions.

In order to construct a theology after the pattern of Barth Bromiley turned to Barth's theology of election. Clearly Bromiley, as a result of Barth's influence, sought to promote this motif by discussing Barth's theological dictum that Scriptural election does not speak of individuals, but of a corporate decree. Bromiley maintained that God's decree of election referred to his desire to enter into a gracious covenant relationship with a chosen people.[45] Indeed, Bromiley proposed that the very "special prudence and care" mentioned in the *Westminster Confession (III, 8)* should lead one not to the sorting of individuals, but to Jesus Christ, "in whom

---

42. "A form of Calvinism which teaches that the decree of the fall logically preceded that of election. The order of God's decrees, then, is: (1) to create human beings; (2) to permit the fall; (3) to save some and condemn others; and (4) to provide salvation only for the elect." Erickson, "Infralapsarianism," 84.

43. Bromiley, "Decrees of God." We recognize that Bromiley's reference to Islam to describe fatalism is inappropriate to contemporary debate on this issue.

44. Ibid., 18.

45. Ibid.

God's grace and wrath are manifested."[46] To support his case Bromiley turned to the Confessions. Given his Barthian approach and agenda this is hardly surprising. In his writing Bromiley revealed Barth's alternative, yet accurate, reading of key historical sources. One might suspect that Bromiley would quote Barth at this point. However Barth's influence is more seen in Bromiley's approach and theological assertions. This is initially seen in the Christological motif he emphasized. Indeed, he came back to the confessions he had only just derided and praises those aspects that suited his Christological emphasis. Hence, for Bromiley, the *Formula of Concord* "puts it well" when it states that "(i)n Christ [. . .] is the eternal election of God sought." Furthermore, the *Remonstrant Articles* "display fine judgment" as they stated that God "hath determined [. . .] to save Christ for Christ's sake." Further "Calvin teaches us to seek our election in Christ." It is an orientation that he saw echoed in the *Belgic Confession,* which asserted that God's eternal and unchangeable council is to elect certain men to salvation in Jesus Christ. In addition, Bromiley maintained that the *Thirty-Nine Articles* stated that it is God's everlasting purpose to deliver "those he hath chosen in Christ." Similar thoughts are expressed in what Bromiley described as "some noble sentences" from Bullinger's *Second Helvetic Confession.*[47] One detects in these comments not only the influence of Barth's Christology but also his historical approach.

As Bromiley knew, Barth's doctrine of election, in his *Church Dogmatics,* also referred to the Confessions and Reformers.[48] Indeed Bromiley, in his *Introduction to the Theology of Karl Barth,* summarized Barth's handling of these historic documents (in the construction of his doctrine of election) by stating that "Barth appreciates the positive elements of these possibilities."[49] Therefore, the article gave clear evidence that Bromiley had the agenda to promote a theology after the pattern of Barth. This is not only reflected in his corporate exposition of the doctrine of election, but also in his Christological and historic approach which contributed toward his agenda of an orthodoxy distinct from fundamentalism and liberalism.

---

46. Ibid., 19.

47. Ibid.

48. Bromiley, *Introduction to the Theology of Karl Barth,* 84–90.

49. Ibid., 86.

An Alternative to Liberalism

Just as it has been affirmed that Bromiley's evangelicalism led him to be critical of fundamentalism's approach, so it is now contended that this same evangelical heritage led him to also use Barth as a source to challenge the claims of Protestant Liberalism. In 1959 Bromiley wrote an article for *Christianity Today* with the title of "Barth: A Contemporary Appraisal."[50] Here Bromiley set out his agenda to define the basic nature of Barth's theology to the evangelical world of 1959. The nature of his agenda is seen as Bromiley asserted Barth's orthodox credentials by stating that Barth had rejected the kind of liberal theology associated with Rudolf Bultmann, particularly his understanding of mythology. According to Bromiley Barth had come to the conclusion that myth does not categorize the literature of the Gospels, for example, because they have to do "with a work of God in time and space, worked out in the actual life and death and resurrection of Jesus of Nazareth and credibly attested by those associated with him as apostles."[51] Barth therefore concluded, reported Bromiley, that the so called "demythologization" demanded by Bultmann was "formally an impossible enterprise."[52] Therefore, since Barth regards Scripture to be taken as read, Bromiley put to the reader Barth's assertion that Scripture is to be read objectively.

Because Barth began with the assumption that Scripture is to be read with genuine objectivity, he consequently thought that Bultmann, in order to sustain his "demythologized" reading of Scripture, "allows abstract and non-biblical concerns to dominate his reading."[53] As Bromiley described it, Barth observed that the result for Bultmann is a hermeneutic based on himself which resulted in the measure of his understanding. "In reaction therefore, Barth insists that theology must rest upon exegesis of the text in terms of itself and not alien categories, problems, or assumptions."[54] Consequently, Bromiley became a champion of Barth's motif of a theology of the Word of God.

According to Bromiley the evangelical should find in Barth an ally who has successfully challenged the approach of liberalism. He believed

50. Bromiley, "Barth: A Contemporary Appraisal."

51. Bromiley, "Decrees of God," 9.

52. Ibid.

53. Ibid.

54. Ibid.

it was a theology bound by the secondary materials associated with an anthropocentric dealing with Scripture, by finding it "possible to relegate secondary materials to their proper secondary rank, to deal once again with Scripture as a primary and authoritative source."[55] Indeed, Barth sought to "subjugate historico-critical analysis to the demands of authentic exposition."[56] Good exposition, claimed Barth, recognized that the biblical authors belong to the event of revelation itself and seek an "interpretation *with* the biblical authors instead of *about* them in an openness that lets them tell us what they have to say rather than trying to force them to say what we want them to say."[57] However, Bromiley was aware that Barth's hermeneutical approach had created concern among evangelicals.

Barth's Approach of the Word of God

Bromiley consistently praised and promoted Barth's approach to constructing theology based on a definitive theology of the Word of God. His appreciation significantly contributed to his agenda of promoting Barth as an important model and worthy mentor, who could enable evangelicals to construct an alternative theology to those already on offer. This would amount to maintaining orthodoxy while engaging constructively with the issues that were pertinent to modernism. This agenda was outlined in a 1956 article for *Christianity Today*. In it Bromiley reflected upon his translation of the second part of Volume I of Barth's *Church Dogmatics*. The work cited the significance of the volume's *Prolegomena*; in this section Barth "lays the foundation with his doctrine of the Word of God."[58] Important for evangelicals to consider, thought Bromiley, was the observation that Barth's motif of the theology of the Word is to be respected for its assertion of biblical authority.[59] Consequently, Bromiley supported Barth's thesis that biblical supremacy is the proper starting point for doing good theology, believing that "(o)nly the Bible is a primary witness and

---

55. Bromiley, *Karl Barth Centenary*, 8.

56. Bromiley adds that in this way Barth was able to "open the door to the strange new world within the Bible which a false approach had for so long closed to any real penetration." Later he adds that the historico-critical method is in fact a useful servant, all-be-it a poor master. Ibid.

57. Ibid.

58. Bromiley, *Barth's Doctrine of the Bible*, 14.

59. Ibid.

therefore the Word of God."[60] Indeed, Barth in his *Prolegomena To Church Dogmatics* stated that the "Church does not claim direct and absolute and material authority for itself but for Holy Scripture as the Word of God." Its power, claimed Barth, comes from the one to whom it bears witness: that is, Jesus Christ, the Word of God.[61] Bromiley knew, however, that Barth's Christological understanding of the Word of God was a stumbling block for many evangelicals.

Bromiley recognized that evangelicals have had doubts about the thesis of Barth that Christ forms the hermeneutical key to the Bible. The result, noted Bromiley, has been a corresponding difficulty with many of Barth's exegetical procedures and conclusions. While Bromiley observed that these are legitimate queries he went on to defend this vital component of Barth's approach. Bromiley forcefully contended that evangelicals do well to consider that one of their own central themes is people finding fellowship with God and final redemption.[62] This being the case, one must note that the

> work of revelation and reconciliation comes to a climax and completion in Jesus Christ, the incarnate Son. For Barth this means that Christ himself is the central theme of theology, the object of the prophetic and apostolic testimony, the object also of the Church's ongoing proclamation, and hence the constant object of all dogmatic enquiry, around whom all the dogmatic *loci* circle, toward whom they all refer, and in relation to whom we must always understand and expound them.[63]

Barth further justified his consistent focusing on Christ since "Scripture itself justifies a reference of all things to Christ, for all the Scriptures bear witness to him."[64] Indeed, church history also pointed in this direction. Barth alluded to the opinion of the Patristics, for whom Jesus Christ was also the key to understanding Scripture. The Reformers also construed the Bible in terms of Christ.[65] Indeed, Bromiley's argument was that Barth was a theologian who stood in the tradition of the Reformation, an

60. Ibid., 15.
61. Barth, *CD I/2*, 538.
62. Bromiley, *Barth's Doctrine of the Bible*, 10.
63. Ibid.
64. Ibid.
65. Bromiley, "Karl Barth and Anglicanism," 20.

endeavor that fundamentalists had manifestly failed to fulfill. Consequently, evangelicals should also be encouraged by Barth's interest in historical theology, particularly that of the Reformers.

Barth's historical approach

Bromiley noted in the 1986 article that some of Barth's historical surveys "will surely count amongst the most brilliant and perspicacious of all his writings."[66] In an earlier article for *The Churchman* Bromiley discussed the importance of historical theology in Barth's approach to constructing theology, contending that "Barth's activity in the field teaches us the need to take historical theology with full seriousness."[67] While Barth's primary concern for a satisfactory approach to doing theology was the exploration of Scripture, Bromiley alluded to Barth's secondary concern for theological history. The result was the emergence of "one of the foremost historical theologians of the century."[68] Indeed, Bromiley made the comment in his *Karl Barth and Anglicanism* that Barth's personal achievements in Reformation scholarship were astonishing. However, while Barth worked hard in patristics, and gave evidence of an "astonishing grasp of modern European development," his second main focus of attention after Scripture was the work of the Reformers. Indeed, Bromiley believed that one of Barth's dominant motifs amounted to a return to the Reformation tradition under the motto: "back to the Reformers."[69] To demonstrate his contention he referred to the sources used in the *Church Dogmatics*. Indeed, Bromiley made the observation that a "glance at the indexes of the succeeding volumes of the *Church Dogmatics* offers a clue."[70] One must remember, claimed Bromiley, that Barth is to be understood as a theologian "thoroughly in the tradition of the Reformation."[71] According to Bromiley, therefore, evangelicals had every reason to remain within their own tradition with the confidence that Barth will enable them to do so with depth and sophistication.

66. Bromiley further claims that Barth's work had rekindled interest in the reformers, fathers, school men, and even the Protestant orthodox of the seventeenth century. Ibid., 9.

67. Bromiley, *Karl Barth and Anglicanism*, 14.

68. Ibid.

69. Ibid., 15.

70. Ibid.

71. Bromiley, *Barth's Doctrine of the Bible*, 14.

CONCLUSION

Bromiley's contribution to the cause of establishing a theology in North America after the pattern of Barth is seen in his work of translation and theological interpretation. His translations of Barth's *Church Dogmatics* into English opened the door for many North American theologians to be able to read and analyze Barth's work for themselves. Bromiley also commented upon Barth's significant theological contribution to evangelicalism. This provided a helpful study of Barth's work and aided readers to grasp its depth and meaning. Bromiley also actively promoted Barth as a theologian who had much to offer. Clearly, Bromiley had an agenda to portray Barth as a friend to evangelicals, who could trust him to be a worthy partner in dialogue and mentor in the construction of a theological alternative to both fundamentalism and liberalism. While it is true to say that Barth was not an evangelical after the pattern of the North Americans, it is certain that he was a theologian of the Word of God and prioritized the theology of the Reformers. He was a theologian of a new kind of orthodoxy which intersected at numerous points with the ambitions of the "new evangelicals." Indeed, many fundamentalist and conservative evangelicals would argue that in doing so the "new evangelicals" cease being evangelical, but sell out to a German form of liberal Protestantism known as *evangelisch*. Bromiley believed otherwise and assiduously made his case.

The core of Bromiley's thesis was an open appreciation of Barth's theology of the Word of God. It was a motif of the Word of God recognized by its Christological hermeneutics and accountability to historical theology; especially that represented by the Reformation. It praised Barth's threefold understanding of the Word that is 1) spoken definitively in Jesus Christ, 2) the Word witnessed to, and 3) the Word proclaimed. Rather than being rationalistic, or speculative and abstract, it was open to the real possibility that the Spirit, in an event of divine revelation, will bring about an encounter between humanity and a personal God that is both objective and existential. Consequently, Bromiley is to be understood as a "new evangelical" since his approach is characterized by an exposition of Scripture free of the constraints of modernist rationalism, so much at the core of fundamentalism, or the anthropomorphic and abstract subjectivism found in liberalism.

James Daane was another significant contributor to Barth's reception among evangelicals. This North American theologian found in Barth the answer to his dilemma of how to preach election in the Reformed tradition.

5

James Daane

JAMES DAANE CAME TO contribute to the promotion of Barth among
evangelicals as a progressive theologian within the Christian Reformed
Church. Earlier in his career he had been a critic of Barth, warning evangelicals to stay clear of a theologian who had veered from the fixed course
of Protestant Orthodoxy. Like other fundamentalist critics, Daane believed that Barth was a theologian more driven by the influence of Greek
philosophy, expressed through dialecticism, than he was by the Bible. His
earlier contention was that God was the Lord of order and consistency and
not of contradiction. Clearly the image of God as orderly and consistent
was a reflection of his fundamentalist culture which sought a theology
comprising of a series of logically ordered propositions. Contradiction
was obviously Daane's early perception of dialecticism. However, Daane
underwent a reorientation in his thinking that led to a dramatic change
of mind-set.

The later Daane became an advocate of Barth and an author influenced by his theology. In fact Daane underwent a shift from fundamentalist critic to new evangelical advocate. It is not clear what brought this
about. One can compare his early critical works with his later appreciative
writing. These provide a helpful comparison and allow one to trace an
outline of Daane's shift. But it is not known what influence or series of
events prompted him to make this change. Indeed, his close colleague
at Fuller Seminary, Ray Anderson, revealed that Daane never spoke of
his reasons for making this substantial turn in his theology.[1] One can
only assume that his progressive tendencies led him to think of Barth
as a helpful source in the pursuit of his agenda to construct a new evangelical theology. Daane's transition from critic to advocate represents his

---

1. Anderson, pers. comm., 12 March, 2004.

own transition from fundamentalist to new evangelical. The evidence suggests that he came to believe that his own Reformed faith contained many inadequacies that needed to be remedied. Indeed, he saw in Barth a theologian who had successfully corrected many misinterpretations of Calvin's theology.

More specifically Daane found, in the motif of Barth's doctrine of election, a means for the preacher of the Gospel to give hope in his or her message. Therefore, Daane's concern for the place of theology in the ministry of preaching had a profound effect on his thinking. The result was a theologian who promoted Barth's work and theology by, in the main, reviewing Barth's work and those who wrote about him.

James Daane was Professor of Pastoral Theology at Fuller Seminary from 1966 until his retirement in 1979. He was also a founding editor and contributor to the *Reformed Journal,* a monthly magazine that has provided, since 1951, a central forum for theological progressives within the Christian Reformed Church.[2] Consequently, Daane played an active and visible role in the Dutch Reformed community, although his influence has extended more widely. "As an associate editor for *Christianity Today* from 1961 to 1965, and then a Professor at Fuller Seminary, Daane participated actively in the larger evangelical world."[3]

EARLY CRITICISMS OF BARTH

Daane's early response to Barth echoed many of the common criticisms leveled against him by most North American evangelicals. This early response was clearly a result of the influence of his Calvinist and fundamentalist background in the Dutch Reformed Church. In a letter to *The Calvin Forum* in 1948, Daane was clearly in agreement with fellow Calvinist and fundamentalist Cornelius Van Til, who accused Karl Barth of distorting a number of Christian doctrines.[4] In an article for *The Reformed Journal* in 1952 Daane further complained that "while Barth, Brunner, Tillich, Bultmann, and many others, differ in various ways, they all have one thing in common. All are dialectical."[5] In this article Daane believed that the church owed it to its own sense of self-preservation to "know the signs of the times" so that it can defend

2. Thorne, *Evangelicalism and Karl Barth*, 112.

3. Ibid., 113.

4. Daane, "As to Barthianism," 48.

5. Daane, "Theological Dialecticism: Explained and Illustrated," 10.

itself against any emerging threats to orthodoxy. Therefore, he exhorted Christian leaders to become familiar with the meaning of dialecticism, since "the dimensions of Dialectical Theology are so great and its scope of influence so broad, that no theology interested in its own existence can safely ignore it."[6] Daane proceeded to warn intrepid theological adventurers to beware of dialecticism's alien ways.

In the name of "knowing the enemy" Daane, in his *Theological Dialecticism: Explained and Illustrated,* lead the reader through the various facets of dialectical theology. The most significant of these was dialectical method. This was an important starting point since Daane's contention at the time was that it is from dialecticism's method "that its most peculiar characteristics stem."[7] In the article Daane proposed that part of the problem with dialectical method lay in its ancient Greek roots. Consequently, he sounded a note of warning when he stated that it 'represents a way of thinking which theology has borrowed from ancient philosophy.'[8] Daane made very clear what the implication of this was. Dialecticism was not a biblical approach to theology, but one influenced by the pre-Christian thought of Socrates (c. 470–399 BC), whose philosophy was guided more by the method one used in finding the truth than in the truth itself.[9] Clearly, this was Daane's most strenuous objection to Barth's theology at the time.

Daane gave an illustration of Barth's particular use of dialecticism by pointing to his doctrinal assertion that "(e)ach person is both reprobate and elect." Daane complained that this is a conception of the truth that could only result in the assertion that the reality about each person 'lies somewhere between reprobation and election.'[10] He reflected on this position with the help of Cornelius Van Til, who believed that the apparent contradictions of Scripture resulted from the "effect of sin upon man's mind."[11] Consequently, Daane concluded that dialectical theology was not the end result of a discerning reading of Scripture but of subjective and finite minds. He argued that the *apparent* contradictions found

6. Ibid.
7. Ibid.
8. Ibid.
9. Ibid., 11.
10. Ibid.
11. Ibid.

in Scripture said more about the mystery of God's self-disclosure that is beyond humanity's grasp, than any truth that God might wish to effectively communicate.[12] He believed that God's wisdom was a mystery to the infinite mind and can't possibly be defined by human philosophical notions, such as those offered by the Greek Philosophers. Clearly, therefore, Daane, at this time, pursued a highly critical and unappreciative reading of Barth that had as its agenda to warn readers against the unsound tone of Barth's theology. However, while it appears that in these early years Daane was clearly an ally of Cornelius Van Til, by the beginning of 1959, while continuing to harbor some reservations,[13] Daane had changed his mind.

FROM CRITICISM TO APPRECIATION

In an article for *The Reformed Journal* Daane reviewed Karl Barth's commentary on *The Apostle's Creed according to Calvin's Catechism*. It is evident in this article that Daane was reading Barth from a new perspective and had developed a totally new approach. Instead of warning readers about the subjective sin bound theology of dialecticism, of which Barth was a major contributor, Daane now praised him and exclaimed that "it is a joy at any price for a Reformed student or preacher to hear Barth give his commentary on Calvin's Catechism."[14] This comment, early in Daane's change of heart, gives significant insight into the reasons for Daane's new direction. Indeed, instead of siding with Van Til's many criticisms Daane obviously concurred with Gabriel Vahanian's analysis that "the present work [of Barth's] is in our estimation perhaps the best simplified and systematic introduction to the theology of Karl Barth in its correlation with the Reformation."[15] Furthermore, Daane praised Barth's work because it dealt with the heart of Christianity, which, he contended, was to be equated with "the heart of Barth's theology."[16] Indeed, Daane commended the Swiss theologian as one who explained the heart of the Christian

12. Ibid.

13. In a 1961 review of Van Til's "Karl Barth and Chalcedon," Daane agrees that Barth's notion of *Geschichte* is ambiguous and elusive. Daane, *Review of C. Van Til*, "Karl Barth on Chalcedon," 21.

14. Daane, "The Faith of the Church," 21.

15. Ibid.

16. Ibid.

faith as a theologian of "equal theological stature" to John Calvin himself.[17] Therefore, Barth was no longer seen as a mistaken apprentice of Socrates, but as a faithful student of the Reformation.

In his new estimation Daane clearly challenged the opinion that Barth is a liberal at odds with evangelicalism. It is evident that Reformed theologian came to see in Barth a theologian who more adequately represented the thinking of the Reformers than the Calvinist's of the modern era, who had developed a sterile confessionalism once removed from the theology of the Reformers. This is seen in Daane's description of Barth as an orthodox theologian who defended the virgin birth and resurrection of Christ. In fact, Daane noted that these traditional soundings led one translator of Barth's work, Gabriel Vahanian, to have the concern that Barth appeared "to lean too conspicuously towards orthodoxy."[18] Furthermore, Daane also highlighted Barth's many appreciations of Calvin's Christology. This included Calvin's Christological assertion that "in the Christian sense, we may speak of God 'in himself' only after we have understood his divine condescension whereby he became man in Jesus Christ."[19] Daane's new appreciation of Barth soon developed into an open promotion of the Swiss theologian. This is seen in an article Daane wrote for *The Reformed Journal* in 1962.

In his introduction to his article, *Can We Learn from Karl Barth?* [20] Daane placed Barth within the context of Reformed and liberal theology of the Western world. Clearly, in an attempt to present Barth as an ally with evangelicals in their contention with liberalism, Daane conveyed Barth's belief "that neither the Reformed nor any of the other theological traditions could meet the crises through which the western world was passing."[21] Indeed, Barth's contention, stated Daane, was that none of these theologies had been able to free themselves of "the de-Christianizing liberal subjectivism bequeathed to Western thought by Schleiermacher."[22] To provide an alternative to Friedrich Schleiermacher's (1768–1834) subjectivism, and to speak with relevance to the world he found himself

17. Ibid., 21–22.
18. Ibid., 22.
19. Ibid.
20. Daane, "Can We Learn from Karl Barth?"
21. Ibid., 7.
22. Ibid.

in, "Barth built a theology on the objective, redemptive action of God in Christ, a theology of revelation, whose truth does not depend on man's discovery of, or his feelings about, God."[23] Believing that a study of Barth *can* help theologians learn more about themselves and their own theologies, Daane turned to his passionate belief in the importance of the doctrine of election.

BARTH'S DOCTRINE OF ELECTION

Previously, Daane had held that Barth's doctrine of election was the result of his flawed dialectical method. However, after his 1959 "turn" his contention was that Barth's doctrine of election is at the heart of all that is good about his theology. Daane began his discussion with the acknowledgement that "(e)lection is of the very structure of Reformed theology."[24] However, he believed that the Reformed doctrine of election had become distorted. It was more a result of the Canon of Dort's declaration in response to the perceived threat of Arminianism, than anything implicit in the teachings of the Reformers. Daane's main concern was that it was a doctrine that amounted to the election of the individual. The result was a theology in isolation "not only from the biblical teaching of the election of Israel, but also quite in isolation from the election of Jesus Christ."[25] To support his case he turned to the theology of John Calvin.

Daane clearly lamented the fact that John Calvin's belief that "Christ is the 'mirror' of our election"—that is the election of the Christian is reflective of Christ's own election—appears to be almost forgotten in Reformed theology. Indeed, Daane asserted that later Calvinist systems, such as Louis Berkhof's *Systematic Theology*, did not even mention it. This is in spite of the fact claimed Daane, that it is profoundly important to the understanding of Calvin's original thought on the topic and "the biblical teaching about election."[26] Furthermore, Daane complained that even though centuries have passed "the election of Christ is still not an integral and structural part of Reformed theology."[27] However he found hopeful signs in the theology of Karl Barth.

23. Ibid.
24. Ibid., 8.
25. Ibid.
26. Ibid.
27. Ibid.

It is evident that Daane saw the strength of Barth's approach of discussing election by observing that Berkhof devoted a large section to individual election or reprobation and sums up election of Israel and Christ in a few sentences. By contrast Barth discussed the election of the individual only in the light of Christ's election. The biblical foundations found in Barth's emphasis on corporate election are understood by Daane to focus on the cross, which is the very centre of the Christian message. Jesus was crucified, claimed Daane, because he claimed to be the elect, the chosen of God. He asserted that election and crucifixion are closely linked and believed that the "election of Christ is the crucial question at that most central of all events, the Cross [. . .] So central is the election of Jesus in the thought of the New Testament that even the unbelievers at the cross recognized its centrality." This is all in stark contrast, believed Daane, to the emphasis that had developed in Reformed theology. Consequently, he maintained that Reformed theologians were unable to respond to Paul's teaching that election occurred "in Christ."[28] However, Daane expressed the conviction that a study of Karl Barth might direct Reformed theologians to realize that aspects of their theology had become erroneous or even dangerous.[29]

Daane, speaking to Reformed evangelicals, claimed that a "study of Barth's doctrine of election may lead us to see our inadequacies and having given us an awareness of these it may drive us back to the important aspect of Calvin's thought which we have all but forgotten, namely, that Christ is the 'mirror' of our election."[30] Daane believed that as this is done individual election is set aside and replaced with a doctrine of election comprehended in conjunction with Christ's election, "so that we discover our election when we discover His and we know our own when we in faith believe that He is God's Elect."[31] According to Daane, the problem with individual election is that it has contributed to a theological sterility in Reformed theology. Furthermore, he lamented the fact that Reformed theologians have applied their "limited doctrine of individual election to the covenant, to common grace, to the general offer of salvation."[32] The

28. Ibid.
29. Ibid., 9.
30. Ibid.
31. Ibid.
32. Ibid.

result is a general dissatisfaction that is accompanied by little hope of anything better. He concluded that "our theological fortunes will not change until we learn to look at our election in the light of the election of Jesus Christ." Indeed, "Barth may open our eyes and give us new hope and energy for our task."[33]

Daane firmly held that Barth's concept of corporate election has the ability to enrich Reformed theology and deliver it from its fruitless dead end.[34] Indeed, as this Christological approach is embraced Daane asserted that other areas of theology, in addition to election, will also be enriched. In fact, he contended that a study of Barth's thought "may jab us awake and give us that new and much needed theological vigor and excitement necessary to look again and learn from our theological history and to thrust out in new avenues of approach so that our theology may again be on the move."[35] James Daane dealt more extensively with the doctrine of election in his 1973 publication, *The Freedom of God: A Study of Election and Pulpit.*[36]

In *The Freedom of God* Daane's contention was that God's election of Jesus is the core of Christian truth.[37] He believed that the election of Christ, as God's chosen one, is affirmed in Scripture on a number of occasions. Indeed, Peter, on the day of Pentecost, "preached on the only thing he could have preached, the subject that lies at the heart of the cross and the resurrection—God's election of Jesus."[38] To be sure, the resurrection was God's elective act, "the act that constituted his election of the man, Jesus of Nazareth."[39] Daane also contended that the Apostle Paul saw the central importance of the election of Christ to the Christian message. He went so far as to state that the apostle was converted with the recognition of the election of Jesus. Furthermore, out "of the basic knowledge of God's election of Jesus arise Paul's knowledge of his own election, his knowledge of his peculiar task as a chosen instrument."[40]

33. Ibid.

34. Ibid.

35. Ibid.

36. Daane, *The Freedom of God.*

37. Ibid., 9.

38. Ibid., 10–11.

39. Ibid., 11.

40. Ibid., 13.

Daane recognized Barth's influence on his own thinking and affirmed that "Karl Barth was correct when he said that election is the sum and substance of the gospel."[41] Daane's conviction was supported by Geoffrey Bromiley who wrote in his *Introduction to the Theology of Karl Barth* of Barth's belief "that election is the sum of the gospel."[42] Indeed, in his *Church Dogmatics* Barth himself declared that the "doctrine of election is the sum of the Gospel because of all words that can be said or heard it is the best: that God elects man; that God is for man the One who loves in freedom."[43]

Daane clearly had the concern that while Christian theologians have never denied the election of Christ, they have generally never explicitly developed a thorough theology of it. He lamented that while every conceivable aspect of the person and work of Christ had been the subject of a detailed study rarely, "except in the thought of Karl Barth," has it been "the object of special theological investigation."[44] In his discussion on Christ's election Daane began with an investigation of the history of the doctrine. His dependence on Barth is seen here, since he used the same approach. Barth believed that traditional Augustinianism or Calvinism "offers no proper basis" for a satisfactory outworking of the doctrine because, fundamentally, their starting point was with humanity rather than God.[45] Barth's conviction was that one can't legitimately understand the doctrine of election "except in the form of an exposition of what God Himself has said and still says concerning Himself. It cannot and must not look to anything but the Word of God."[46] Barth came to this conclusion after hearing a paper delivered in Geneva by the Parisian Pastor, Pierre Maury, at the 1936 "Congrès international de théologie calviniste."[47] Daane also criticized the approach of Augustine and Calvin by regretting, as Barth had done, their mistaken

41. Ibid.

42. Bromiley, *Introduction to the Theology of Karl Barth*, 84.

43. Barth, *Church Dogmatics*, II/2, 3.

44. Ibid., 116.

45. Bromiley, *Introduction*, 85; Barth *CD 2/2*, 14, 17.

46. Ibid., 35.

47. The conference coincided with the 400th anniversary of the arrival of the Reformation in the city. The theme of the conference was Calvin's doctrine of predestination. McCormack, "Karl Barth's Critically Realistic Dialectical Theology," 455.

starting point. Daane further followed Barth's approach by relating the centrality of Christ's election to the election of Israel.[48]

Barth held that the centrality of the doctrine of election in Jesus Christ necessitates that the discussion must consequently flow to the election of Israel. He made the connection by asserting that Israel, as God's elect, becomes narrowed down to "Jesus Christ as the one true Israelite."[49] Daane clearly followed Barth's pattern in his declaration that Jesus Christ is the "fulfillment and actualization of Israel's election."[50] Daane claimed that one must assert this because Jesus Christ was Jesus of Nazareth, the Jew who was the seed of Abraham, the son of David, and the elect of God. Indeed, Mark Lindsay, in his *Covenanted Solidarity: The Theological Basis of Karl Barth's Opposition to Nazi Antisemitism and the Holocaust*, pointed to Barth's conviction that there is an intrinsic solidarity between Christians and Jews which is integral to Barth's formulation of the doctrine of election.[51] Barth saw this doctrine as being founded on the exposition of the Word by relying heavily on Romans, chapters 9–11. In this passage Israel is pictured by Barth as the old community, while the church is the new community in the election of Jesus Christ. Indeed, the existence of Jewish Christians confirms God's transference of the old community through Jesus Christ and into the new.[52] Bromiley summarized Barth's discussion in the following comment:

> As the old man passes in Jesus Christ, and the new man comes, so the one differentiated community has a passing form and a coming form. Israel as the passing form renders the special service of praising God's mercy in the death of the old man and of the showing what God elects for himself in electing fellowship with man,

---

48. Daane, *Freedom of God*, 117; Bromiley, *Introduction*, 85.

49. Ibid.

50. Daane, *Freedom of God*, 119.

51. Lindsay, *Covenanted Solidarity: The Theological Basis of Karl Barth's Opposition to Nazi Antisemitism and the Holocaust*, 223. Barth believed that the "Church . . . as the gathering of Jews and Gentiles . . . is at the same time the revealed determination of Israel." Barth, *CD II/2*, 199.

52. Barth wrote that God's election of Israel provided an essential foundation for his future work of electing a people through Jesus Christ: "The Israelite of the community of God reveals that when in His eternal election of grace God elects fellowship with man, He has Himself assumed in relation to man the indestructible position of Leader, Disposer and Giver." Ibid., 234.

namely, the death of Jesus Christ with a view to his resurrection, in
which Israel itself is dead with a view to its rising again.[53]

Daane is clearly influenced by Barth as he also relied on Romans for
his discussion and, like Barth, connected Israel and the Church through
Jesus Christ. For Daane the "exclusive feature of God's election of the
nation of Israel, together with the inclusion of Gentiles in the church,
belongs inherently and inextricably to the election of the church."[54] Daane
followed Barth's approach in his assertion that the "election of Israel and
its relation to the salvation of Gentiles is nowhere more fully discussed
than in Romans 10 and 11."[55] Certainly it appears that Barth again influences North American theologian in his discussion of the election of the
community.

Barth explained that while the primary subject of election is the
election of Christ,[56] this election included the election of the community. In Barth's system the community is a Christological entity. For him
the election of the community does not take place outside the election
of Christ. Indeed, in his *Church Dogmatics,* he stated that "the election of
Jesus Christ is simultaneously the eternal election of the one community
of God."[57] This is quite different from the theology of election and reprobation affirmed in fundamentalist Reformed theology.

Daane clearly objected to the theological assertion that election and
reprobation are simply two sides of the same coin. He began this discussion by outlining the problem he had with the kind of Reformed theology that had been represented by Herman Hoeksema and Cornelius Van
Til. They both regarded the doctrine of election and reprobation as the
distinct feature of the Reformed faith. Their theology asserted that God
loves the elect because they are righteous in Christ and hates the repro-

---

53. Bromiley, *Introduction,* 92.

54. Daane, *Freedom of God,* 140.

55. Ibid., 141.

56. "The election of grace is the eternal beginning of all the ways and works of God
in Jesus Christ. In Jesus Christ God in His free grace determines Himself for sinful man
and sinful man for Himself. He therefore takes upon Himself the rejection of man with
all its consequences, and elects man to participation in His own glory." Barth, *CD II/2,* 94.
Barth also wrote: "In its simplest and most comprehensive form the dogma of predestination consists, then, in the assertion that the divine predestination is the election of Jesus
Christ." Ibid., 103.

57. Ibid., 195.

bate because they are sinners. "The elect alone are the object of grace; for them alone the gospel is good news. For the reprobate God has no blessing at all but only an eternal hatred."[58] The problem that Daane had with this theology was in its relationship to the preaching of the gospel. Clearly he came to be deeply concerned about what it meant to preach election. He firmly believed that once "one commits himself to the decree of decretal theology, it is theologically impossible for him to allow, justify, or explain preaching the gospel to all men. So, too, it is impossible for him to bring election into the pulpit."[59] Daane's contention, simply stated, was that "reprobation gets in the way of every attempt to take election seriously because in traditional Reformed theology *reprobation is always there.*"[60] Daane clearly found the solution to his conundrum in the theology of Karl Barth.

In Barth Daane found a different theology of election and reprobation and summarizes the Basel theologian's doctrine with the observation that Barth believed that "all men are both reprobate and elected in Jesus Christ, who is both reprobate and elect."[61] Indeed, Barth stated that Christ demonstrated that he is "the Son of God who is rejected for their sakes (that is, sinful and disobedient humanity) and yet who is still the Elect of God even in His rejection."[62]

CONCLUSION

James Daane became an important advocate of Barth's theology in the Christian Reformed Church and as a member of the faculty at Fuller Seminary. His interaction with Barth provides a helpful insight into North American responses to Barth since his own writing represented a transition of thought from criticism to appreciation. From believing that Barth was guided more by Socrates than the Bible, Daane turned to become one of Barth's most faithful evangelical advocates. Daane came to view Barth as a true exponent of Reformation theology. His doctrine of election was clearly Daane's primary point of contact and dominant motif. He saw Barth as reinvigorating the best aspects of Calvin's theology, which

58. Daane, *Freedom of God*, 24.
59. Ibid., 33.
60. Ibid., 35.
61. Ibid., 37.
62. Barth, *CD II/2*, 126.

he believed had been distorted over time. Indeed, Daane's agenda was to reaffirm Barth's assumption: that election is the sum of the Gospel, and he followed Barth's affirmation that election is fundamentally collective. Clearly, Daane's latter approach distinguishes him as a theologian seeking a new evangelicalism freed of the rationalist constraints imposed by fundamentalists.

Having studied early significant encounters with Barth the concern now moves to consider another significant period of response beginning in the 1970s. A study of this second period begins with David Mueller's important interpretative work. Like Daane, Mueller also saw the significance in Barth's doctrine of election, but also pursued a wide range of other motifs; most notably, Barth's theology of the Word of God and Christocentric approach.

6

David Mueller

THIS CHAPTER IS CONCERNED with the influence of Karl Barth in the
theology of David Mueller. It is contended here that Karl Barth became an important theological source for Mueller as a result of the influences of his father (who had been a Barthian scholar), his doctoral studies
on Barth's method and a period of post-doctoral research with Barth in
Basel. The result of these influences has been a significant contribution
to the understanding of Barth's theology in the English-speaking world.
Although fluent in German, Mueller was not a translator of Barth's works,
as Geoffrey Bromiley had been, but became an important promoter of
Barth's work and a perceptive interpreter of some of the key motifs of his
theology. Mueller was a teacher of theology and had a vocation to promote
knowledge and understanding of Barth in North America. Indeed, it will
become evident that Mueller's agenda was to promote Barth's theology
as a key source for future theological work. He presented the American
Christian scene with Barth's theology and challenged the church of his
time with issues he believed needed to be addressed.

Mueller, like the other theologians investigated here, discovered in
Barth a source of theological depth and power that enabled the establishment of a new evangelical theology free from the rationalistic constraints
and limitations of both fundamentalism and liberalism. He was able to
do so by thoughtfully engaging with Barth's writings and presenting his
arguments in the context of North American evangelicalism. It will be
shown in this chapter that Mueller's alternative approach was based on the
motifs of Barth's theology of the Word of God, Christology, and election.

David Mueller was first introduced to Barth's thought by his father,
William A. Mueller, who had written a doctoral dissertation in the early

1930s dealing with the dialectical theology of the early Barth.[1] The senior Mueller also preceded his son as a teacher of historical theology at the Southern Baptist Theological Seminary.[2] Phillip Thorne pointed to this significant early influence as he noted that the "elder Mueller also raised his son in a bilingual home, providing the young scholar not only with an early acquaintance with Barth, but also with an essential tool for serious study of German-speaking theology."[3] David Mueller acknowledged these early influences when he stated that his own "theological development was strongly influenced by neo-orthodoxy and more particularly by the theology of Karl Barth."[4] A further influence is seen when the younger Mueller completed, in 1958, a doctoral dissertation at Duke University on Barth's theological method. Mueller confessed that it was an experience that remained the most decisive influence in his thought.[5] This endeavor was followed in 1959–1960 by "an 'unforgettable' year of postgraduate studies in Basel," during which time he heard some of Barth's final lectures.[6]

BARTH'S CHRISTOLOGY

In his 1990 publication, *Foundation of Karl Barth's Doctrine of Reconciliation*, Mueller revealed his long-term interest in the theology of Barth by declaring that during the previous three decades he had been intensively involved with Barth's theology. During this time he had completed a doctoral dissertation assessing Barth's theological method and later taught courses and graduate seminars on Barth's theology.[7] Mueller's agenda is clearly seen in the hope that an increasing number of English speaking theologians would contribute to a critical engagement with Barth and in particular his doctrine of reconciliation, which, Mueller contended, char-

---

1. Mueller, "Karl Barth," 12.

2. Thorne, *Evangelicalism and Karl Barth*, 160.

3. Ibid., 160.

4. Mueller, "Changing Conceptions of 'Christian Experience,'" 165. In 1987 David Mueller dedicated a paper to his "father and theological mentor, William A. Mueller" who he states had introduced him to the theology of Karl Barth. Mueller, "The Contributions and Weaknesses of Karl Barth's View of the Bible."

5. Ibid.

6. Ibid., 160.

7. Mueller, "Foundation of Karl Barth's Doctrine of Reconciliation," iii.

acterized the contemporary German theological scene.[8] His own part in this endeavor was his publication of *Karl Barth*, in 1973.

In this instructive work Mueller directs the reader to Barth's Christocentric theology. The core understanding of this motif is explained by Mueller's proposal that Barth "consciously went beyond the Reformers in regarding Jesus Christ as the final criterion of every theological statement."[9] It appears that Mueller's interest in Barth's Christology assisted in his agenda to promote an evangelicalism distinct from fundamentalism's rationalist understanding of Scripture as the inerrant Word of God. Mueller achieved his agenda by directing the reader to an alternate view. He rightly contended that Barth's deepening Christocentrism, which came to shape his entire doctrinal system,[10] resulted in a Christocentric understanding of revelation in which Jesus Christ is God's revelation and therefore the basic text of all theology.[11] Therefore, instead of discovering God's revelation in a series of propositions extracted from sacred literature, as with fundamentalism, revelation was to be found in Jesus Christ. Clearly, by taking this path, Mueller was able successfully to undercut fundamentalist's claims by dismantling the foundation on which their thesis was set. Indeed, in a chapter dedicated to this topic Mueller stated his purpose for writing the book as being to "illustrate how the centrality of God's revelation in Jesus Christ determines both the structure and content of various doctrines in the *Church Dogmatics*."[12] In addition to his doctrine of revelation Mueller found that Barth's Christocentrism was particularly evident in his doctrine of election (*CD* II/2), published in 1942.

Mueller clearly had the agenda to promote Barth as a true student of Scripture and to depict fundamentalists as erroneously repeating Calvin's failure to construct a coherent doctrine of election that accurately reflected the biblical witness. Mueller's alternative was to promote Barth as a theologian who, unlike Calvin, was faithful to Scripture in a way Calvin never was. Consequently, Mueller also believed that Barth was totally justified in pointing out the deficiencies in Calvin's doctrine of election.

8. Ibid., vi.

9. Ibid., 48.

10. Ibid., 49.

11. Mueller cites Barth, *Church Dogmatics: I/2*, 122. Mueller particularly notes Barth's doctrine of grace which based itself on the alien righteousness of Christ. This is a motif found in Luther, but carried further Barth. Ibid., 48.

12. Mueller, *Karl Barth*, 94.

Indeed, Mueller pointed to Barth's contention, in his *Church Dogmatics* (II/2), that Calvin had failed to interpret "God's eternal election apart from God's revealed will in Jesus Christ."[13] It is in the doctrine of election that Mueller noted that Barth's "intensification of his Christocentrism is evident."[14] Indeed, Mueller understood this part of the *Dogmatics* to be the jewel in the crown of the entire system. He believed it to be Barth at his best and most profound, being in agreement with Balthasar's estimation that Barth's doctrine of election "is the most magnificent, most unified and most carefully formulated part of the entire system; it is composed with the greatest love and represents the heart of Barth's theology."[15] To support his claim he quoted Barth's declaration that

> (t)he doctrine of election is the basic witness to the fact that the gracious God is the beginning of all the ways and works of God. It defines grace as the starting-point of all subsequent reflection and speech, the common denominator which should never be forgotten in any statement which follows, and which should, if possible, come to expression in some way in every subsequent statement.[16]

Mueller believed that the central component of Barth's doctrine of election was God's election in Jesus Christ.[17] Clearly, Barth affirmed that God has decided to be "for man" in Christ. That is, God has decided to elect humanity to life and salvation through his Son.[18] As a result of this foundational affirmation Barth was able to declare that the doctrine of election is the "sum of the Gospel." However, in order to make this claim he must disagree with the "classical doctrines of election from Augustine to Aquinas and Calvin." Mueller believed that Barth was able to do so since

13. Ibid., 48. Barth believed that Calvin's doctrine of double predestination was a distortion of biblical teaching that resulted in a "fatal parallelism" of election and rejection. Barth, *Church Dogmatics: II/2*, 17.

14. Ibid., 96.

15. Ibid.

16 Ibid., 96–97.

17. Ibid., 97.

18. Barth states in his *Church Dogmatics*: "The election of grace is the eternal beginning of all the ways and works of God in Jesus Christ. In Jesus Christ God in His free grace determines Himself for sinful man and sinful man for Himself. He therefore takes upon Himself the rejection of man with all its consequences, and elects man to participation in His own glory." Barth, *CD II/2*, 94.

Scripture had spoken to him on these matters. As he meditated on what he had heard he found himself "driven irresistibly to reconstruction."[19]

Mueller rightly contended that a crucial paragraph found at the beginning of the section, "The Election of Jesus Christ," best summarized Barth's Christocentric doctrine of election:

> The election of grace is the eternal beginning of all the ways and works of God in Jesus Christ. In Jesus Christ God in His free grace determines Himself for sinful man and sinful Man for Himself. He therefore takes upon Himself the rejection of man with all its consequences, and elects man to participation in His own glory.[20]

Mueller, undoubtedly aware of the concern of his evangelical readers that all theology be based on an accurate reading of the Word, described Barth's approach as being based on biblical exposition. This, claimed Mueller, is demonstrated as Barth constructs his theology of election on the basis of an exegesis of John 1:1–2,[21] Ephesians 1:4ff., and other New Testament passages.[22] The result of his exegesis demonstrated that the decision of the triune God is to bring about his saving purposes in the world through his Word, the eternal Son of God.[23] Yet Mueller found a surprising and challenging aspect to Barth's conclusion, since it departed from the entire history of the doctrine of election by way of a rigorous refusal to speak of God's decree of election apart from Jesus Christ. Mueller's dilemma was resolved when Barth's doctrine was put within the context of theological history. Mueller knew the dilemma that was inherent in presenting Barth to his readers as being at odds with the Reformers. However, the dilemma was resolved by Mueller with his assertion that while Barth was in disagreement with the Calvin in some respects, he was in agreement with Calvin's (and Luther's) belief that Jesus is the head of the elect.[24] In this sense Barth's doctrine is seen both to build upon the Reformers and correct their deficiencies where they are seen to be at odds

19. Mueller, *Karl Barth*, 99.

20. Ibid., 100.

21. Barth States: "in the name and person of Jesus Christ we are called upon to recognize the Word of God, the decree of God and the election of God at the beginning of all things, at the beginning of our own being and thinking." *CD II/2*, 99.

22. E.g., Eph 1:10, 23; 3:9; 1 Cor 15:20; Col 1:18; 2:10; Gal 4:4; Heb 1:2. Ibid., 100, 163.

23. Mueller, *Karl Barth*, 100.

24. Ibid., 102.

with Scripture. According to Mueller the significance of Barth's theology is seen in the first major thesis of his doctrine of election: the decisive affirmation of Jesus Christ as electing God.[25] Mueller further discussed the motif of election with what he termed "the second major thesis of Barth's doctrine of election": Jesus Christ, the elected man.[26]

Mueller rightly pointed out that in Barth's Christological doctrine of election Jesus Christ is not only the electing God, but also the *object* of the election. He further contended that Barth comes to this conclusion on the basis of his exegesis of Ephesians 1:4, which maintains, claimed Barth, that "we are elected only 'in' Jesus Christ, who is the elected man. All other men are elected because God foreordained their election through the humanity of his Son."[27] According to Mueller Barth saw his theology of election as finally providing clarity to a doctrine that had never been properly defined, but, as Barth put it, had always remained an "enigma wrapped in a mystery." According to Barth the problem had never been properly solved since traditional theology could never seem to cover the breach it had created between Christology and predestination.[28] To this effect Mueller made the comment that "Barth's purpose in viewing Jesus Christ both as electing God and the electing man[29] is to dispel the obscurity which has characterized doctrines of election at the point of identifying both the God who elects (or his decree) and the elect."[30] Barth's Christological emphasis is also found in his doctrine of man.

Mueller noted that Barth's anthropology consists of a massive 600 pages in his Volume III/2 of the *Church Dogmatics*. His starting point

25. Ibid., 102. Barth stated that "(t)he election of Jesus Christ is the central choice and decision of God." Furthermore, Christ is not only the electing God but the elected in whom "our election can be known to us and contemplated by us only through His election." *CD, II/2,* 115.

26. Ibid., 102.

27. Ibid., 103.

28. Barth makes the comment that it was not only Thomas Aquinas, but also the Reformers, who never developed the doctrine, but ignored it altogether. *CD II/2,* 110. It is important to note, however, that Barth did make a significant connection with what he regarded as Augustine's important contribution. *CD II/2,* 119.

29. Barth states: "In its simplest and most comprehensive form the dogma of predestination consists . . . in the assertion that the divine predestination is the election of Jesus Christ. But the concept of election has a double reference—to the elector and to the elected . . . Thus the simplest form of the dogma may be divided at once into two assertions that Jesus Christ is the electing God, and that He is also elected man." *CD II/2,* 103.

30. Ibid., 104.

was that "man is made an object of theological knowledge by the fact that his relationship to God is revealed to us by the Word of God."[31] Mueller pointed to Barth's agreement with Calvin that true self-knowledge and knowledge of God are correlates. Indeed, humanity can only truly understand its nature as creatures of God by listening to the Word of God revealed in Jesus Christ.[32] This is a point that Mueller later takes up in an article for *Perspectives in Religious Studies*. Here he compared Barth to Ritschl and Schleiermacher and reminded the reader that Barth opposed all talk of religious experience that is not rooted in Jesus Christ. For this reason he rejected natural theology and any attempt to elevate the religious person to a place of pre-eminence in theology. Barth remained insistent that "God's revelation of himself takes precedence over man's appropriation of that unveiling."[33] The foundational element in this theology arose from Barth's assumption that God's ultimate revelation has been in Jesus Christ. Consequently Mueller asserted Barth's orthodox credentials as he summarized his "starting point" as the "concrete revelation of God in the history of the covenant climaxing in the Word made flesh (John 1:14)." As a result, Barth always accentuated—in agreement with the Reformers and in contrast to Ritschl and Schleiermacher—the priority of God's initiative above all human responses. Indeed: "The final authority for interpreting man's relationship to God is not man's reason or his moral or religious consciousness."[34] Mueller also discussed Barth's Christocentrism in his theology of the Word of God.

BARTH'S VIEW OF THE BIBLE

In 1987 David Mueller delivered a paper at the "Conference on Biblical Inerrancy," under the title: *The Contribution and Weaknesses of Karl Barth's View of the Bible*.[35] It is an interesting title since nowhere in his paper did he discuss any weaknesses. However, what Mueller did do was introduce Barth's doctrine of the Word of God with an outline of Barth's theology of the threefold Word of God: the revealed Word, the written Word, and

---

31. Ibid., 113.

32. Ibid., 114. Barth's assertion was that "Jesus is Himself the revealing Word of God." Barth, *Church Dogmatics: III/2*, 3.

33. Mueller, *Changing Conceptions*, 168.

34. Ibid., 167.

35. Mueller, "The Contributions and Weaknesses of Karl Barth's View of the Bible."

the proclaimed Word. Mueller noted that the sole foundation of Barth's system of revelation is God's revelation of himself. This is expressed firstly in a statement that the "speaking and action of God is attested in the old and new covenants with their centre in Jesus Christ, the Word made flesh, who unites the two covenants."[36] Indeed, Mueller further observed that Barth "consciously seeks to reassert the primacy of the Reformer's Scripture principle."[37] It was Barth's claim that the authority of the Bible is axiomatic for all Protestants who seek to stand in the tradition of the Reformation.[38] Barth's third form of the Word of God, the preached Word, also stood within the tradition of the Reformers. However, it was with the nature of the written Word, the topic of the conference, that most attention was given.

To illustrate the nature of Barth's thesis Mueller turned to Barth's *Dogmatics*, where the description of Scripture as "a witness to God's revelation in Christ is likened to the figure of John the Baptist. Standing midway between the covenants, John was 'sent from God [. . .] for testimony, to bear witness to the light [. . .]' namely, to Jesus Christ (John 1:6–7)."[39] However, the Biblical witnesses are not directly identical with God's revelation of himself. Mueller therefore restated Barth's conclusion that the Bible cannot be equated with the Word to which it attests. This pointed to the Bible's limitations. Yet Mueller was undoubtedly keen to present Barth as a theologian who asserted the Bible's authority. Mueller did this well when he pointed to Barth's contention that this limitation in no way denies the Bible's uniqueness. Mueller quoted Barth's comment:

> In this limitation the Bible is not distinguished from revelation. It is simply revelation as it comes to us—to us who are not ourselves prophets and apostles, and therefore not the immediate and direct recipients of the one revelation, witness of the resurrection of Jesus Christ.[40]

In order to successfully promote Barth among evangelicals Mueller needed to address the theory of inspiration which had long been at the forefront in the defense of their views. Mueller did this well by accurately depicting Barth as a theologian who stood firmly in the tradition of the

36. Ibid., 423.
37. Ibid.
38. Ibid., 424.
39. Ibid., 425.
40. Ibid.

Reformers. To illustrate this point Mueller initially referred to Barth's 1918 commentary on Romans in which he declared his own indebtedness to the Reformation emphasis on the divine inspiration of the biblical witness. This is again emphasized in the *Church Dogmatics*.[41] From this emphasis Mueller pointed to Barth's distinctively Reformed affirmation of the pre-eminent authority of Holy Scripture above the preached Word and the sacraments.[42] However, Barth's definition of the authority of Scripture is to be distinguished from fundamentalist definitions of inspiration. The authority of Scripture, claimed Barth, is on the basis of ability to act as a witness to the real event of revelation that took place at a certain point in history in the person and work of Jesus Christ. Again, in order to appeal to his evangelical audience, Mueller prudently recalled that Barth supported his thesis on the basis of a careful exegesis of classic Scriptural passages. Mueller referred to Barth's treatment of 2 Tim 3:14–17 and 2 Pet 1:19–21. In reference to his exegesis Mueller emphasized Barth's comment that both of these passages speak of the Holy Spirit as the author of what is written in Scripture in his capacity as a witness to revelation. Consequently, the writers of these passages, indeed all Scripture, speak as *auctores secundarii* [secondary authors].[43] In following this path Barth distinguished himself from both liberal and fundamentalist theology.

In opposition to the rationalistic basis of fundamentalism Mueller asserted that faith is neither the intellectual acceptance of the Bible as the Word of God nor intellectual assent to certain doctrines. Indeed, Barth followed the Reformers (a path that fundamentalists incorrectly claim as their own), especially Calvin, when he asserted "an inextricable unity between Jesus Christ, the revealed Word, the testimony of Holy Scripture, and the Word of the Holy Spirit as the *Teacher of the Word*."[44] Mueller elaborated on this further when dealing with Barth's response to Protestant Orthodoxy. Here Mueller referred to Barth's contention that the seventeenth century Protestant Orthodox view of inspiration (from which contemporary fundamentalism draws much of its thinking) was a departure from the Reformers. Mueller joined Barth's lament when he noted that Protestant Orthodoxy lost appreciation for the Reformer's

41. Barth, *Church Dogmatics: I/1*, 463.

42. Ibid., 426.

43. Ibid., 427.

44. Ibid., 431.

view that "faith's confession that the Bible is the Word of God confesses God's sovereignty and his mysterious working through his Spirit enabling the human word of the biblical witnesses to mediate his presence."[45] In contrast Protestant Orthodoxy had followed a process of secularization through which the biblical authors became clerks, secretaries or short hand writers, who wrote what was dictated to them. The result was a docetic dissolving of the concept of the Bible's witness to revelation. Mueller further pointed to Barth's concern that this process produced a mechanical view of Scripture used as an instrument of its interpreters to assert what cannot be maintained in the face of serious exposition. In Barth's view it was a path devoid of spiritual force and a marked departure from Calvin's description of the biblical witnesses as servants and the Reformation's theology of inspiration, which understood Scripture as the mediation of God's saving presence.[46] On the basis of this argument Mueller referred to Barth's theology of Scripture as a human document.

Mueller pointed to the value of emphasizing Barth's theology of the humanity of Scripture. It was Barth's contention that the Bible could not truly be understood without viewing it in its human dimension. Mueller summarized Barth's thought when he stated that "the exegete takes the text seriously not in by-passing its humanity or literary form, but in submitting to it as the sole place in which God mediates his presence."[47] On these grounds Mueller cautioned evangelicals against divinizing the Bible, since this only undermines Scripture and sets it apart from Jesus Christ. In Barth's logic a totally divine Scripture does not have the capacity to communicate with humanity unless it possesses its own humanity. Indeed, this is the case with the humanity and divinity of Jesus Christ. If Scripture is to have authority as a witness to God's revelation it must itself possess the same characteristics. Therefore, while being divine, the written Word must also be fully human.

To illustrate his point Mueller discussed Barth's comment that "Holy Scripture is like the unity of God and man in Jesus Christ. It is neither divine only or human only [. . .] (I)n its own way and decree it is very God and very man, i.e., a witness of revelation which itself belongs to revela-

---

45. Ibid., 443.

46. Ibid., 444–45.

47. Ibid., 428.

tion, and historically a very human literary document."[48] Barth further looked to the total lack of necessity to discount the humanity of Scripture since this contradicts the biblical witness that "all of God's dealing with Israel and the Church and humanity as a whole involve God's accommodation of himself to finite, mortal, erring and sinful human beings."[49] As a result of these reflections evangelicals have complained that Barth's theology undermines Scripture. Yet Mueller once again challenged this assumption on the basis of Barth's insistence that the "Word of God cannot be known apart from engagement with Holy Scripture."[50] Again Mueller's contention is here asserted, that Barth's theology can be described as a theology of careful biblical exegesis. Mueller highlighted this by quoting from Barth's parting counsel to his Bonn students on being banned from Germany by Hitler in 1935: "Do exegesis, exegesis, exegesis!"[51] On the basis of this kind of conviction Mueller insisted that Barth was a true evangelical and a worthy mentor for future theological work.

In assessing the importance of Barth to the contemporary evangelical situation Mueller asserted that Barth's doctrine of Scripture established him as an evangelical in the tradition of the Reformers. More specifically, Barth's theology has benefited the American evangelical scene which will be further enriched if it continues to engage in dialogue "with both his doctrine of Scripture and his interpretation of the major doctrines of evangelical theology in the tradition of the Reformers."[52] Indeed, Mueller was in agreement with Bernard Ramm's thesis that Barth's doctrine of Scripture provides the best model for evangelical theology today.[53] Mueller further advanced Barth's credentials by pointing out that he stood against the "German Christians" who regarded German National Socialism as a legitimate second source of revelation along with God's revelation in Jesus Christ. Against this "illicit merger" Barth stood as a key figure reaffirming for the Confessing Church, in its Barmen Declaration, that the "inviolable foundation of the German Evangelical Church is the Gospel

48. Barth, *CD I/2*, 501; Ibid., 429.
49. Ibid., 429.
50. Ibid.
51. Ibid.
52. Ibid., 437.
53. Ibid.

of Jesus Christ as it is attested for us in Holy Scripture."[54] This stood in direct contrast to the legacy of nineteenth-century liberalism.

BARTH'S INTERACTION WITH NINETEENTH CENTURY LIBERALISM

In an article for *Religion and Life*[55] David Mueller studied Barth's interaction with nineteenth century liberalism. Mueller began by noting that one way to interpret Barth's theological method was to compare and contrast it with that of the nineteenth century. Indeed, the North American theologian proposed that Barth's critique of Cartesianism, (and its synonyms: anthropological, or liberal theology) provided a clue to understanding his methodology and system.[56] Barth's analysis stipulated that Cartesianism was a product of humanism and the Renaissance and that it found classical expression in Descartes (1596–1650), "who based the certainty of the existence of God on man's certainty of his own existence."[57] Barth believed that "Cartesianism reached its zenith in Schleiermacher and his followers, and its denouement in Feuerbach, Harnack, and Troeltch."[58] However Mueller noted that it was to Schleiermacher that Barth gave most of his attention.[59]

Mueller revealed that Barth's prefaces to the successive editions of *The Epistle to the Romans* describe his disdain for the method of liberalism which he perceived as elevating humanity to the level of God. In it he regarded Schleiermacher as demonstrating genius, but nothing, so Barth believed, to indicate that he was a good teacher since "he is disastrously dim-sighted in regard to the fact that man as man is not only in *need* but beyond all hope of saving himself."[60] Mueller made the important observation that Barth found this philosophically orientated theology overly subjective, leading him to create a theology of the objective Word of God. Mueller's astute observation was that like Anselm, Barth believed that the

---

54. Ibid., 438.

55. Mueller, "The Theology of Karl Barth and the Nineteenth Century."

56. Ibid., 81.

57. Ibid.

58. Ibid.

59. Ibid.

60. Mueller further notes that Barth's contention with Liberalism continued after his transition from a theology of dialectics toward a theology of the Word of God. Ibid., 84.

only secure starting point in theology "was the objective revelation attested in the Word of God and the credo of the church; to begin elsewhere meant the possibility of remaining caught within the subjective circle."[61]

Barth outlined his theology of the Word no where more clearly than in his 1932 revision of *Church Dogmatics* (CD I/1). Mueller observed that Barth responded to Schleiermacher's (and others) subjective "pietistic-rationalistic Modernism" by focusing on the objective pole of revelation. Mueller asserted that Barth developed his objectively based theology by constructing a Christology that "consciously goes beyond the Reformers in making Jesus Christ the final criterion of every theological statement."[62] On this basis Mueller contended that Barth increasingly found that he was successfully able to do battle with anthropological theologies, and noted that the creation of the Nazi orientated German Christians led by Bishop Ludwig Müller, served as a critical catalyst for further theological work.

Mueller discussed Barth's opposition to natural theology, which he saw as the grounding for the theological distortions of the German Christians. His primary objection was that it perceived itself as a further source of revelation to the central revelation in Jesus Christ.[63] In response Barth wrote his heated *Nein!* to Brunner in 1934, for he feared that any assent to natural theology would spell disaster. It was for this reason that Barth opposed the *analogia entis* and pursued the *analogia fidei*. Mueller recalled that Barth did so because it emphasized that knowledge of God was dependent on God's self-revelation which could only be appropriated through faith. In this analogy the problems of anthropological theologies are overcome as the incongruity between God and humanity, knower and known, are overcome. Further, as Barth pursued this line of thought the foundations of naturalism which had been utilized by the "German Christians," were dismantled. In describing these events Mueller skillfully pointed to the issues surrounding Barth's well-known and significant shift from dialectics to analogy.[64] Mueller contended that Barth, as he wrestled with these issues, came to see that his earlier dialectical theology had the capacity to lead to a denial of any knowledge of God. Further, Mueller rightly made the observation that Barth must have come to see the com-

---

61. Ibid., 85.

62. Ibid., 86.

63. Ibid., 87.

64. Here Mueller refers to Urs Von Balthasar's description of Barth's transition. Ibid., 89.

parisons between his early dialecticism and the emphasis of nineteenth-century theology.[65] Mueller also contended that another consequence of Barth's debate with naturalists, his horror at the Christianity of National Socialism, and his shift to *analogia fidei*, contributed to the construction of his Christocentric method.

As we have seen, Christocentrism is understood by Mueller to be particularly evident in Barth's doctrine of election.[66] Mueller's contention was that it was an approach that enabled Barth to counter the issues he debated because in it Jesus Christ "determines Himself for sinful man and sinful man for Himself."[67] It gives no consideration to the decision of the person since all has been determined in Jesus Christ, who has acted on behalf of all. Mueller therefore noted that a large proportion of Barth's later theology was constructed in response to nineteenth-century anthropological theology. Indeed, Mueller observed that "Barth's method is in part a response to the taunt of Ludwig Feuerbach that 'all theology is anthropology.'" In contrast Mueller made the observation that Barth's Christological dogmatics enabled him to refer to true theology as "theoanthropology."[68] This placed Barth clearly in the heritage of the Reformation.

KARL BARTH AND THE HERITAGE OF THE REFORMATION

As has been demonstrated, Mueller often made comparisons between Barth and the Reformers. Indeed, Mueller made the observation that to "interpret Barth above all else as a neo-Reformation theologian seeking to reaffirm and extend the theological heritage of the sixteenth-century Protestant Reformers[69] [...] accords with his own self-understanding at the

65. Mueller makes the further observation that "Barth's view of faith and the language of faith runs counter to the tendency of nineteenth-century theology at important points." Ibid., 89.

66. Mueller further believes that this doctrine "is the most important single work for understanding the scope of Barth's Christocentrism." Ibid., 89.

67. Ibid., 90.

68. Ibid., 93.

69. In 1988 David Mueller constructed a hypothetical dialogue between Rudolf Bultmann and Karl Barth. Clearly Mueller used his extensive knowledge of German theology to construct this dialogue. Its purpose, as with Mueller's other works, was to educate and inform. During this hypothetical discussion Barth, after making the comment that he found Bultmann's interpretation of the gospel to be inadequate, shared a moment of biting sarcasm. "Have you heard the following joke about modern theologians? 'Bonhoeffer is good beer; Tillich is beer; Bultmann is foam!'" To this Bultmann replied: "Your humor

close of his career."[70] Mueller believed that any attempt to interpret Barth without reference to his intention to reclaim and extend the Reformation's theological heritage will misrepresent him. Mueller contended that, "(a) ny perusal of Barth's citations of Calvin, Luther, and other Reformers as well as Reformation themes in the *Church Dogmatics* makes this claim abundantly clear."[71] Mueller further supported this claim as he alluded to the fact that the heritage of the Reformation was at the heart of Karl Barth's religious upbringing and therefore a significant influence on his thinking. According to Mueller this accounted for a significant number of references to the Reformers, and others of that heritage, which appeared in Barth's writing. Significantly, while most interpretations of Barth's theology concentrate on Barth's shift from liberalism to neo-orthodoxy, Mueller pointed out that Barth's important initial transition to liberalism was *from* the Reformed heritage of his childhood.[72] Therefore, Mueller made the important observation that Barth's roots lie deeply embedded in the Protestant Reformation.

Barth's Reformational roots were largely attributed to the influence of his father, who was a professor of New Testament and Church History at the University of Bern and known for his conservative theological position. Reflecting on his background, Karl Barth later commented that his "faith was nourished in positive evangelical theology."[73] This influence was further strengthened when Barth was called upon at the age of sixteen to prepare for confirmation into the Swiss Church. He recalled that he was not only challenged to "know something of the content of the Swiss Reformed Confessions, but also to be able 'to understand them from within.'"[74] Out of this encounter Mueller observed that "Barth resolved to become a theologian."[75] While his theological training led him

---

is better than your understanding of me. At least the theology which I brew is not a stale beer which is just a rehash of old dogmas thrown at people with the demand: 'You've got to swallow all of it.'" These comments give an indication of the kind of tensions that existed between different branches of the German church, highlighted even more when one considers that Barth and Bultmann where both adherents of the Confessing Church. Mueller, "The Whale and the Elephant: Barth and Bultmann in Dialogue," 199.

70. Ibid., 45.

71. Ibid.

72. Ibid.

73. Ibid.

74. Ibid.

75. Ibid., 46.

away from his Reformed roots his experience of preaching to his congregation at Sanfenwil (1911–1921) led to a struggle with the subject matter of the Bible. Mueller believed that through this struggle Barth increasingly found the historical-critical commentaries inadequate. However, he did not reject this approach, but rather the historical critic's failure "to confront the real subject-matter of the text; that is, they failed to seek the Word of God to which Scripture pointed."[76] Mueller further commented that as Barth searched for guides for comprehending Paul's epistle to the Romans he found help from the commentaries of Luther, Calvin and interpreters like J. T. Beck and Adolf Schlatter, whose perspective was informed by the Reformers. Mueller also pointed to Barth's reference to Calvin as his exegetical guide for the writing of his Romans commentary.[77] However, it is contended here that Mueller overstated the importance of the Reformers and their descendants at this early stage of Barth's theological reorientation.

Mueller retold the events of Barth's change in orientation in terms of a rediscovering of his Reformed roots while at Sanfenwil, during which time he wrote his commentary on Romans. T. F. Torrance would agree that Barth did indeed begin his change of orientation during this time. Torrance believed that Barth became "determined to hear the Word of God out of itself, as it came straight from above, unfettered by a [. . .] general frame of thought already worked out by modern man."[78] Torrance further commented that the powerful influence upon Barth at this time was the eschatological teaching of Christoph Blumhardt,[79] Franz Overbeck, and Søren Kierkegaard.[80] Indeed, the attraction of Overbeck came from his quest for a return to the original history of the church in the lifetime of Christ himself. However, there is disagreement with aspects of Mueller's thesis. Torrance believed that theologically and philosophically, during these early years, "it was undoubtedly Kierkegaard who had the greatest impact" on Barth.[81] McCormack would seem to concur with Torrance's observations, describing Barth's change as a discovery of the otherness

76. Ibid.

77. Ibid.

78 T. F. Torrance, *Karl Barth: An Introduction to His Early Theology*, 35.

79. Ibid., 36.

80. Ibid., 42.

81. Ibid., 44.

of God.[82] McCormack's theory further challenged Mueller's contention that Barth relied heavily on Calvin for the writing of his Romans commentary. McCormack maintained that up until the time of his professorship at Göttingen Barth's main encounter with Calvin had been at Geneva (1909–1911), when he had read the *Institutes* "through the lens provided by his Herrmannian theology."[83] However, Torrance and McCormack would agree with Mueller's acknowledgement that when Barth became the honorary professor of Reformed theology at the University of Göttingen his Reformed and Reformation heritage became his own.[84] Consequently, there are doubts about Mueller's thesis that Barth made a speedy return to his Reformed roots while at Sanfenwil at some time between 1911 and 1921. Torrance and McCormack are seen, therefore, to be correct in their estimation that Barth turned direction during the summer of 1924 when he was preparing for his lectures on Reformed dogmatics and came across Heppe's volume. Mueller most likely developed his thesis in order to avoid discussion on Barth's dialectical period, by making a comment on Calvin into a decisive moment of theological conversion that did not actually take place, as Mueller described it, until a number of years later. This reservation is supported by the observation that when Barth wrote his commentary on the epistle to the Romans the Reformers are hardly mentioned. It is worthy of note that Calvin is only cited five times, whereas Dostoyevsky is referred to on nineteen occasions. Luther is referred to on nine occasions, while Kierkegaard is cited over twelve times.[85] However, Mueller was right that when Barth commenced his *Church Dogmatics*, in the period after 1932, he developed a theology "grounded in the Word of God attested in Scripture." Furthermore, by that time he had sought to write "a confessional theology true to the Reformers' heritage."[86]

82. McCormack, *Karl Barth's Critically Realistic Dialectical Theology*, 125.

83. Ibid., 293.

84. Mueller undercuts his own argument by making this observation, particularly since he makes Reformed dogmatics synonymous with the theology of the Reformers. *The Heritage of the Reformation*, 47.

85. Barth, *Epistle to the Romans*.

86. Ibid., 47.

CONCLUSION

The discussion leads to the conclusion that Karl Barth was a significant influence in the construction of David Mueller's new evangelical approach. Indeed, Mueller's appreciation of Barth led to a body of work dedicated to the promotion of Barth's doctrine and theological approach. He believed that Barth's theology could form the basis of a new alternative for North American evangelicalism. The influences that led Mueller to this endeavor are clear and discernible. His father's interest in Barth led Mueller to pursue a similar interest. His PhD studies and time in Basel further strengthened and clarified his direction. However, Mueller was not primarily concerned with constructing his own theological system after the pattern of Barth. Rather, it would appear that Mueller was concerned to teach others about the many possibilities that Barth's theology provided. He did so by providing summaries of Barth's work, introductions to his thinking and papers on key aspects of his theology. Clearly his agenda was to educate others in the basics of Barth's work. Behind this lay Mueller's agenda to present Barth as an evangelical theologian of the Word who had contended with liberalism and fundamentalism and, while remaining deeply indebted to the Reformers, sometimes saw the need to go beyond them when compelled by the Word of God. Mueller presented Barth as a Christocentric theologian for whom Jesus Christ was himself the Word of God who constituted church authority and the basis of every doctrine. He also discussed with interest, the motif of Barth's doctrine of election.

While Mueller provided North Americans with an important introduction to Barth's theology it is true to say that Donald Bloesch has proven to be a significant model in the construction of a theological system influenced by Barth at most points. Bloesch, in a similar vein to Mueller, also had a number of influences, which led to Barth being an important source in his theology. Consequently, the discussion now turns to Bloesch.

7

Donald G. Bloesch

KARL BARTH REMAINS A significant influence in the theology of Donald G. Bloesch. It will be shown in this chapter that Barth was a significant influence in Bloesch's theological development from childhood to adult academic life. This is apparent in Bloesch's theological writing in which Barth's work is constantly used in the construction of his theological motifs. It will be argued here that while Bloesch differed from Barth in a number of areas,[1] it is true to say that he saw Barth as a respected mentor and valuable conversation partner who could enable one to effectively construct a new evangelical theology, free of the rationalist constraints of fundamentalism and liberalism.

Barth is clearly behind Bloesch's theology of the Word of God. Here he developed a theology of the Word significantly influenced by Barthian Christology. Indeed, Barth is seen as a stalwart mentor who enabled Bloesch to fulfill his agenda of upholding the authority of Scripture, without becoming entangled in all the impossibilities he saw associated with contemporary fundamentalism's propositional rationalism. Barth is also an ally who assisted Bloesch in his battle with immanentalism which he believed reduced God to being a passive collaborator with humanity. In contradistinction Bloesch advocated Barth's understanding of transcendence, in which God is active as redeemer and healer. Also, Bloesch preferred the guidance of the reformed theologian Karl Barth to Martin

1. While Barth's objectivism locates salvation completely outside the self in the decrees of God and also in the work of Christ, Bloesch tries to balance the objective and subjective dimensions of salvation. Barth deemphasizes the sacraments in Christian devotion and indeed reinterprets them as signs of Christian commitment rather than means of grace, whereas Bloesch speaks of sacraments as means of grace. Barth sometimes gives the impression that all are saved through Christ's universal statement. However, Bloesch prefers to say that all are invited to salvation through God's electing grace. pers. comm. (April 6, 2005) 1.

Luther and post-Reformation Lutheranism. Consequently, this chapter explains that Bloesch proposed a theology heavily grounded in Barth's theology of the person and work of Christ. It is further contended here that the influence of Barth in Bloesch's Christology flows as a natural corollary into the influence of Barth in his soteriology. It is also to be observed that Barth was appreciated by Bloesch for his objectively based approach to theology and for his doctrine of predestination which finds all of humanity predestined in Christ. Clearly, Bloesch also preferred Barth's reappraisal of the atonement which replaced the traditional emphasis of satisfaction with a theology of the triumphant love of God. The discussion now turns to an account of Bloesch's life, where the influences that led to his theological output are clearly seen.

Donald G. Bloesch's grandparents traveled from Switzerland to the United States as missionaries to German speaking migrants. Herbert Bloesch, his father, became a minister to their sponsoring group, the Evangelical Synod of North America,[2] which, in 1943, joined with the General Synod of the Reformed Church in the United States to form the Evangelical and Reformed Church (ERC).[3] In 1957 the ERC joined with the Congregational Christian Churches, itself an amalgamation of various groups, to form the United Church of Christ.[4]

Bloesch's difficulty with fundamentalism was consistent with his denominational background. Indeed, it is true to say that Bloesch's mature theology had its roots in both the church and the home. The denominations which came together to form the United Church of Christ (UCC) were ecumenical and open; they were not fundamentalist or dogmatic. They were founded on distinct theological foundations: Lutheran Pietism, evangelicalism, and Reformed theologies. The ERC's doctrinal standards, the denomination of Bloesch's youth, included both Reformed and Lutheran confessions, together with the freedom of interpretation that where these standards differed the norm was to be guided by the Word of God.[5] Bloesch recalled that his two-year preparation for confir-

---

2. As a denomination the ESNA was a product of several Midwestern immigrant congregations of the Evangelical Union of Prussia, itself a German Lutheran and Reformed amalgamation brought about by King Frederick III (1770–1840). Wilshire, "The United Church of Christ," 1199.

3. McKim, "Donald Bloesch," 388.

4. Wilshire, "United Church of Christ," 1200.

5. Steinmetz, "Evangelical and Reformed Church," in *The New International Dictionary of the Christian Church* (Exeter: Paternoster, 1974) 360.

mation in the Evangelical and Reformed Church involved a long study of the Evangelical Catechism, an experience, he noted, which had a lasting influence.[6]

After graduating from high school in 1946, Bloesch entered Elmhurst College, the preparatory school for pre-theological students in the Evangelical and Reformed Church. Elmer Colyer, a colleague of Bloesch at Dubuque University, noted that, "(m)ost students at Elmhurst College intent on entering the ministry in the ERC continued on to Eden Theological Seminary. Instead, Bloesch chose Chicago Theological Seminary (CTS), partly because of his growing interest in the sociology of religion but also due to his desire to pursue PhD studies."[7]

At CTS Bloesch came across a faculty who described themselves as neo-naturalists. However, as a result of being deeply influenced by his more conservative confessional and pietistic background he could not accommodate to their thinking. It was at this time that Barth came to play a significant role in Bloesch's theology. Looking for a satisfactory way forward he began to read the major works of Kierkegaard, Brunner, Barth, Tillich, and Bultmann, with interest and appreciation.[8] Bloesch came to find in Barth a clear conservative alternative to the theology on offer at CTS. It is without doubt that Barth fitted well with Bloesch's background in confessionalism and upheld the great themes of the Reformation, such as the Word of God, salvation by grace alone and the atonement.[9] In addition, Barth clearly provided an intellectual avenue for Bloesch to engage these themes in dialogue with contemporary theological thought. He wrote that "Barth has given to the modern church an alternative that makes it possible to maintain continuity with the teaching of the church through the ages and yet be in fruitful dialogue with modernity."[10] Bloesch's background also contributed to his ready interest in neo-orthodoxy. Indeed, he finally wrote his PhD thesis on the theology of the American neo-orthodox theologian, Reinhold Niebuhr, who had also been a significant figure within the Evangelical

6. Keylock, "Evangelical Leaders you Should Meet: Meet Donald Bloesch," 62.

7. Colyer, "Donald G. Bloesch and His Career," 12.

8. Ibid., 13.

9. Bloesch, "The Legacy of Karl Barth," 6.

10. Bloesch, "Karl Barth: Appreciation and Reservations," 127.

Synod of North America.[11] These influences have been enhanced by Bloesch's neo-orthodox colleague at the University of Dubuque, Arthur Cochrane, whom Bloesch has regarded as one of his mentors.[12]

In Bloesch's view Karl Barth was the foremost Protestant thinker of the twentieth-century and "the most profound and influential theologian of our age."[13]

Clearly Bloesch, bringing the influence of his early years to Chicago University, and in contrast to his lecturers, turned to Karl Barth. He was to be Bloesch's influence of choice and a constant source as he expounded his theological motifs. Indeed, in relation to contemporary Protestant thought Bloesch contended that while he would have reservations with parts of Barth's conclusions, much of Barth's work was to be applauded, appreciated, and embraced as "novel and daring formulations of the age-old truths of the Bible."[14] Furthermore, Bloesch asserted that Barth had a significant part to play in formulating a new kind of evangelicalism in North America. This belief led to the agenda of promoting Barth among evangelicals, a conviction expressed simply yet profoundly in his article, *The Legacy of Karl Barth*, where he announced that "(w)e should see Barth first of all as an evangelical." Bloesch's conviction was clearly based on the belief that Barth was "committed to the gospel of reconciliation and redemption, the message that we are saved by the free grace of God alone as revealed and confirmed in Jesus Christ. For Barth, this entailed an acknowledgment of the authority of Holy Scripture as the primary witness to God's self-revelation in Christ."[15] Bloesch further cultivated Barth's evangelical credentials by asserting Barth's upholding of the grace of God and in "his ardent espousal of the substitutionary atonement of Christ" and "his defense of the Virgin Birth of Christ and His bodily resurrection." Bloesch also noted appreciation for what he believed to be Barth's "brilliant exposition of the doctrine of the trinity," and his understanding of prayer, which he contended must surely be "recognized as biblical and evangelical."[16]

11. Like Bloesch, Niebuhr's father, Gustav, had been a minister in that denomination. Fox, *Reinhold Niebuhr: A Biography*, 2.

12. Colyer, *Donald Bloesch and His Career*, 14.

13. Bloesch, *Evangelical Renaissance*, 80–81.

14. Bloesch, *Legacy of Karl Barth*, 6.

15. Ibid., 17.

16. Bloesch, *Evangelical Renaissance*, 82–83.

BLOESCH WRITES ABOUT BARTH

It is to be acknowledgement that Bloesch's appropriation of Barth into a new kind of evangelicalism began with Bloesch writing *about* Barth. Bloesch's early work, his 1976 publication *Jesus is Victor! Karl Barth's Doctrine of Salvation*, amounted to an outline of Barth's soteriology. In the foreword Bloesch revealed his agenda by stating that he wrote the book "partly in order to counteract popular misunderstandings of Karl Barth's theology," and yet to also share his thoughts on where he believed Barth fell short.[17] Clearly Bloesch's agenda was to highlight those motifs within Barth's theology that confirmed his orthodox credentials and hence his appeal to evangelicals. Furthermore, these motifs form the basis of Bloesch's use of Barth as a source in his theological writing. However, it is also apparent that the influence of evangelicalism and Bloesch's intention to remain within that group led him to have reservations about aspects of Barth's theology.

Barth was seen by Bloesch to fall short of constructing a theology that is fully in accord with his own evangelical and catholic approach.[18] However, Bloesch's "principle criticism of Barth's theology is that he ever and again fails to hold together the objective and subjective poles of salvation."[19] Nevertheless, while being critical of some of Barth's theology Bloesch expressed a great deal of indebtedness. Clearly his approach was to depict Barth as a theologian standing in the tradition of the Reformers, yet having the ability to develop their theology in areas that seemed to fall short. This is seen when he noted that while Barth's doctrines of God and the person of Christ have been a noteworthy and positive influence on his theological development, his exposition of the being and perfections of God "surpasses that of the Reformers in comprehensiveness, clarity, and biblical fidelity." Bloesch has also revealed that he greatly benefited from Barth's doctrine of Scripture and praised Barth's reliance on the Reformers and Anabaptists,[20] while also being in tune with the modern world.[21]

---

17. Bloesch, *Jesus is Victor! Karl Barth's Doctrine of Salvation*, 9.

18. Ibid., 9.

19. Ibid., 10.

20. Bloesch believes that in regard to the ministry, the sacraments, and perhaps eschatology, Barth has a closer affinity to the left-wing Reformation, particularly the Anabaptists, ibid., 15.

21. Ibid.

Bloesch clearly contended that it is with Barth's objective soteriology that one notes the most obvious tension with evangelical orthodoxy. Barth's affirmation, stated Bloesch, was that all are elected by God and adopted into Sonship, just as all are predestined to salvation in Christ.[22] It is a sentiment Bloesch repeated some ten years later in his contribution to Donald McKim's work, *How Karl Barth Changed My Mind*, where he again counted Barth, along with Luther and Calvin, as one of his principle theological mentors. However, it is Bloesch's agenda for evangelicalism that must be highlighted here. Clearly, Bloesch depicted Barth as an heir of the Reformation who had the ability to advance their theology in the light modern theological insights. In this sense Bloesch depicted Barth as a true evangelical holding within his own genius the best of both worlds, without falling victim to the extremes of fundamentalism or liberalism.[23]

THE INFLUENCE OF BARTH UPON BLOESCH'S THEOLOGY

Theology of the Word

Bloesch was greatly influenced by the motif of Barth's theology of the Word and in particular his understanding of biblical authority. It is asserted here that Bloesch perceived in Barth an ally of evangelicals who was willing to promote the "primacy of biblical revelation over church tradition and religious experience."[24] Clearly Bloesch was impressed with Barth's biblical fidelity[25] and saw him as a theological mentor who enabled one to dialogue constructively with issues related to higher criticism, yet maintaining that such criticism only has the ability to take one so far. Consequently, one sees in Bloesch the belief that Barth's gift to the modern church is in his provision of a hermenuetical alternative to both fundamentalism and liberalism since he "makes it possible to maintain continuity with the teaching of the church through the ages and yet be

---

22. Ibid., 32.

23. Bloesch also reveals that what he appreciates about Barth is his strong affirmation of the freedom and sovereignty of God. While this theme is also found in Calvin, Bloesch prefers Barth's understanding of the sovereignty of God, of God's sovereign love, to Calvin's emphasis on his sovereign majesty and holiness. Bloesch, *Appreciation and Reservations*, 126.

24. Ibid., 127.

25. Bloesch, "Soteriology in Contemporary Christian Thought," 133.

in fruitful dialogue with modernity."[26] Therefore Barth, who frequently utilized the sources of theological history, enabled Bloesch to fulfill his agenda of standing in the tradition of the church while also engaging in the interpretation of Scripture in a creative and innovative fashion.[27] Here one finds in Bloesch an appreciation of Barth as a valuable source in his agenda to find a middle ground between fundamentalism and liberalism. Indeed, in contrast to both fundamentalism and liberalism Bloesch followed Barth when he stated: "We know what we say when we call the Bible the Word of God only when we recognize its human imperfections in face of its divine perfection, and its divine perfection in spite of its human imperfection."[28]

In dealing with the doctrine of the Word in his *Holy Scripture: Revelation, Inspiration and Interpretation,* Bloesch set the tone of his argument in motion by referring to Scripture as that which "bears the imprint of divine revelation." While what he meant by this is expanded on later, the clear implication is that the words of Scripture are not totally divine, but somehow holding the image of God within them. Later he referred to John Wesley to assist his argument against those believing the Bible to be inerrant by stating that Wesley, so much part of the heritage of evangelicalism, recognized the possibility of error in the genealogies.[29] Yet Bloesch referred to the rise of historical and literary criticism to argue the point that one is left with no choice but to consider with earnestness the human authorship of Scripture. Bloesch, who has sought to convince evangelicals of his argument, prudently pointed out that this was a reality not lost on the Reformers, but one that has become lost among the assertions of fundamentalism. It was Protestant Orthodoxy, claimed Bloesch, and not the Reformers, who reacted polemically against their surrounding environment to produce overtly rationalistic statements concerning the inerrancy of Scripture. Its most distorted form has come in the shape of

---

26. Bloesch, *Appreciation and Reservations,* 127.

27. Bloesch, "Soteriology in Contemporary Christian Thought."

28. Bloesch, "Holy Scripture: Revelation, Inspiration and Interpretation," 39. Barth, in his *Church Dogmatics,* makes this point when he describes Scripture as a witness of divine revelation and states: "A witness is not absolutely identical with that to which it witnesses . . . In the Bible we meet with human words written in human speech, and in these words, and therefore by means of them, we hear of the lordship of the triune God." Barth, *Church Dogmatics, I/1,* 463.

29. Bloesch, *Holy Scripture,* 86.

contemporary fundamentalism's view that the Bible has scientific as well as spiritual authority. Indeed, one sees that Bloesch's agenda is advanced in his declaration that their concern is for the accuracy of a book more than the God who stands as its subject.[30] This being the case, one must ask what influence lay behind Bloesch's conclusions. Fundamentalists also quote the Reformers, yet with a quite different result. As one progresses through Bloesch's carefully plotted argument the answer is discovered in the influence of Karl Barth.

It is certainly true to say that Barth, in his *Church Dogmatics,* understood the Word of God in much the same way as Christian theology has traditionally understood the unity of the divine and human natures of Jesus Christ. That is, in the case of Scripture, "a witness to revelation which itself belongs to revelation, and historically a very human document."[31] In Bloesch's understanding Barth gave the topic of biblical authority depth and scope by claiming that God has chosen to communicate his Word through the instrument of human authors. Bloesch quoted him as saying that "(t)he miracle of God takes place in the text formed of human words."[32] Therefore Bloesch also followed Barth in affirming the divine nature of Scripture,[33] since it is the work of God that is done in the text. Indeed, "the miracle of God takes places in this text formed by human words."[34]

Bloesch asserted that the Bible can be said to be correct and infallible concerning the real questions of life that God addresses and therefore is the authoritative and truthful Word of God whatever its external flaws might be. Indeed, he encouraged the following of Barth's assertion that while every text carries the mark of human imperfection, every text also carries with it the potential for being a "vehicle of divine grace."[35] Consequently, one must conclude that Bloesch concurred with Barth's

---

30. Ibid., 101.

31. Barth, *CD, I/1,* 501.

32. Bloesch, *Holy Scripture.*

33. Mueller points out that one of the reasons Bloesch is attracted to Barth's theology is because of his view on the authority of Scripture. Mueller, "Review of Jesus is Victor! Karl Barth's Doctrine of Salvation," 575.

34. Bloesch, *Holy Scripture.*

35. Bloesch also writes: "Barth would probably say that even the apostolic proclamation that 'God was in Christ reconciling the world to himself' is not faultless unless it is perceived through the eyes of Trinitarian faith." Ibid., 102. Barth, *CD, I/1,* 115–16.

affirmation that the Bible contains both divine infallibility and human fallibility. Sure enough, in his *Church Dogmatics*, Barth stated that the prophets and apostles, due to their unique place in history as recipients of a revelation event, were able to proclaim that "God is with us." Clearly Bloesch reiterated Barth's claim that the biblical authors, although they did not seek authority, "even with their fallible human words, they can continually claim and enjoy the most unheard-of authority."[36] As Bloesch followed Barth's concern to view the Bible as both fallible and infallible it is evident that he endorsed Barth's theology of paradox.

Bloesch's agenda of promoting Barth as a significant source for evangelicals, in contrast to liberalism and fundamentalism, was enhanced by his declaration that Barth's view of the Bible, while being at odds with these two groups, was firmly in accordance with the Reformers. This is seen in Bloesch's exhortation to consider Barth's affirmation, in contrast to Tillich's dialectical method,[37] that a paradox exists between divine infallibility and human fallibility.[38] Bloesch declared: "The paradox is that Scripture is the Word of God as well as the words of mortals. It is both a human witness to God and God's witness to himself."[39] He furthered this argument with the help of the mainline Reformers who, he claimed, affirmed the divinity of Scripture together with statements acknowledging its frailty and humanity.[40] One can only truly hear the Word of God in the form of verbal inspiration. However, this cannot be duplicated within the subjective disposition of the writers who carried within them the marks of their cultural conditioning.[41] Clearly Bloesch saw Barth as affirming the Reformer's assertions. However, Bloesch also saw Barth as

36. Ibid., 115–16.

37. Bloesch comments: "Theological authority is paradoxical in the Barthian sense rather than dialectical in the Tillichian sense. It is not based on a dialectic between the Spirit of God and the human Spirit, because this would make the self-understanding of fallen humanity the criterion for the validity of the message." Bloesch, *A Theology of Word and Spirit*, 190.

38. Bloesch, *Holy Scripture*, 103.

39. Ibid., 87.

40. Bloesch goes on to state that "Calvin accounted for the limitations in world view evident in the Bible by the concept of accommodation ... He suspected that Matthew, in describing the journey of the wise men, improperly labeled as a star what was probably a comet ... Luther allowed for exaggerations in the Bible ... He could express doubt regarding the Mosaic authorship of the Pentateuch, the apostolic authorship pf Jude and the redeeming value of such books as Revelation and James." Bloesch, *Holy Scripture*, 89–90.

41. Ibid., 108.

constructively going beyond the Reformers in his theology of paradox. Indeed, Barthian paradox can be seen as a significant influence as Bloesch drew upon Barth's theology of God's eternity. Indeed, Barth is described as having made "a valiant effort to bring the philosophical concept of eternity into the service of biblical revelation."[42] Bloesch applauded Barth's contention with Protestant orthodoxy's portrayal of God as being *without time and beyond time*, by replacing it with the conception that "God includes time within himself while still remaining eternal."[43] Bloesch consolidated his allegiance to Barth in this matter by restating the Basel theologian's view that "God is supratemporal rather than nontemporal." This idea, said Bloesch, "corresponds to the biblical distinction between *Chronos* and *Kairos*. The first indicates what is fleeting and transitory. The second denotes the fulfillment of time in an enduring relationship with the eternal."[44] Consequently, it is believed here that Barth enabled Bloesch to pursue his agenda for a more moderate approach to exegesis that maintains what he believed to be key aspects of Christian Orthodoxy, while having the freedom to engage constructively with issues of contemporary theological debate. Therefore it is evident that Bloesch, following Barth, did not endorse the authority of Scripture on the basis of inerrancy but in its capacity to bear witness to God's self-revelation in Jesus Christ.

Barth did not advocate, said Bloesch, a rigid adherence to the letter of Scripture, nor a belief in biblical inerrancy. However, he did acknowledge the authority of Holy Scripture as the primary witness to God's self-revelation in Christ.[45] Indeed Barth, in his *Church Dogmatics*, asserted the centrality of Christ in the event of divine revelation, with Scripture having authority only to the extent that it bears witness to God's self-revelation in Christ. Barth succinctly summarized his thesis when he stated: "In general, therefore, the witness of Holy Scripture to itself consists simply in the fact that it is witness to Jesus Christ."[46] Barth understood Biblical authority in terms of its function to not claim authority for itself but to attest to the "living" canon of Jesus Christ.[47] What the writers offer is not

42. Ibid., 86.
43. Ibid.
44. Ibid.
45. Bloesch, *Legacy of Karl Barth*, 6.
46. Barth, *CD, I/1*, 485.
47. Ibid., 115.

the revelation itself but a witness to the revelation expressed in human terms.[48] No doubt Bloesch found inspiration from Barth's assertion in his *Church Dogmatics* that the Bible "is the concrete means by which the Church recollects God's past revelation [. . .] The Bible, then, is not in itself and as such God's past revelation [. . .] The Bible [. . .] bears witness to past revelation."[49] It is agreed here that Bloesch's theology clearly followed Barth's when he steadfastly maintained that there is no other way to know God other than as God has chosen to reveal himself, and what "this God has done exclusively and finally in Jesus Christ, as witnessed to by the Holy Bible."[50] Bloesch further alluded to Barth's wise assertion that the authority of Scripture lies in its writers who bear witness to the infallible Word of God found in Jesus Christ.[51] It is on these grounds that Bloesch concluded that Scripture is a document of divine authority and discusses the issue of inspiration.

According to Barth there are two moments of inspiration: the enlightenment of the writers and the illumination of the readers.[52] The influence of this upon Bloesch is clearly seen when he expressed that in his view "inspiration is the divine election and superintendence of particular writers and writings in order to ensure a trustworthy and potent witness to the truth. The Spirit of the Lord rests not only on the prophet but also on his words. Illumination is the inward awakening of the believer to the truth that is revealed."[53] Bloesch supported Barth's emphasis on the importance of the work of the Holy Spirit in making the believers reading of the Bible a true divine encounter between God and humanity. As Jesuit scholar Avery Dulles rightly observed, "Bloesch's doctrine of the Word represents that which comes from the outside; the Spirit, that which emerges from within, enabling recipients to recognize and interpret

---

48. Bloesch, *Essentials*, vol. 1, 52.

49. In his discussion Barth goes on to define witnessing as that which points in a specific direction beyond itself to another. "Witnessing is thus service to this other in which the witness vouches for the truth of the other, the service which consists in referring to this other." Barth, *CD, I/1*, 111.

50. Rohrer, "The Theologian as Prophet: Donald Bloesch and the Crisis of the Modern Church," 212.

51. Bloesch, *A Theology of Word and Spirit*, 190.

52. Bloesch, *Holy Spirit*, 102.

53. Ibid., 119.

the external Word."[54] Indeed, Bloesch believed Barth to be closer to the Reformers in this regard than modern fundamentalism.[55] The question then arises concerning the nature of authority.

Bloesch was in agreement with Barth that the norm of faith or basis of authority is outside us (*extra nos*) "in the objective self-revelation of Jesus Christ."[56] The influence of Barth upon Bloesch's theology led him to use Barth's three-fold understanding of the Word of God as the basis of his own approach to theology. Indeed, he believed Barth to have "made a helpful distinction between the three forms of the Word of God—the revealed Word of living Word (Christ), the written Word (Scripture) and the proclaimed Word (the church)." Indeed, Barth, in his *Church Dogmatics*, summarized a lengthy discussion on his three-fold theology of the Word in the following description. "The revealed Word of God we know only from the Scripture adopted by Church proclamation or the proclamation of the Church based on Scripture. The written Word of God we know only through the revelation which fulfils proclamation, or through the proclamation fulfilled by revelation. The preached Word of God we know only through the revelation attested in Scripture or the Scripture which attests revelation."[57] The effect of this influence upon Bloesch's thinking is seen when he described the Word of God synonymously with Jesus Christ who is the living water of life. This living water, claimed Bloesch, can only be received through the faucet, which is the Bible, and the glass, which stands for the Church.[58] Through these means one encounters God.

Doctrine of God

In his work on the Doctrine of God, *God The Almighty*, Bloesch expressed concern about the path contemporary debate on the issue is taking. He wrote that,

> (it) is becoming increasingly clear that a palpably different understanding of God and his relationship with the world is steadily pressing itself upon the modern consciousness. A new immanen-

54. Dulles, "Donald Bloesch on Revelation," 61.

55. Bloesch, *Essentials*, vol. 1, 53.

56. Bloesch, *Theology of Word and Spirit*, 186.

57. Ibid., 190. See also Barth, *CD, I/1*, 121.

58. Bloesch, *Theology of Word and Spirit*, 197.

talism is displacing the transcendentalism that has hitherto characterized both Catholic and Protestant theology.[59]

In regard to contemporary debate Bloesch lamented the theology of
Jürgen Moltmann and Wolfhart Pannenberg who, in their theologies of
hope, located transcendence in the future. Consequently the Christian's
hope no longer looks to a transcendent realm beyond history but to a
series of undisclosed possibilities in the unfolding of history. Bloesch also
expressed concerns about process theology's proposal of a finite God who
strives to realize full potential alongside humanity's striving to do the
same. Representative of this movement is the hymnody of Brian Wren
who in the hymn, *Bring Many Names*, celebrates "strong mother God,"
"warm father God," "old aching God," and "young growing God, eager, on
the move, saying no to falsehood and unkindness crying out for justice,
giving all you have." Bloesch undoubtedly struggled with the sentiment
of these words which appeared to him to be replacing a majestic holy
God with a heroic figure, pathfinder and innovator, who elicits our sym-
pathy and admiration and challenges us to work and grow with him/her
in making a better society.[60] Yet another philosophy on offer was deism,
and Bloesch saw no comfort from this school of thought either. In deism,
claimed Bloesch, God is supreme, but totally detached.[61] Against these
inroads of philosophically based immanentalism Bloesch would have us
follow Barth's (and Brunner's) rediscovery of "the utter transcendence of
the living God over his earthly and human creation."[62]

Indeed, it is without doubt that Bloesch's own unearthing of the doctrine of God is thoroughly influenced by Barth. Bloesch's argument is to
be seen as a precisely orchestrated juxtaposition between philosophical
subjectivism and Barthian objectivism. In this way Bloesch continued
Barth's own crusade against the theology of the German philosophical
school in favor of what he has described as a theology of the Word. Barth
wrote of the hidden God who cannot be known in any other way than as
he chooses to make himself known, by his grace, in the event of revelation. He held that our knowledge of God must never depart from this
basic premise. In asserting this claim Barth stated that "God is always the

59. Bloesch, *God The Almighty: Power Wisdom, Holiness, Love*, 17.

60. Ibid., 20.

61. Ibid., 22.

62. Ibid., 23.

Lord, over whom man (that is, humanity) has no power, nor can have, except the power to be his child, trusting and obedient to him."[63]

Bloesch's Barthian approach to handling a philosophy of God, which he referred to as arising out of the immobile and self-sufficient God of the Hellenistic philosophical tradition, is summarized in the comment: "As theologians we should not use biblical images to illustrate and support philosophical vision, but we may use philosophical concepts to clarify the biblical vision."[64] In contradistinction, Bloesch would have us concur with Barth's living God whose omnipotence means that while he is immutable he is not trapped within an existence of unchangeable powerlessness.[65] Indeed, Barth believed that the omnipotent God is distinct from the unchangeable, "whose unchangeableness inevitably means utter powerlessness, complete incapacity, a lack of every possibility, and therefore death."[66]

Bloesch drew a clear distinction between the passive God of philosophy and the active God of Barth's theology which he believed to stand in the biblical tradition. In this endeavor Bloesch encouraged the reader to embrace Barth's approach of transcendence and paradox. God does not arise out of ourselves (aseity) but acts in history to address humanity in its brokenness, despair, pain, and suffering. A God who is the passive observer of our own making is a far cry from the "God who loves and judges, who gives grace and withholds grace, who agonizes over human sin and seeks to rescue the human creature from sin."[67] Thomas Torrance was right in his observation that "Bloesch is indebted [. . .] to Karl Barth who sought to correct classical and Reformed tradition by viewing God's power in the service of his love, and recovered the biblical focus on God's infinite readiness to redeem and heal."[68] In developing this thesis Bloesch, in *God the Almighty*, enlists the support of German Barthian scholar Otto Weber and Barth's German counterpart, Dietrich Bonhoeffer. Bloesch referred to Weber as one who resisted the notion of absolute power associated with classical theism and encourages one to consider the think-

63. Barth, *CD, II/1*, 210.

64. Bloesch, *God the Almighty*, 35.

65. Bloesch, *Essentials*, vol. 1, 27.

66. Barth, *CD, II/1*, 523.

67. Bloesch, *God the Almighty*, 35.

68. Torrance, "Bloesch's Doctrine of God," 142.

ing of Bonheoffer who, in his *Letters and Papers From Prison*, "spoke of the need to conceive of God in terms of his powerlessness rather than almightiness. God has power, but this is paradoxically the power of the powerlessness of his love."[69]

In desiring to appear conversant with current debate, without losing the Barthian foundations of his approach, Bloesch extended his repertoire of theologians to include contemporary theologians of the Barthian school. In Bloesch's *God the Almighty* the first to gain mention is Eberhard Jüngel, whom Bloesch quite deliberately described as one "who draws heavily on Barthian theology."[70] It would appear that Jüngel is described in this way in order for the Barthian character of the discussion to remain in the minds of the reader. Jüngel, as one who stands in the tradition of Barth, also sought to draw one away from thinking of oneself as a subject in the centre of things and into a position of thinking of oneself in terms of one's relationship with God. Jüngel stipulated that God, in his Trinitarian communion, can only be known objectively, as he reveals himself from the centre of his being.[71] Against the philosophy of Fichte, who conceived of an impersonal God, and the philosophically influenced theology of Paul Tillich, who held that God is in the process of overcoming the non-being within him with his own character of being, Bloesch concurred with Jüngel "who does not speak of God who becomes but of a God whose being is dynamic." Furthermore, Bloesch agreed with Jüngel's assertion that "God is a personal being who is ever active."[72] This is in contrast to Hegel, who conceived of God in idealistic and impersonal terms. The influence of Barth here is seen as Bloesch appeared to be continuing Barth's argument against Hegel's idealistic doctrine which saw God as a projection of human subjectivity.[73] The Scottish Barthian theologian Thomas Torrance was also used by Bloesch as a useful ally in delivering a theology influenced by Barth. Torrance is described as giving "cogent articulation to the insuperability of God's action and being."[74] His thesis was that "God's *energeia*, or act, inheres in his being." Bloesch also

---

69. Bloesch, *God the Almighty*, 105.

70. Ibid., 35.

71. Ibid., 38.

72. Ibid., 38.

73. McCormack, *Karl Barth's Realistic Dialectical Theology*, 354.

74. Bloesch, *God the Almighty*, 37.

found Barth helpful in correcting non-personal aspects of the Christian tradition that specify that God is timeless or spaceless.[75]

In agreement with Barth Bloesch stated that describing God as timeless and spaceless "reduces God to a force or power that upholds the universe as its ground rather than a personal being who enters into real relationships with the human creature."[76] God is being, action, and personhood, in relationship with humanity. This is in contrast to Reformed orthodoxy in which God's predestinating decree has come more and more to be interpreted in terms of causal determinism, rather than the gracious initiative of a loving God. Bloesch's argument was aided by the Barthian influenced Reformed theologian James Daane. The Barthian character of Bloesch's thesis is kept well and truly alive as Daane became, in Bloesch's argument, a friend who helps to reinvigorate Barth's contention with orthodoxy. Bloesch correctly viewed Daane's proposal as being that the Reformer's concept of sovereign grace has been distorted and reinterpreted by Reformed Orthodoxy. This means that God accounts for whatever comes to pass in history as a matter of fact, rather than the one who responds in grace to whatever might occur in history. From this Bloesch drew the same conclusion as Daane that if Reformed Orthodoxy is consistent with its assumptions then God must be responsible for sin and evil. Bloesch encouraged the reader to consider Daane's bold invitation to return to the more biblical outlook of a God who is free both to be himself and to go out of himself into history. Bloesch therefore concluded that grace is not the coming to a realization that everything has been determined. Indeed, God is not bound by the rigors of human logic, but is free to relate lovingly with his people. Bloesch continued his exposition of the doctrine of God with an outline of his Christology and soteriology in his work, *Jesus Christ: Savior and Lord.*

Christology

In the opening of his first chapter of his *Jesus Christ: Savior and Lord,* Bloesch clearly set forth his Christological orientation by asserting that Christology constitutes the heart of his theology. He stated that Christ is the means by which one might truly know God. Indeed, "(t)o know

75. Ibid., 52.
76. Ibid., 58.

the nature of God we must see his face in Jesus Christ."[77] Foundational to Bloesch's Christology is his doctrine of the two natures. Under the heading, "The Mystery of the Incarnation" Bloesch drew upon an array of Biblical passages and gave a brief survey of the orthodox position, primarily with the aid of the early church, before giving a fuller theological exposition of the topic under the guidance of Karl Barth. It appears that Bloesch most likely chose Barth as his conversation partner in order to comprehensively respond to modern philosophical trends in theology, containing elements in which the theologies of the early church or Reformation were ill equipped to respond. Furthermore, as Bloesch relied on Barth to construct his Christology he created an epistemological bridge to other aspects of his theology influenced by Barth's general Christological approach.

Bloesch, in a more thorough treatment of the issue than in his earlier *Essentials*,[78] drew upon Barth's conception of *anhypostasia* (impersonal humanity) and *enhypostasia* (personality in God). Through Barth's thesis Bloesch made the assertion that "Jesus Christ is visible as 'true man' and invisible as 'true God' (Karl Barth). He is both the God who has become human and the human who is exalted to God (Barth)."[79] Bloesch further employed Barth to advance his argument by extracting assertions from Barth's *Church Dogmatics*. The result is Bloesch's declaration that what one finds in Jesus Christ "is an irreversible union between the Word of God and Jesus as man."[80] Bloesch reminded the reader that Barth correctly interpreted the Word as becoming flesh in terms of assuming flesh,

> for the Word of God remains even in the incarnation. For Barth the Word became not merely a human but also a particular man. He stoutly maintained this position against the view of some sectarian Christians, including the German Christians, that Christ was not a Jew but the "universal man." Barth also contended that Jesus Christ does not take on simply human nature. He identified fully with our sinful predicament even though he never succumbs to sin, thereby becoming a sinner. Against Nestorianism Barth strongly affirmed

77. Bloesch, *Jesus Christ: Savior and Lord*, 15.

78. In his earlier Essentials, Bloesch also alludes to Barth to assert that Jesus Christ "is both Revealing God and Representative Man. He is invisible as true God and visible as true man (K. Barth)." Bloesch, *Essentials*, vol. 1, 127.

79. Bloesch, *Jesus Christ*, 56.

80. Ibid.

the *theotokos*—Mary as God-bearer or Mother of God. That is, he refused to separate the human and divine natures.[81]

Bloesch also drew heavily upon Barth for his discussion on kenoticism. He agreed with Barth, who censored the Nestorian tendency of many kenoticists who failed to recognize "that it is precisely in the humiliation of Christ that his divinity is manifested and demonstrated."[82] Bloesch was also in agreement with Barth's contention that kenosis does not amount to Christ renouncing his divinity, as found in post-Reformation Lutheranism, but in his being in the form of God alone. The North American theologian, as he dealt with this topic in his *Essentials*, drew this conclusion from Barth's proposal that while Christ's heavenly glory during his incarnation was only dimly reflected, and that while consequently his majesty was not immediately evident, he remained fully God.[83]

In contending with the issue of the Lordship of Christ Bloesch was also able to draw significantly upon Barth, who "stressed the transcendent character of the Kingdom of God."[84] Bloesch appeared favorable to Barth's theology of the Lordship of Christ by asserting that he had followed church tradition when he "hailed Jesus in both his humanity and his divinity as the king of all the nations of the world."[85] In contrast to Luther's apocalyptic eschatology, Bloesch also preferred Barth's Christological eschatology that laid stress on the lordship of Christ. Bloesch consequently related Christ's lordship to his victory over evil powers. Indeed, "Jesus Christ is already king and the powers have been subjugated, though (they have already been disarmed)[86] they fight on through the strength of deception."[87]

---

81. Ibid., 66. See also Bloesch's earlier argument in volume one of *Essentials* where he states: "Barth contends with some biblical support that Christ assumes fallen human nature and not simply human nature." Bloesch, *Essentials*, vol. 1, 130.

82. Bloesch, *Essentials*, vol. 1, 137.

83. Ibid., 138. Barth states: "He humbled Himself, but he did not do it by ceasing to be who He is. He went into a strange land, but even there, and especially there, He never became a stranger to Himself." Barth, *CD, IV/1*, 180.

84. Bloesch, *Jesus Christ*, 220.

85. Following Barth, Bloesch goes on to assert: "The kingdom of darkness is a pseudo kingdom that claims to have power but has actually been divested of its power not only in the cross and resurrection victory of Christ but already in creation." Ibid., 220.

86. Bloesch, *Jesus is Victor*, 61.

87. Bloesch, *Jesus Christ*, 220.

Bloesch also alluded to Barth who outlined in his *Church Dogmatics* that while the Nothingness is still in the world it is in virtue of the blindness of humanity's eyes and the cover which is still over the world.[88] In his earlier *Jesus is Victor!* The North American theologian led one to consider Barth's view that we do not live in "a world in slavery but a liberated world, one that wholly and solely belongs to its only Lord and master, Jesus Christ."[89] Yet Bloesch also led one to consider Barth's pronouncement that the kingdom under the lordship of Christ cannot be merged or united with any existing kingdom or social structure.[90] Clearly, Bloesch preferred Barth's distinguishing between the kingdom of grace, which now includes the whole world, and the kingdom of glory, which refers to the future of the world as redeemed.[91] Indeed, the North American scholar, in *Jesus Christ,* urged careful consideration of Barth's contention that the kingdom of Christ exists within two dimensions: church and state.

> The civil community is the outer circle and the Christian commu-
> nity the inner circle of the kingdom of God. Their common centre
> is Jesus Christ—God incarnate, crucified and risen. For Barth the
> state is based not on natural law or on the rule of force made nec-
> essary by sin but on the justice of God revealed in Jesus Christ.
> Barth introduced the concept of a "political service of God," which
> consists in the proclamation of Christ's lordship over all of life.[92]

Having established his Christology Bloesch built upon it with a Christologically based soteriology.

Soteriology

The objective characteristic of Barth's soteriology is clearly appreciated by Bloesch who accepted it as "a valuable corrective to many other theologians, past and present."[93] Indeed, Bloesch's appreciation of many aspects of Barth's thought was further enhanced when he stated that "Barth has performed a real service to Christian theology by reminding us that sal-

---

88. Bloesch, *Essentials,* vol. 2, 145.

89. Bloesch, *Jesus is Victor,* 61.

90. Bloesch, "The Lordship of Christ in Theological History" 30.

91. Bloesch, *Essentials,* vol. 2, 146.

92. Bloesch, *Jesus Christ,* 220.

93. Ibid., 194.

vation is originally and essentially objective."[94] Yet Bloesch is concerned to stress that his following of Barth on this matter is confined to the later Barth, at which point his maturity, as Bloesch perceived it, led him to elevate the significance of the subjective pole of salvation.[95] Barth was insistent, claimed Bloesch, that though God's grace is free, it is not cheap. "It demands from us lives of self-sacrificial and abundant service."[96] Indeed, it is to be noted that Bloesch applauded Barth for the fact that he did come to balance some of the extreme statements of objectivism with the recognition that the person of faith is one who participates if he or she is to benefit from it.[97] Indeed, while Bloesch is not totally in agreement with all that Barth had to say on this topic he did convey with some enthusiasm that in Barth's discussion of the Holy Spirit "a real place is made for the subjective pole of salvation."[98]

Bloesch can also be said to be in agreement with Barth's reinterpretation of predestination "as the universal election of humankind to redemption." Fully consonant with Barth's emphasis on divine love is his contention "that Jesus Christ is both the elected one and the reprobate."[99] Following Barth, Bloesch declared that "in Jesus Christ, in his sacrificial life, death and resurrection, all humankind is elected, justified and sanctified."[100] Bloesch was also clearly in agreement with Barth's Christological reappraisal of the soteriology of the Reformation. He contended that Barth rightly saw "that salvation must be grounded in Christ [. . .] According to Barth the election, justification, and sanctification of all people (men)

94. Ibid., 195. Barth in his Church Dogmatics, under the heading "God with us," makes as his starting point the assumption that at the heart of the Christian message is the description of an act of God. Therefore it is not for humanity to come to conclusions on the basis of observation, consideration, investigation, or speculation. Indeed, "'God with us' tells us that we ourselves are in the sphere of God. It applies to us by telling us of a history which God wills to share with us and therefore of an invasion of our history-indeed, of the real truth about our history as a history which is by Him and from Him and to Him." Barth, *CD, IV/1*, 6–7.

95. Bloesch, *Jesus Christ*, 196.

96. Ibid., 195.

97. Barth could say that the atonement is "both a divine act and offer and also an active human participation in it: the unique history of Jesus Christ; but enclosed and exemplified in the history of many other men of many other ages." Ibid., 165. Barth spoke of the essentiality of the act of faith in Barth, *CD, IV/1*, 758.

98. Bloesch, *Jesus Christ*, 165.

99. Bloesch, *Karl Barth: Appreciation and Reservations*, 126.

100. Bloesch, *Jesus Christ*, 194.

took place in the life and death of Jesus Christ."[101] While Bloesch never makes much of Barth's doctrine of election he did restate Barth's conception that all are "elected by God and adopted into sonship in his eternal decree that comes in the historical realization of Jesus Christ." Indeed, "all are predestined to salvation in Christ."[102] Therefore Bloesch closely followed Barth's contention that salvation is an event that has already taken place for all of humanity in the redeeming work of Jesus Christ.[103] Bloesch reminded the reader that in Barth's theology "faith is not included in the event of redemption but rather is an awakening to the redemption already accomplished in Jesus Christ."[104] Therefore, humankind has already been elected to salvation in Jesus Christ.[105]

One must also conclude that Barth gave to Bloesch a perceptive restatement of the doctrine of the atonement. The evidence for this is in his statement that for Barth the "emphasis is on God's vicarious identification with the sin and plight of humanity in Jesus Christ rather than on the satisfaction of the requirements of God's law."[106] Bloesch clearly agreed

101. Bloesch, *The Christian Life and Salvation*, 24.

102. Bloesch, *Jesus is Victor*, 32. This theme is also restated in Bloesch's comment that while we are elected before the creation of the world, we are elect in Christ. Bloesch, *Christian Life*, 48.

103. In his *Church Dogmatics* Barth contends that even if the individual were to decide to reject God this rejection would be void, since he or she has already been chosen in Christ. Barth describes a person's rejection of God as a perversion that God conceals by his own divine decree that has included all in the election of Christ. "(The person) belongs eternally to Jesus Christ and therefore is not rejected which (such a person) deserves on account of (this) perverse choice is borne and cancelled by Jesus Christ." Barth, *CD, II/2*, 306.

104. Bloesch, *The Christian Life*, 25. Later in this work Bloesch reiterates this sentiment by stating that "we can affirm that our salvation has its beginning not in the moment of decision . . . but rather on the Mount of Calvary." Ibid., 47.

105. D. Bloesch, "Sin, Atonement, and Redemption," 175. In his *Church Dogmatics* Barth clearly states his belief that between God and humanity there stands the person of Jesus Christ, himself God and himself a human, and so mediating between the two. In Christ, according to Barth, God reveals himself to humanity and in Christ humanity sees and knows God. Barth, *CD, II/2*, 94. In this context one may assert, claims Barth, that Jesus Christ is the electing God and elected human. "In its simplest and most comprehensive form the dogma of predestination consists, then, in the assertion that the divine predestination is the election of Jesus Christ. But the concept of election has a double reference—to the elector and the elected . . . Thus the simplest form of the dogma may be divided at once into two assertions that Jesus Christ is the electing God, and that he is also the elected man." Barth, *CD, II/2*, 103.

106. "The themes of penal substitution and satisfaction are nonetheless present in Barth, but they are placed in a new context." Bloesch, *Appreciation and Reservations*, 127.

with Barth in holding to the notion that through the sacrifice of Christ on the cross, and by his glorious resurrection from the grave, the human situation has been decisively overcome.[107] Bloesch saw in Barth many signs of the mainline views on the atonement that have been taught by the church, such as his ardent espousals of the substitutionary and universalist views of the atonement of Christ,[108] and of his priestly role of one who intercedes in sacrifice to satisfy God's justice.[109] Nevertheless, the North American Theologian also saw Barth as bringing something new into the picture, since he did not abandon traditional concepts but saw them in a new context, and in so doing radicalized their meaning.[110] Bloesch alluded to the fact that in Barth's thought there was a clear divergence from the satisfactionist, or judicial, view. "The cross is to be understood primarily not as the fulfillment of a legal contract calling for the shedding of innocent blood but as the triumph of sovereign love over enmity and alienation, which invariably resulted in the shedding of blood."[111]

The opinion expressed here is that Bloesch also related well with Barth's concept of wrath. In Christ's sacrifice God's wrath is revealed, but as the obverse side of his love. Indeed, the cross, so much at the heart of the gospel, is a revelation of divine love.[112] Clearly Bloesch also followed Barth in the assertion that "(t)he wrath of God is the purity and holiness of his love [. . .] (which is), therefore, a means of grace as well as of judgment."[113] It is to be concluded, therefore, that Bloesch concurred with Barth in spurning popular notions of God's wrath turning into love via the sacrifice of the cross, in favor of a sacrifice that predisposes his gracious love. Bloesch's strong agreement with Barth was also evident when he asserted that the atonement amounts to an incursion of vicari-

---

107. Bloesch, *Jesus Christ*, 169.

108. Bloesch, *Evangelical Renaissance*, 82.

109. Bloesch, *Christian Life*, 52.

110. He does not abandon concepts such as substitution, satisfaction, and penal redemption. Bloesch, *Jesus is Victor*, 45.

111. Bloesch, *Jesus is Victor*, 46. In his Church Dogmatics Barth clearly diverges in his argument away from Anselm's "Latin theory" of the substitutionary atonement and asks: "Why should not this pure and free forgiveness which God has accomplished in His incarnation itself be His saving reaction to the sin and guilt of man, the restitution of that which has been stolen from him, the satisfaction of the hurt done to his honor, the forceful overcoming of the consequent disturbance of the relationship between Himself and man?" Barth, CD, IV/ 1, 486–87.

112. Bloesch, *Evangelical Renaissance*, 60–61.

113. Bloesch, *Jesus is Victor*, 46.

ous, triumphant love into history as he comes into the world identifying with its guilt and shame.[114] Consequently, one must describe Bloesch as holding to a Barthian view that necessitated a rejection of cold legalisms and an embrace of a substitution resulting from the heart of God for all creation. Christ received the penalty of the sin of the world,[115] and yet it was self-sacrifice in love for the sake of reconciliation, rather than an act of furious rage by a spurned God.[116] Bloesch was in agreement with Barth's conclusion that

> (t)he substitution is not a work that takes place outside of us and is then subsequently applied to us but a work in which our dying and rising again is enacted. It is not that Christ has borne the judgment of God in our place, thereby enabling us to escape judgment. Instead the judgment has been executed upon us in Christ, and therefore we and all (people) have already passed through this judgment.[117]

The reconciliation Barth has in mind did not so much result in a change of attitude in the person but "a change in the human situation resulting from a new initiative on the part of God toward humanity."[118] Consequently, Barth's theology of the atonement fits into his objective understanding of soteriology, in that salvation has already taken place for humanity in the reconciliation already given in Jesus Christ. What is required of the person is an inner awareness. Barth described this as inner history (*Geschichte*) which is to be differentiated from objectively discern-

---

114. Bloesch, *Essentials of Evangelical Theology—Volume 1*, 154.

115. In his work, *The Christian Life and Salvation*, Bloesch makes the point that the one who is estranged from God is in dire need of reconciliation with God [...] Humanity needs a priest who will intercede before the throne of God . . . (because a) sacrifice must be offered that will satisfy the justice of God, 52. Barth, in his *Church Dogmatics*, states that the sinner is rejected by God, "that he not only stands under the wrath and accusation of God, but because this wrath is well founded and this accusation is true, he stands under His sentence and judgment." Barth, *CD, IV/1*, 173–74. Barth also correlates God's wrath with his love when he states that God's consuming wrath is that of his love. Barth, *CD, IV/1*, 563.

116. "The cross is basically to be understood not as a ritually prescribed instrument of propitiation directed to eternity but as an incursion of divine grace into the arena of human history." Bloesch, *Jesus is Victor*, 51.

117. Ibid., 50. Bloesch comments further by adding that Christ "suffers the punishment of sin on our behalf, but only in a qualified sense can it be said that he suffers and dies in our stead, since we suffer and die in and with him." Ibid., 51.

118. Ibid., 49.

ible history (*Historie*). Bloesch has followed Barth's assertion that only faith creates the eyes to see, apprehend, and receive the work of Christ for humanity. Indeed, one must conclude that Bloesch's strongest affirmation of Barth's theology is to be seen when he described Barth as "profoundly biblical in his asseveration that only faith can discern the supernatural reality and mystery that lie within and behind the historical events related to Jesus' life, death, and rising again."[119] Barth's influence is also seen in Bloesch's theology of law and Gospel.

In Bloesch's understanding Barth, in contradistinction to the mainstream of Reformation tradition, gave priority to the gospel in the determination of the content of the law. The Reformers considered the law as that which could lead one to the truth of the gospel.[120] Yet Barth taught that to know the law one must first know the gospel. In agreement with Barth, Bloesch stated that "(i)f we are to understand the demand of the law rightly, we must first have been confronted by the promise of the gospel. Therefore the law serves to direct one to the gospel but can only direct us as we have encountered the gospel."[121] Consequently, Bloesch also followed Barth as perceiving the law in terms of the love of God. Bloesch has reminded us that "(in) Barth's view the kingdom of God is not a new world order bringing another set of mandates and obligations but the invasion of an entirely new reality into the structures of human existence, infusing them with the motivating power of love."[122] Along with Barth, Bloesch proposed that love fulfils the imperatives of the law. "Love liberates us from the burden of the law and empowers us to keep the command embodied in the law."[123]

Finally, Bloesch made it clear that he is "remarkably close to Karl Barth in his affirmation of the universality of calling and election."[124] He was also in accord with that aspect of Barth's thinking affirming that all

119. Ibid., 53. Also see Bloesch's comment: "A renewed evangelicalism will reread Karl Barth in order to learn from his profoundly biblical insights [. . .]" Bloesch, "Soteriology in Contemporary Christian Thought," 132.

120. For Luther the law was the hammer of God's judgment, which brings about a conviction of sin, with the gospel offering the balm of forgiveness. For Calvin the law prepared one for faith in Christ. Bloesch, *Jesus Christ*, 200.

121. Ibid., 201.

122. Ibid., 204.

123. Ibid.

124. Although Bloesch believes he differs from Barth by emphasizing the particularity of how these are realized in humanity. Bloesch, *Essentials*, vol. 1, 168.

are ordained for fellowship with Christ, yet with only some realizing their destiny to be sons and daughters of God. Yet all will finally be overcome by the invincible and sovereign love of Jesus Christ.[125] It is evident that Bloesch drew a close parallel between Barth's doctrine of election and his teaching on universalism. While Bloesch perceived Barth as stopping short of affirming a universal final salvation and allowed for the "impossible possibility" of self-damnation, he still maintained that we can sincerely hope for a universal final salvation, and we have grounds for such hope because of the promise of Scripture that "God is faithful even while (we) are faithless and that the gifts and call of God are irrevocable."[126] Bloesch, therefore, came to the conclusion that while God is never under any binding obligation to offer grace we can, as a consequence of his love, view everyone with hope.[127] This is not to say, however, that Bloesch saw Barth as a Universalist. Indeed Bloesch, who clearly sought to address the concerns of conservative evangelicals, was adamant that "Barth is not a universalist [...] for he does not affirm that the church of God will necessarily include all persons, even unbelievers." Bloesch conveyed his affinity to Barth in this area. Indeed, in a comparison between himself and Barth Bloesch affirmed that "both of us oppose universalism while still affirming Christ's universal triumph over the powers of darkness."[128]

CONCLUSION

Barth has been an instrumental figure in Bloesch's theology. Indeed, Barth's thinking has been a constant influence during Bloesch's theological development. Furthermore Barth constituted a significant source as the North American theologian constructed his theology and pursued his theological agenda of a new moderate approach within North American evangelicalism. One must conclude that this produced a theology containing elements of liberalism and conservatism, without permitting their extremes. Indeed, one does not find in Bloesch the influences of either contemporary philosophical liberalism, based on subjective reasoning, or Christian fundamentalism which he contended to be held captive by the impositions of reason and logic upon God's majesty and transcendence.

125. Ibid., 168.

126. Bloesch, *Jesus is Victor*, 62.

127. Bloesch, *Appreciation and Reservations*, 129.

128. Bloesch, per. comm., April 6, 2005, 1.

Indeed, it has been demonstrated that along with Barth one will not find in Bloesch's work a God in constant change, but a God who is characterized by consuming love.

It is evident that Barth's Christological emphasis has been the centerpiece of his motifs. Indeed, Bloesch adopted a theology of paradox based on the divine and human natures of Christ; a theology of the Word which has recognized both the authority of the text, as that which bears witness to God's revelation in Christ, as well as its humanness. Bloesch also produced a soteriology bearing many of the marks of Barth's theology. In particular, it is clear that Bloesch's theology of predestination and atonement closely followed Barth's Christological emphasis. In contradistinction to the majority evangelical view, Bloesch followed Barth in proposing the predestination and reconciliation of all in Christ. The marks of Barth's theology are also evident as Bloesch contested that God's wrath can in no way be separated from his love. Overall the result is a construction of a theology which has provided a striking contrast to both liberal and fundamentalist evangelicalism in North America. It is an evangelicalism very much influenced by the theology of Karl Barth.

Donald Bloesch represents the best of North American systematic theology after the pattern of Barth. However, Barth's writings were extensive and covered a wide range of interests and topics. As a pastor, Barth was also concerned with human existence and ethics. Ray Anderson utilized Barth's work in his contribution to theological praxis. Indeed, more substantially than any other North American theologian.

8

Ray Anderson

R AY ANDERSON IS A North American theologian indebted to the thought of Karl Barth. Anderson's search for an incarnational theology, applicable to the pastoral setting, led him to search for an alternative approach. His search ultimately resulted in the significant influence of Thomas Torrance in Scotland, a major interpreter of Barth's theology in the English-speaking world. There are signs of the Swiss theologian's influence in Anderson's doctoral thesis and it can be said with certainty that the influence of Torrance became apparent in Anderson's publications. However, there were other influences that deepened Anderson's appreciation of Barth. Included in these were Anderson's reading his works while teaching at Westmont College (1972–1976), his discussions with Bernard Ramm concerning the importance of Karl Barth to evangelical theology, and the joining of the Fuller Seminary faculty which proved to be a significant step in consolidating Anderson's appropriation of Barth. At Fuller, Anderson came in contact with Geoffrey Bromiley, a major translator and interpreter of Barth's work. The evidence is that the combination of these influences led Anderson to consider Barth as a major theological source who could significantly help in the construction of his theological works. Consequently, Barth came to be the significant influence in how Anderson pursued his theological motifs.

The principal influences of Barth in Anderson's writing are firstly discussed in relation to his construction of a theological anthropology. Anderson's interest in this arose from his early ambition to construct an alternative theological praxis for the pastoral setting. His anthropology followed Barth's criticism of anthropologies based on modernist rationalism which he described as being based on "Cartesian assumptions." Following Barth, Anderson pursued an agenda of a theological anthropology that defined humanity as determined by the Word of God. It will also be argued here that Barth's influence is to be found in Anderson's Christology, his definition of humanity and his understanding of Christian ethics.

THE SEARCH FOR A NEW DIRECTION

When Ray Anderson was a student at Fuller Seminary (1956–1959) he did not have the opportunity to read the works of Karl Barth, since virtually none of the *Church Dogmatics* had been published in English. Even when Dr. Geoffrey Bromiley joined the faculty, during Anderson's last year as a student, he "really did not get introduced to Barth's theology, although Anderson became aware that Barth's works were being translated."[1] Anderson's journey to becoming a theologian influenced by Barth started during his eleven years as a pastor with the Evangelical Free Church (1960–1970). In his pastoral setting he found it difficult to apply the traditional Calvinist theology that had been taught to him at Fuller by Paul Jewett[2]. Searching for an alternative Anderson preached a series "on the life of Jesus from the Gospels based on Paul's statement in Colossians that in Christ 'the fullness of the godhead dwelt bodily.'"[3] This began Anderson's "turn" to a new direction in theology. During this early stage of change Anderson developed what he has come to call "an incarnational theology."[4] He revealed that he came more and more to realize "that the incarnation was the critical point from which to do theology, and that Christology was the key to our understanding of God."[5]

However, believing that he needed to deepen his theological foundations Anderson sought the advice of Dr. David Hubbard, who was the president of Fuller Seminary at the time and who had done his doctoral work at St. Andrews in Scotland. Hubbard responded to Anderson's enquiry by suggesting he go to Edinburgh to study under Professor Thomas Torrance, a major British interpreter and champion of Barth's theology. Anderson followed Hubbard's advice and left for Scotland in 1970 before returning in 1972 with a PhD. He wrote his dissertation on *The Historical*

1. Anderson, pers. comm., March 19, 2003.

2. Paul Jewett was installed as Professor of Systematic Theology at Fuller Theological Seminary in 1955. He began his career with a critical analysis of *Emil Brunner's Concept of Revelation* (1954). He maintained a rather conservative Calvinism throughout his tenure at Fuller. Thorne, *Evangelicalism and Karl Barth*, 107.

3. Anderson, pers. comm., April 30, 2003.

4. Loc.cit.

5. Ibid., 107.

Transcendence and the Reality of God. While his dissertation was not influenced by Barth to the same extent as his later works, it is evident that his time with Torrance gave him a substantial introduction to Barth's thought.[6] Indeed, through the mediation of Thomas Torrance Karl Barth became a significant source in Anderson's future writing.

The North American theologian became more familiar with Barth when he began teaching at Westmont College (1972–1976). There he read Barth in greater depth and discovered that much of his writing resonated with his own incarnational theology.[7] It would appear that Anderson found in Barth a valuable mentor whom he saw as an important source in pursuing an agenda of incarnational praxis. The significance of this period is seen in Anderson's recollection that by the time he was appointed to the faculty at Fuller Theological Seminary on the spring of 1976 he was "quite deep into Barth."[8] And this was further encouraged by his new colleague at Fuller, Geoffrey Bromiley, who was teaching a seminar on Barth's theology.

A THEOLOGICAL ANTHROPOLOGY AFTER THE PATTERN OF BARTH

In addition to Bromley's stimulation at Fuller Anderson received further inspiration in conversations he had with Dr. Bernard Ramm about Barth's impact on evangelicalism. These discussions reinforced Anderson's conviction "that Barth's theology offered real substance for a contemporary evangelical theology."[9] Anderson followed these discussions by publishing, in 1982, *On Being Human: Essays in Theological Anthropology.*[10] This major work relied significantly on Karl Barth.

In *On Being Human* Anderson discussed the problems of non-theological anthropologies and revealed his indebtedness to Karl Barth in his pursuit of an alternative, particularly his *Church Dogmatics,* III/2.[11] Anderson's observation was that a more classical anthropology of the church must be considered a theological anthropology since it is founded

6. Ibid.

7. Ibid.

8. Ibid.

9. Ibid.

10. Anderson, *On Being Human: Essays in Theological Anthropology.*

11. Ibid., 8. Barth, *Church Dogmatics: III/2.*

on the presupposition "that the human person is created and sustained by the Word and grace of God."[12] However, Anderson contended that these basic assumptions had been undermined by modernism, which he saw as the prevailing mood among both his secular and religious contemporaries. He described such scholars as Cartesian, "because like Descartes they seek to explain the mystery of the human in terms of the human subject."[13] Descartes, stated Anderson, affirmed the discontinuity between the self, as existing as the object of divine grace, and the self which determines reality for itself. Hence the dictum: *I think, therefore I am.*[14] Following Barth, Anderson found this assumption to be problematic, since it proceeds from *anthropos* rather than from *theos.* Consequently, Anderson pointed to Barth's assertion that anthropologies based on this Cartesian assumption are "symptoms of real humanity, not real humanity itself."[15] Indeed, Barth referred to these symptoms as observations made by natural science which can only constitute attempts to understand the nature of humanity. Therefore it is to be observed that Anderson followed Barth in finding a tragic element in non-theological anthropologies, since they did not reflect the true person.[16] Indeed, Barth contended that true humanity, as man and woman, "stands before God and is real as he receives and has the Spirit and is thus grounded, constituted and maintained by God."[17]

In his construction of a theological anthropology Anderson referred to Barth's assertion that "if we know man only in the corruption and distortion of his being" there can be no true understanding of humanity's

12. Ibid., 8.

13. Ibid.

14. Ibid., 11.

15. Ibid., 14. Anderson quotes Barth's *Church Dogmatics, III/2*, 200. In this section of the *Dogmatics* Barth counters the arguments of non-theological anthropologies by arguing that man has the potentiality to be endowed as "the *partner* of God and therefore no merely the sharer in a transcendence immanent in human existence itself." Barth, CD, III/2, 201–2.

16. Barth, *CD, III/2*, 14. Anderson refers to Barth, *CD, III/2*, 429.

17. Ibid., Barth, 430. Earlier Barth protested that: "In face of the whole discussion we can only declare our fundamental objection that the soul and the body of the man of whom they (anthropologists and natural scientists) speak are the soul and body of a ghost and not of real man. To dispute concerning these and to throw light on their co-existence and relationship is necessarily a waste of time and effort. We can only be opposed to all these theories that the soul and body of real man are not two real series or sides existing and observable in isolation [...] We do not have the body here and the soul there, but man himself as soul of his body." Ibid., 429.

true creaturely nature.[18] While Anderson acknowledged that a theological anthropology must begin with humanity itself, he insisted that it must take into account the Word of God that has come to humanity. The influence of Barth in Anderson's theology is very evident in his contention that God's proclamation has already occurred in Jesus Christ, the Word made flesh. Indeed, Anderson pointed to Barth's assertion that Christ is not only the one who brings the Word and bears it fully, but he is also the one who lives in obedience to that Word.[19] While this Word may be distorted in the process of becoming the written Word, it nevertheless reveals the true form of that which is human. Here Anderson clearly followed Barth's concern for a subjective "this worldly" understanding of the human person by advocating an objective view of humanity that comes from the revealed Word. Further, it is evident that Anderson followed Barth's Christological orientation in also defining humanity in terms of God's self-revelation in the humanity of Jesus Christ, particularly his crucifixion and resurrection. In Christ's crucifixion one can see the grave situation that humanity is in and yet in the resurrection one perceives God's original intention for humanity. Indeed, Anderson believed that it has been Karl Barth, more than any other theologian, who correctly and comprehensively developed a theological anthropology by beginning with the humanity of Jesus Christ as both crucified and risen.[20]

It is also to be noted that the influence of Barth's Christological anthropology is seen as Anderson concurred with Barth that one must first go to Christ to learn about humanity and then to Adam. "Both Adam and Christ are part of the human story which makes up redemptive history. But even though Adam precedes Christ chronologically, Christ precedes Adam as the true form of humanity."[21] In addition one must observe that Anderson followed Barth's theology of analogy in the statement that "the form of humanity as revealed through the crucified humanity of Jesus Christ cannot be grasped directly, either by speculative or scientific anthropology [. . .] In order to penetrate the truth of humanity under judgment, one must himself come under judgment [. . .] It is truth

18. Ibid., 15–16. Anderson refers to Barth, *CD, III/2*.

19. Anderson, "A Theology for Ministry," 19.

20. Ibid., 18.

21. Ibid.

which comes by way of repentance and faith."[22] Anderson also discussed humanity in relation to Christ's attributes. Humanity, he claimed, in his *Historical Transcendence and the Reality of God,* which was reproduced under the heading, "The Man who is for God' in *Theological Foundations for Ministry*"[23] also finds its identity in Christ's self-renunciation. In this work Anderson referred to Christ's kenosis and the importance of kenoticism. He took from Barth the observation that when we see God *for* us, that is, his "way of *kenosis*," we "see him *as he is.*"[24] Consequently, when humanity is bound into community by being bound to God himself the "mind of Christ [...] forms the ontic structure of the community to which men are called to Christ."[25] Barth further led Anderson to conclude that this "way" is not ethical self-renunciation, but an actual appeal to the kenotic way of life.[26] Consequently, Anderson discussed humanity's need to "respond to the creative divine Word."[27]

In his earlier *The Shape of Practical Theology: Empowering Ministry with Theological Praxis* Anderson asserted that the Scriptural understanding of covenant is such that the creature to who God speaks is in a position to be able to respond to him. Here Anderson pointed to Barth, who described the "real man" as being determined "by God for life with God and existing in the history of the covenant which God has established with him."[28] In this covenant the human creature has the ability to be aware of God and to be approached by him. In the event of this approach one becomes aware of the divine summons to be human. This self-consciousness becomes the person's mark of differentiation from other

22. Ibid., 16.

23. Anderson, "The Man Who is for God."

24. Ibid., 242.

25. Ibid., 248.

26. Anderson directs the reader to further read Barth, *Church Dogmatics, IV/1,* 188ff, which he recommends as a commentary on the "law of humbling" found in the New Testament and which reflects "the kenotic way of Divine Sonship." Ibid., 248. Here Barth claimed that Christ's wisdom "proclaims itself in what necessarily appears folly to the world; His righteousness in ranging Himself with the unrighteous as One who is accused with them, as the first, and properly the only One to come under accusation; His Holiness in having mercy on man, in taking his misery to heart, in being willing to share it with him in order to take it away from him." Barth, *Church Dogmatics: IV/1,* 188.

27. Anderson, *On Being Human,* 37.

28. Anderson, *The Shape of Practical Theology,* 37–38.

creatures "which places us in direct contact with the very soul[29] of a person, and hence, apprehends that which differentiates the soul—the reality of the divine creative Word of God."[30] Consequently in Anderson's belief the human's proper response to the Word leads to a new way of life. That is, the presence of this creative Word leads to praxis. Indeed, Anderson stated that the purpose of this book was to "define more clearly the shape of practical theology as truly a theological enterprise rather than mere mastery of skills and methods" and to "demonstrate the praxis of practical theology as critical engagement with the interface between the word of God as revealed through Scripture and the work of God taking place in and through the church in the world."[31] In demonstrating one of the tasks of this engagement Anderson turned to Barth's understanding of ethics as theological anthropology.

THEOLOGICAL ETHICS

In *The Shape of Practical Theology* Anderson began his description of Barth's ethics by explaining it as a task to be understood within theology, rather than an independent philosophy arising out of human speculation, reason and logic. Consequently, Anderson, as he interpreted Barth's theological anthropology, described an ethics that is free from what is believed to be the distortions, indeed idolatry, that is found in abstract ethical reasoning that grounds itself in philosophical, and therefore speculative, principles. In contradistinction, Anderson pointed to Barth's agenda of understanding ethics as primarily an act of God upon humanity. Indeed, it was an act in Jesus Christ which has to do with humanity's existence in Christ. Consequently, Anderson spoke of theological anthropology which has as its aim "to expound the grace of God as given in Jesus Christ and the command of God as the sole ground on which theology as well as anthropology rest."[32] Indeed, Anderson pointed to Barth's rejection of abstract, philosophical and naturalistic ethics which views human beings as self contained. Barth contended that these subjective and idealistic views

---

29. Anderson earlier describes "soul" as a term "to denote that awareness or openness to God which is distinctive to the human and impossible for the non-human, the basic spiritual dimension of a human person's animated existence." Ibid., 38.

30. Ibid., 39.

31. Ibid., 8.

32. Ibid., 132.

must be transcended, overcome, and radically discarded by viewing people as the object of divine grace, and consequently a totally new subject- "the subject who is established as the object of God's grace." Anderson pointed out that in this understanding Barth is clearly setting aside general ethics as an independent and autonomous moral law grounded in human moral reason.[33] In contrast, Anderson was clearly convinced by Barth's Christologically grounded ethics.

Anderson concurred with Barth that it is humanity's existence in Jesus Christ that is the true basis of ethical behavior. He pointed to Barth's argument that there "can only be one real form of humanity [...] and Jesus Christ has revealed that form of humanity as it was originally and finally determined to be."[34] Indeed Barth concluded, stated Anderson, that when the true form of humanity has been discerned then the true criterion for theological ethics has been discovered. This form of true humanity is observed in the incarnation, where God establishes the nature of right ethical response in hearing and obedience. The concept of neighbor was important to these assumptions.

Humanity as co-humanity

Anderson was clearly influenced by Barth when he asserted that in Christ God becomes neighbor to humans as creature "and summons persons to become the neighbo(u)r of God and to fellow humanity."[35] Indeed, Barth's assertion that the basic form of humanity is found in Jesus Christ, in whom Barth found humanity expressed as fellow humanity (*Mitmenschlichkeit*). However, this is not a new form of humanity in Jesus Christ, but rather real humanity as determined by God, the "humanization" of humanity (*Vermensehlichung*).[36] The influence of Barth is also seen in Anderson's discussion of humanity as determined in relationship with others. Anderson clearly followed Barth when he made the assertion that humanity is a determination of the Word of God: "a determination of being with others, and the determination of one person with the other."[37] He developed

---

33. Ibid., 133.

34. Ibid., 134.

35. Ibid., 135.

36. Ibid., 138.

37. Anderson, *On Being Human*, 45. Indeed, in his *Church Dogmatics* Barth describes "humanity as a being of man with others." Barth, *CD, III/2*, 243.

this point as he engaged with Barth's social thesis that "individuality as a form of human being is a result of differentiation through relation with another."[38] Indeed, the determination of humanity in its singularity "is a *history* of self in encounter."[39] The influence of Barth in Anderson's thinking is further seen in Anderson's referral to Barth's assertion that "to say man is to say history, and this is to speak of the encounter between I and Thou."[40] Indeed, Barth stipulated that the encounter between I and Thou "is not arbitrary or accidental [. . .] but essentially proper to the concept of man."[41]

Anderson believed that humanity is able to attain that for which it was created by God as it comes to the realization of its co-humanity. To explain this in biblical categories he pointed to the biblical narrative where Adam is not a "completed human" before he exists in differentiation from another in reciprocity, and in the context of a social response that defines existence.[42] Therefore, Anderson also followed Barth in stipulating that "the *imago Dei* is fundamentally a structure of co-humanity." Here Anderson stood with Barth in opposition to the *imago Dei* being defined in soteriological terms as the "function" of relating. This is in contrast to the more favored description of the *imago Dei* portrayed as the ontological structure of the human being.[43] Therefore Anderson concurred with Barth that we "cannot say man without saying male or female."[44] Anderson developed this thesis to the point of discussing "the cure of souls" from a theological perspective. Clearly following Barth, Anderson contended that the cure of the soul takes place within the context of community, where the individual is able to exist in relatedness to others. To illustrate his pastoral theology Anderson initially referred to the medieval church and the *mutua consolatio fratrum*. That is, humanity "is to exist fraternally, in mutual consolation, so as to nurture and sustain humanity in particular."[45] This reference led to Barth's assertion, claimed Anderson, that the cure of souls means "the actualization of the participation of the

---

38. Anderson, *On Being Human*, op.cit., 46.

39. Ibid., 47.

40. Ibid., 47. Anderson refers to Barth, *CD, III/2*, 248.

41. Barth, *CD, III/2*, 248.

42. Anderson, *On Being Human*, 48.

43. Ibid., 75–76.

44. Ibid., 51. Anderson quotes Barth, *CD, III/2*, 286.

45. Ibid., 195.

one in the particular past, present and future of the other, in his particular burdens and afflictions."[46] Therefore, in the incarnation the humanity who exists in Adam is given a particular humanity "as the object of divine grace."[47] In this event real humanity, which is humanity in Christ, is discovered out of "sinful humanity," which is humanity in Adam. Out of this understanding of real humanity defined by humanity in Christ who exists in co-humanity, Barth was able to propose a description of real humanity as under the "saving determination of God."[48] Consequently, following Barth, Anderson proposed that our neighbor is not an ethical construct based on an ethical principle, or even a duty to love. This real, or true, humanity is manifest in Jesus Christ who serves to ground moral responsibility. It cannot be described as moral reason alone, but as "co-humanity as determined by God."[49]

Anderson made the observation that Barth's concept of neighbor is "the material content of the command of God through Jesus Christ."[50] In Jesus, Barth found the "man-for-others." Indeed, Anderson further pointed to Barth's assertion that the "neighbor is both God and the other." To "deny the other is to deny God" and therefore to "recognize the other as neighbor is to recognize the good and the right as the demand of God on me through the neighbor."[51] This is made a reality within the experience of humanity, not because of a choice to follow a particular moral reasoning, but because in "the humanity of Jesus Christ the actual humanity of every person has been taken up, judged, put to death and justified."[52] This Christological orientation is further seen as Anderson stipulated that the Word is the basis for ethical thinking.

Anderson firmly placed the basis of his discussion upon Barth's insistence that theological ethics ought to be grounded in dogmatics. Anderson contended that this is clear in the development of Barth's lectures on ethics at Münster and Bonn in 1929 and 1930. The genesis of this

---

46. Ibid., 195. Anderson quotes Barth, *CD, IV/3*, 885. Indeed, Barth claimed that the cure of souls "has to be understood and exercised as a form, and indeed basic form, of the divine and human service of the community." Barth, *Church Dogmatics: IV/3*, 885.

47. Ibid., 135.

48. Ibid., 138.

49. Ibid.

50. Ibid., 132.

51. Ibid., 138.

52. Ibid., 139.

thought is believed by Anderson to have begun between 1921 and 1925 when in the course of his Göttingen Dogmatics Barth was able to say that "(t)he Word of God is the basis of ethics."[53] In fact, it is in the right hearing of the Word, and in an obedient response, that one's personal and social life constitutes the basis for theological ethics. The consequence of this is that the question of the goodness of human conduct is found in the Word of God[54] which is where one must seek to ground ethics. Furthermore, from the Word comes the command of God which is to be heard and obeyed. Consequently, Barth was quick to see that "the command of God unites love of God and love of neighbo(u)r in a single ethical movement."[55] It is evident that in Anderson's analysis Barth's contention was that the ethical principle of loving one's neighbor could not be thought of independently from the command of God. Therefore, Barth "grounded both dogmatics and ethics in the divine self-revelation that has as its object the goodness of humans in their social, political and historical existence."[56] However, according to Anderson Barth did not seek to define ethics in terms of a formal demand of God, but rather as actions resulting as a consequence of our union with Christ. It is an issue of existence in co-humanity in that as "God assumed humanity in the person of Jesus of Nazareth the human person becomes the neighbor to whom God turns in his freedom as Creator, Reconciler and Redeemer." [57] It is a Christological orientation also found in Barth's understanding of natural theology.

BARTH'S NATURAL THEOLOGY

In a volume marking the centenary of the birth of Karl Barth in 1986, Anderson contributed an essay with the title: *Karl Barth and New Directions in Natural Theology.*[58]

Anderson began his discussion with a reminder of Barth's now famous response to Emil Brunner on the matter of natural theology.

53. Ibid., 141.

54. Anderson further comments that this "is brought out more clearly in his later treatment of ethics as dogmatics, where the *hearing* of the Word of God involves the *doing* of the Word of God, and where the command of God upholds the practice of doing the will of God." Ibid., 142.

55. Ibid.

56. Ibid.

57. Ibid.

58. Anderson, "Karl Barth and New Directions in Natural Theology."

Anderson rightly observed that Barth's *NEIN!*, "written in response to Brunner's tract on *Nature and Grace* in 1934, still stands as a monument to Barth's rejection of natural theology."[59] Indeed, Anderson contended that Barth's primary objection to Brunner's natural theology was its potential to play directly into the hands of the "German Christians."[60] Brunner proposed a "point of contact" outside of special revelation which resulted in a "new combination" of sources for theology. Barth countered this proposal with the declaration of Jesus Christ as the "one Word of God [. . .] which calls us back to the single task of theology."[61] It is Scripture itself, declared Barth, that "gives us 'another strand' of witness to the Word of God as found in nature."[62] In contrast to Brunner's proposition Barth advocated a natural theology based on Scripture. That is, the nature Psalms (111, 113–16), together with relevant passages in Romans 1 and Acts 17. However, Anderson further contended that Barth did not understand this "second line" of witness in Scripture to be a parallel witness to that of the gospel. Nor, claimed Anderson, "will Barth allow that these passages teach that there is knowledge of God which stands independently of God's revelation in Christ."[63]

Anderson developed his analysis of Barth's stance on natural theology by referring to Thomas Torrance's observation that Barth did not reject natural theology because of its rational structure, but because of its "*independent* character, developed on the basis of 'nature alone,' in abstraction from the active self-disclosure of God in Christ."[64] However, Anderson

59. Ibid., 241.

60. Ibid.

61. Ibid., 242. In this section of the *Church Dogmatics* Barth is writing in the context of the "German Christians" and the subsequent writing of the Barmen Declaration. He concludes and summarizes this section with a resolute affirmation: "When the Church proclaims God's revelation, it does not speak on the basis of a view of the reality of the world and of man, however deep and believing; it does not give an exegesis of these events and powers, forms and truths, but bound to its commission, and made free by the promise received in it, it reads and explains the Word which is called Jesus Christ and therefore the book which bears witness to Him. It is, and remains, grateful for the knowledge of God in which He has given Himself to us by giving us His Son." Barth, *Church Dogmatics, II/1*, 178.

62. Ibid.

63. Ibid.

64. Anderson points to Torrance's observation that Barth's commitment was "to one coherent framework of theological thought that arises within the unitary interaction of God with our world in creation and Incarnation." Ibid., 243.

clearly believed that Barth experienced a later change in direction. He further contended that there are hints in the later writings of Barth that "invite us to consider the fact that he did indeed wish to preserve a correspondence between knowledge of God in creation and knowledge of God through Christ."[65] Anderson saw this in Volume Four of Barth's *Church Dogmatics* where he argued that "the creaturely world, the cosmos and even the nature of man is given in an authentic speech and word."[66] Indeed, Anderson saw a more emphatic statement on this subject by Barth which he declared in the posthumously published *The Christian Life*, which stated that God, in creating humanity, "has made himself known to man and therefore to the world."[67] However, Anderson clearly believed that Barth, even in these later years, preferred to speak of an "analogy of relation *(analogia relationis)*" in which the "basis for a positive natural theology lies within the interaction of God as Creator and Redeemer with creation."[68] Indeed, Barth perceived that natural theology had the ability to serve the church "in its witness to the transforming and sustaining power of the Word of God."[69] This opinion, however, stood in stark contrast to Barth's belief that two centuries of Protestant theology in Germany had totally failed in its attempt to create a synthesis.[70] In relation to Barth's strong conviction Anderson asked the important and necessary question: "can we find in Barth's transformation of theology itself a new direction for natural theology?" It was Anderson's conviction that we can.[71]

Anderson interpreted Barth's new direction in natural theology by comparing it to "the older natural theology," which defined as a movement from "being-to-being" with the nature of created being providing a clue to the synthesis. However, the new direction of Barth is described by Anderson as "from 'act-to-being,' with God's act of Incarnation and

65. Ibid., 246.

66. Ibid.

67. Ibid.

68. Ibid., 247.

69. Ibid., 248. In his *Church Dogmatics* Barth states that the "pedagogic necessity of a 'natural' theology as a prelude to real theology will obviously force itself upon us. Man will have to be incited and instructed to make the right use of this position of his, i.e., to make a general survey of his different possibilities and perhaps their gradation, in order finally to discover the possibility from which he can be told that it is not only his, but that as his it is the divine possibility attested in God's revelation." Barth, *CD, II/2*, 90.

70. "This was the battle cry of his *Epistle to the Romans*." Ibid., 248.

71. Ibid., 248.

creation seen in unitary action of grace by which creaturely being is determined and upheld."[72] Anderson further concurred with Barth that the problem with the older natural theology was its attempt to understand the being of God as Creator "in abstraction from his revelation as Father, Son and Holy Spirit." Barth challenged this older form on two counts. Firstly, Anderson referred to Barth's judgment that it established the notion that the being and Word of God could be understood outside the act of God's revelation. Secondly, Anderson pointed to Barth's contention that it destroyed the freedom of God to remain as the 'Wholly Other' in his relation to the world.[73] Consequently, Anderson turned to Barth's insistence that the Incarnation is "the criterion by which creation itself is understood."[74] Indeed, since the created world is contingent upon the objectivity of God as its source, its own nature does not define or determine it.

> Through sin, the created order experiences contingence away from God as negative contingence, experienced as disorder. Through the incarnation of God in Jesus Christ, the ontological status of the created order is returned to its contingence toward God through the humanity of Christ, which is bound up with the essential and eternal relations of Christ as the Son of the Father.[75]

The immediate implication of Barth's new direction in natural theology is in the realm of theological ethics, particularly as an extension of the thought with respect to the interaction of Incarnation and creation.[76] According to Anderson the resulting first task of theological ethics must be the displacement of the notion that ethics works within an autonomous sphere moored in "orders of creation," such as Barth saw in Brunner's "other task of theology."[77] Anderson observed that Barth responded to Brunner's thesis by creating a theological ethics based on theological anthropology. That is, one that is able to provide "a new ontological structure for the consideration of moral theology and human life."[78]

72. Ibid., 249.

73. Ibid., 250.

74. Ibid., 251.

75. Ibid. Anderson later adds that the incarnational (and Trinitarian) "thrust in Barth's theology enabled him to sever the artificial link which natural theology had attempted to construct between humanity and deity as a 'being-to-being' synthesis." Ibid., 252.

76. Ibid., 253.

77. Ibid., 254.

78. Ibid., 255.

CONCLUSION

This chapter has maintained that Ray Anderson's pastoral setting led him to search for a new approach to theology and a subsequent agenda to construct an incarnational theology. Further, the influence of Thomas Torrance led Anderson into a deeper engagement with the works of Karl Barth, as did his discussions with Bernard Ramm concerning the importance of Karl Barth to contemporary evangelicalism. Later, Geoffrey Bromiley served as an additional influence which consolidated Anderson's appreciation. However, by the time he was lecturing at Fuller Seminary appreciation had turned to appropriation. This came about because Anderson found in Barth a valuable source and mentor who was able to assist him in fulfilling his original incarnational agenda. Anderson did this by pursuing an approach to theology borrowed from Barth's criticism of Cartesianism. This is expressed in Anderson's understanding of humanity based on a motif of theological anthropology defined by the Word of God.

Barth's theological anthropology also led to Anderson's motif of defining humanity in terms of co-humanity. He applied this to the pastoral setting as he constructed a theology of the church community and its ministry. It has also been found that his motif of ethics was also highly influenced by Barth. The result was a theological ethics based on humanity's existence in Christ. Consequently, it has been determined that Anderson followed Barth in grounding ethics in dogmatics. In addition, Anderson's agenda for an Incarnational theology led to a positive critique of Barth's development in natural theology.

Barth was a Reformed theologian and the theologians studied to this point have all been from that tradition. However, Barth was also influenced by pietism. It is for this reason that interest has also been expressed by the Wesleyan theologian Donald Dayton. Dayton's encounter with Barth provides an interesting contrast to the theologians studied to this point. Yet he also possessed a number of similarities, including a transition from fundamentalism to new evangelicalism and an appreciation of Barth's theology of the Word of God.

9

Donald Dayton

Donald Dayton has been a Wesleyan evangelical influenced by Karl Barth. Dayton grew up in the theological environment of the Wesleyan and holiness branch of fundamentalism. However, during his early years of adulthood he cut himself off from these roots and embraced an anti-religious ideology that put its trust in the rationalism of science. Yet later, during his early twenties, this too proved unsatisfactory and he returned to the Christian faith. However, he soon came to the conclusion that there was no returning to the theological environment of his upbringing. Searching for new approach to his faith he enrolled at Yale University where he came across Karl Barth's *Church Dogmatics*. As he read it he began to reflect on its meaning and content. The impact was so strong that it sparked a theological awakening that re-kindled Dayton's theological interest, which became an enduring influence in his theology. This expressed itself in several ways.

In all of Barth's work the Wesleyan theologian discovered a new understanding of the Word of God and the incarnation. He also appreciated Barth's theologically grounded politics which provided Dayton with solid and satisfactory foundations for his political convictions. Clearly, Dayton sought to return to the faith of his childhood, yet in a modified form. These modifications were essential since the fundamentalism of his childhood faith could not accommodate his socialist convictions and the insights he had gained from his scientific education. The encounter with Barth, then, enabled Dayton to fulfill his theological agenda in a way that the Wesleyan and holiness fundamentalism of his childhood was unable to do.

A large amount of Dayton's work regarding Barth was concerned with the motif of his reception in North American evangelicalism. No doubt seeking to analyze his own background and transposition for the benefit of the wider evangelical community, Dayton carefully and thoroughly analyzed the reasons why different branches of evangelicalism responded to Barth in the way they did. He clearly perceived a vocation to provide an incentive for other evangelicals to follow the same path he had trod. He sought to do so by clearing up early misconceptions and upholding Barth as mentor for the future of North American evangelicalism. Indeed, he observed that evangelicalism's generally negative first reactions gave way to a more accepting dialogue in the 1970s. This was due, claimed Dayton, to the changing nature of American society, as well as a growing understanding, interest, and promotion, of Barth's theology among evangelicals and the wider theological community. At the same time, however, while abandoning the fundamentalism of his youth, Dayton retained a commitment Wesleyanism. This is clearly seen in his desire to draw attention to the pietistic motifs present in Barth's theology.

While it is true to say that Dayton abandoned the theological orientation of his upbringing, it is significant to note that he has remained a member of the Wesleyan Church of America. One may therefore conclude that Dayton's modified Wesleyanism, both guided by Barth and searching for a new evangelicalism, amounted to a unique and distinctive contribution to North American evangelicalism. To be sure, Dayton's continued membership of the denomination and appreciation of Karl Barth led him also to emphasize and investigate pietistic strands and influences in Barth's theology, since pietism is also at the root of Wesleyan theology.

Donald Dayton is currently Professor of Historical Theology at the Caspersen School of Graduate Studies, Drew University, New Jersey. He is also a member of the Wesleyan Church of America. The place of Barth in his thinking can be clearly traced to his university education. In 1963 he began study at Houghton College, New York, with majors in Philosophy and Mathematics. In that year he also enrolled at Columbia University and Union Theological Seminary. In 1969 he commenced a Bachelor of Divinity at Yale University and in 1983 began study for a Doctor of Philosophy at the Department of Christian Theology, Divinity School, University of Chicago. His emphasis was on contemporary theology and ethics, with a dissertation entitled: *Theological Roots of Pentecostalism*.[1]

Dayton's appreciation for Barth's theology is evident in a chapter he contributed to an edited work entitled: *Christianity and the wider*

---

1. Dayton, Curriculum Vitea, pers. Comm. (Thurs. October 9, 2003).

Ecumenism. He began his contribution with the estimation that Karl Barth "towers above twentieth century Protestant theology." Indeed, even "those who have sought to evade his influence and articulate alternative positions have quite often had to do that in direct dialogue with him."[2] Dayton revealed his own indebtedness to Barth when, in a 1978 article for *Sojourners,* he recalled that Barth had been one of the most determinative influences in his life and theological development.[3] The significance of Barth to Dayton's theology is best understood in the context of his theological background.

A BACKGROUND IN HOLINESS FUNDAMENTALISM

Dayton recalled that he grew up in a Christian context "rooted in an experientially oriented revivalism" that sought refuge in rationalistic fundamentalism.[4] It was the Wesleyan Methodist wing of the present Wesleyan Church. Dayton asserted that by the mid-twentieth-century the Wesleyan Methodist group had become a holiness/fundamentalist movement, having lost its radical heritage.[5] While elements of this denomination influenced Dayton's mature theology his early opinions were far from positive. He came to believe that the holiness brand of fundamentalism that had been persuasive during his upbringing was no longer satisfactory. Indeed, he saw it as intellectually sterile, unduly conservative and out of touch with the issues that confronted the world. It would appear that all he had at his disposal, as he faced the issues of life as they were presented to him, was a theology that was not able to respond with depth or sophistication. He consequently abandoned these roots and replaced them with "a hardnosed scientific and anti-religious perspective." However, this rationalistic way of thinking eventually faltered whilst he was in his early twenties, "as larger questions of meaning and purpose emerged."[6]

2. Dayton, "Karl Barth and the Wider Ecumenism," 181.

3. Dayton, "Breaking Down the Barriers to Faith: Karl Barth's Determinative Influence on My Life," 25.

4. Ibid.

5. Dayton recalls that this group was "forced out of the American Methodist Episcopal Church for agitating the slavery question (and decided that both slavery and the episcopacy were 'unscriptural' because the bishops used their authority to destroy the abolitionists)." They also founded Wheaten College but lost control of it. Dayton, pers. comm, (February 23, 2004) 1.

6. Dayton, "Breaking Down the Barriers," 25.

DISCOVERING KARL BARTH

Having believed that he had rediscovered his Christian beliefs, Dayton "went off to Yale Divinity School to seek content" to his faith and to "discover which variety of Christianity made the most sense."[7] He recalled that it was during this time that he started reading Barth, who soon became a real force in his life and thought. Dayton recalled: "I can still sense the excitement with which I devoured *Church Dogmatics* in my dorm room. I often had to pace around the room or take long walks around New Haven to dissipate the spiritual energy that had built up."[8] He contended that previously he had been taught to view the Christian faith as "a sequence of spiritual experiences." However, Barth unfolded for him a cosmic vision of the universe, centered in Christ, which radically relativised his own struggles with faith.[9] Dayton consequently found himself reveling in Barth's exalted Christology, "in which Christ is portrayed not only as the head of the church but also as the ground of creation and the source of all that exists."[10] Barth was appreciated by Dayton as a theologian who gave direction to his new theological agenda, indeed made it possible. It amounted to an assertion that one could remain an evangelical while becoming liberated from the fundamentalist rationalism that he had previously abandoned and could never return to.

Dayton's reading of Barth also led him to a new understanding of the Word of God. Barth showed Dayton a way beyond his fundamentalist heritage which taught that a belief in the inerrancy of Scripture was adequate to sustain the truth of Christianity. Indeed, Dayton recalled the feeling of exhilarating liberation at realizing that fundamentalist assumptions had misled him by "elevating Scriptures to the place of Christ."[11] Yet most importantly was Barth's ability to instruct Dayton in the true meaning of the incarnation which radically transformed his inherited theological categories. He confessed that he "began to understand the greatness and glory of God to be best expressed in the divine condescension of God in Jesus Christ."[12] Instead of the theology of his upbringing which

7. Ibid., 25.
8. Ibid.
9. Ibid.
10. Ibid.
11. Ibid.
12. Ibid.

understood such things as some distant negotiations to ensure eternal life, Dayton "began to see the incarnation and death of Christ as events pregnant with meaning and guidance for the shape of his life."[13] Barth was also helpful as Dayton sought to shape his understanding of Christianity and activism.

The Politics of Barth

As a child of the 1960s Dayton had been swept up into its activism, particularly the civil rights movement. While the disinterest that his childhood church exhibited towards civil rights issues contributed to his initial alienation from the Christian faith, Dayton later came to find in Barth one who was able to show that "concerns for social justice were appropriate to biblical faith and not in violation of it."[14] Dayton therefore contended:

> Just as the incarnation of God in Christ represents the Divine condescension in grace and mercy to the undeserving and sinners, so must the life of the church (and of individual Christians) reflect that same downward movement toward those less fortunate, both spiritually and physically.[15]

Dayton later built upon his interest in Barth's politics in an appreciative review of *Karl Barth and Radical Politic,* edited and translated by George Hunsinger.[16] The central concept of the work, which was subsequently debated in a series of articles, is one proposed by Friedrich-Wilhelm Marquardt. His thesis was that "Barth's early involvement in socialist political action and labor union organizing in the second decade of this century was not a false start that culminated in the massive *Church Dogmatics*, but was actually the key to understanding the whole of Barth's theology."[17] While Dayton found this work to be of significance not only to Christians in Europe, but "for Christians in every social and

13. Ibid.

14. Ibid.

15. Ibid.

16. The publication includes the writing of Friedrich-Wilhelm Marquardt, entitled, "Socialism in the Theology of Karl Barth"; a 1911 "socialist" address by Barth on "Jesus Christ and the Movement for Social Justice"; a piece by Helmut Gollwitzer sympathetic to Marquardt's thesis; a critique by Herrmann Diem; and a more general essay by Dieter Schellong, "On Reading Karl Barth from the Left"; an essay by American Joseph Bettis; and a concluding essay by the editor. G. Hunsinger, ed. and trans., *Karl Barth and Radical Politics.*

17. Dayton, Review of G. Hunsinger, ed. and trans., "Karl Barth and Radical Politics," 32.

political context," he essentially agreed with Hunsinger that Marquardt overstepped the mark.[18]

To support his contention Dayton referred to the general index to all of the thirteen volumes of the "Church Dogmatics" in which there is only one reference to socialism. However, while it is clear that an entry in a general index is not a satisfactory means of determining the content or orientation of a work, it is evident that Dayton believed that Barth clearly understood the Scriptures as pushing the Christian in a leftist direction. Yet in contrast to leftist ideology Dayton contended that Barth spoke of a scriptural socialism that transcended subjective political systems, with all their inherent weaknesses and the poverty of their cultural accommodation.[19] Indeed, he sought to proclaim a God who always takes a stand against the lofty and on behalf of the lowly; "against those who already enjoy right and privilege and on behalf of those who are denied it and deprived of it."[20]

Barth's political conviction ran along the same lines as his theology. He sought to expose the problems and inadequacies found in subjective theories by advocating the need to embrace more objective understandings of reality. Hence the belief that God's socialism was infinitely superior to whatever human thinkers can create as socialism.[21] While Dayton continued his interest in politics it is Barth's relationship with North American evangelicalism that comprised the greater part of Dayton's work.

THE RECEPTION OF KARL BARTH IN NORTH AMERICAN EVANGELICALISM: FROM NEGATIVE REACTION TO POSITIVE OUTLOOK

In his 1985 publication, *Karl Barth and Evangelicalism: The Varieties of a Sibling Rivalry*, Donald Dayton studied the growing interest in the Theology of Karl Barth that was developing among evangelicals. Dayton contended that the complexity of dealing with this issue was derived from the variety of opinions that have been expressed. On the one hand was the

18. Ibid., 33.

19. Dayton points out that Barth sought to promote a socialism that was eclectic and pragmatic rather than theoretical and ideological. Ibid., 33, 34.

20. Ibid., 32.

21. Consequently, Barth is "even more radical than Marx—in that the kingdom of God carries a critique even of the Marxian vision." Ibid., 33.

Reformed theologian Cornelius Van Til, who "consistently polemicized against Barth." In an essay published in 1954, *Has Karl Barth Become Orthodox?* Van Til "judged that of all the heresies that have evoked the great creeds of refutation, 'no heresy that appeared at any of these was so deeply and ultimately destructive of the gospel as is the theology of Barth.'"[22] Dayton also noted that the dispensationalist Charles Ryrie found "Barthianism" to be a "theological hoax," "because it attempts to be both critical and orthodox."[23]

Dayton was not surprised by the diverse responses that came from among the evangelical camp. His own response, however, was to promote Barth by arguing that past interpretations were seriously flawed. He did so by acknowledging that the huge task of reading all of Barth's work had made the task of interpretation a lifetime work. The nature of Barth's writing also produced difficulty. "The dialectical and multifaceted character of his thought means that one is always in danger of reading and extrapolating from one facet or another."[24] More significantly Dayton contended that "Barth's profound doctrine of sin, Christocentric orientation, and exegetically oriented theological method have been an offence to the more pragmatic, empirical, and philosophical styles of American theology." Furthermore, Dayton sadly reflected that dialogue with Barth, with only a few exceptions, "have been based on stereotypes so grossly distorted as to be unrecognizable to the careful reader of Barth,"[25] a situation that has arisen out of a misreading of the Basel theologian. Furthermore, Dayton complained that Barth "has often been interpreted from caricature or on the basis of fragmentary readings."[26]

However, while Barth has received a number of negative responses it appears that Dayton's agenda to promote Barth among evangelicals is seen in his highlighting of Barth's positive reception in North America, and his enduring relevance to North American evangelicalism. Dayton's observation was that when Barth began to write the fundamentalist/modernist controversy was at its peak in North America. "His effort to find a new

22. Dayton, "Karl Barth and Evangelicalism," 18.

23. Ibid.

24. Ibid. Dayton also notes that the changes in Barth's thought, from the earlier dialectical period to the later Christocentric orientation have always provided problems for interpreters. Ibid., 18.

25. Ibid., 17.

26. Ibid., 18.

path through these questions was too critical for conservatives [. . .] and too comfortable with classical and biblical language for the liberals who were fighting for the right to use critical tools."[27] However, Dayton believed that by the 1970s both the evangelical heirs of fundamentalism on the one hand and liberalism on the other were showing their intellectual bankruptcy. Dayton asserted that Barth had much to offer those seeking an alternate path.[28] Indeed, Dayton sought to address this very issue in two earlier articles he had written for *The Reformed Journal*.

In 1974 Dayton wrote two journal articles with the same title: *An American Revival of Karl Barth?* In the first Dayton declared that "Barth stands out with a stature that cannot be easily dismissed."[29] To stress the significance of this observation Dayton quoted Klaas Runia's prediction that when Bultmann and Tillich have been forgotten "Barth will still be with us, just as Augustine and Thomas and Luther and Calvin are still with us."[30] In 1974 Dayton was beginning to see the signs of change.

Indeed, Dayton predicted that cultural forces would augment, rather than stunt, a growth in Barth's impact on American theology. He listed seven indications for this. The first was a "new depth in the American understanding of Barth." Dayton contended that this came about with the publication into English of the *Church Dogmatics*.[31] The impact of these was significantly enhanced in the spring of 1962 when Barth made his first trip to America. Furthermore, Dayton recalled that it was also around this time that the "first substantial indigenous secondary literature on Barth"

27. Ibid., 26.

28. Ibid., 26.

29. Dayton, "An American Revival of Karl Barth? (I)," 17. The second part was entitled, "An American Revival of Karl Barth? (2)."

30. Ibid., 17.

31. "The first volume was published in 1936; the second did not appear until 1956. But seven of the thirteen volumes (including those treating the doctrines of creation and Christology—in many ways his most productive discussions) were published between 1960 and 1962." Ibid., 17.

was produced.[32] A few years later, during the mid to late 1960s, a number of popular introductions were also published.[33]

Secondly, Dayton observed that along with the publication of new material in English came "a new appreciation of Barth" and the dropping of old stereotypes. This was particularly seen in Reinhold Niebuhr's reversal and later by a change of perspective among many evangelical leaders. Niebuhr was appreciative of some of Barth's contributions but was primarily critical. This was evident in the 1950s when Niebuhr attacked Barth's silence in the face of the Russian suppression of the Hungarian rebellion. Barth's thought was believed to be morally bankrupt because "he could not sustain the same critique of Communism that he had of Hitler."[34] However, Dayton contended that Niebuhr, like others at this time, failed to see that while Barth was not uncritical of Communism, "he was more concerned with the idolatrous confusion of the church with the nation or culture."[35] Dayton observed that Niebuhr came to understand this shortly before his death. It was a change of heart with considerable impact. A similar situation occurred within evangelicalism. Dayton believed that Cornelius Van Til's polemic against Barth was typical of evangelicalism's early responses. However, Dayton observed that by 1973 Bernard Ramm, a Baptist and evangelical, attacked Van Til's understanding of Barth, suggesting that Barth should be read "to learn how theology should be written."[36] Even more effective, claimed Dayton, has been Donald G. Bloesch, who pronounced that "Karl Barth himself is

32. Presbyterian Arnold Come introduced Barth's *Dogmatics* to preachers in 1962. Lutheran Robert Jenson began a significant series of volumes in 1963. From Evangelicals came attacks like Cornelius Van Til's *Christianity and Barthianism* (1962) and Gordan Clark's study of *Karl Barth's Theological Method* (1963), as well as more appreciative *The Significance of Karl Barth* (1961) by Fred Klooser. Other significant works include John Howard Yoder's *Karl Barth and the Problem of War* (1970), Robert Willis' *The Ethics of Karl Barth* (1971) and Gene Outka's *Agape* (1973). Dayton also notes that in the 1960s there was a rush to provide classical studies from abroad. This list includes: G. C. Berkouwer's *The Triumph of Grace in the Theology of Karl Barth* (1956), Klaas Runia's *Karl Barth's Doctrine of Holy Scripture* and Jerome Hamer's *Karl Barth*. Ibid., 18.

33. First was Robert McAfee Brown's translation of George Casalis' *Portrait of Karl Barth* (1963). Herbert Hartwell's *Theology of Karl Barth* (1964), Colin Brown's *Karl Barth and the Christian Message* (1967), Thomas Oden's *The Promise of Karl Barth* (1969), T. H. L. Parker's *Karl Barth* (1970) and David Mueller's *Karl Barth* (1972). Ibid., 18.

34. Ibid.

35. Ibid.

36. Ibid., 19.

an evangelical theologian." According to Dayton, Bloesch "clearly views Barth as the most exciting and appropriate dialogue partner for the forging of a modern evangelical theology and confesses the profound impact of Barth on his own thought."[37]

Thirdly, Dayton understood the forming of the *Karl Barth Society of North America* to be the "most visible sign of a substantial interest in Barth." Out of the founding of this society came an effort to cultivate support for Karl Barth in North America. This has been assisted, noted Dayton, by the publication of a series of papers and the establishment of a major research collection.[38]

Fourthly, Dayton observed a new concern for biblical studies. He alluded to a feeling among many biblical scholars that historical biblical criticism had become bankrupt. Dayton contended that this opened the way to a more positive reception to the "post-critical" exegetical and theological stance of Barth.[39] Dayton made special mention of the New Testament scholar, Brevard Childs, who contended in his 1970 publication—*Biblical Theology in Crisis*—that "Barth remained invulnerable to the weaknesses that beset the Biblical Theology Movement." Furthermore, Dayton observed the influence of Barth in Childs' concern for "doing theology in the context of the canon" by "recovering an exegetical tradition."[40]

Dayton's fifth indication of Barth's growing impact in North America was his belief that there was a "new cultural situation."[41] Dayton rightly observed that the "impact of a mode of theological thinking like Barth's is determined not only by the logic of theological discussion or analysis, but also by the extent to which it speaks to underlying social and psychic needs that may never rise to consciousness."[42] Indeed, Barth's theology had such a powerful impact on the continent because he spoke germanely "to the unique cultural context of early twentieth-century Europe."[43] Dayton

37. Ibid.

38. Ibid.

39. Dayton refers to the publication by a New Testament Professor at Union Seminary in New York, Walter Wink, *The Bible in Human Transformation*. Dayton also noted two Yale scholars, Paul Minear and Hans Frei. Ibid.

40. Ibid.

41. Dayton, "An American Revival of Karl Barth? (2)," 24.

42. Ibid.

43. Ibid.

believed that optimistic North America was not ready for what Barth had to offer. To be sure, within their context Barth came across as unduly pessimistic. However, Dayton observed that this situation began to change when, in the 1960s and early 1970s, a new malaise began to permeate the American self-consciousness. Dayton noted a number of issues that had changed American optimism into a deep concern and growing pessimism. Indeed, he observed in 1974 that "the optimistic, pragmatic temperament of the American mind and experience has been profoundly shaken." To explain this change Dayton listed a number of defining issues and incidents, including the energy crises, ecological pollution, the Vietnam War, Watergate, and the failure of the reform of the 1960s to effectively deal with social evil.[44] Dayton contended that this fundamental shift in the American psyche might have had an effect on the reception of Barth in North America. His theory was that what appeared "pessimistic" to earlier generations might come to be seen more as "realistic" in America's new cultural setting.[45]

Sixthly, Dayton referred to "a controversial new interpretation of Barth." During the 1970s Dayton observed a retreat from the radical activism of the 1960s and the beginning of a new turn to conservatism. During these times of change Dayton contended that "(t)heologians and churchmen alike seek new and different interpretations of religious thought and life."[46] Furthermore, Dayton believed that Barth became a theologian of significant relevance in America because of the striking parallels between the changes of the 1970s and those experienced by Barth. As Dayton stated: "The decade before Barth's publication of the explosive commentary on Romans was his great period of involvement in social reform."[47] Indeed, Dayton contended that as "the American theological world seeks to understand its own movement from the 1960s to the 1970s, it may well turn to the paradigm of Barth's transition from the 1910s to the 1920s."[48]

Lastly, Dayton, in the 1970s, called for an American "Barmen Declaration."[49] He noted that one of the most important periods in Barth's

44. Ibid.

45. Ibid.

46. Ibid.

47. Ibid., 25.

48. Ibid.

49. Dayton goes on to note that "much of the discussion has emerged from a fall 1973 convocation at Yale Divinity School devoted to the topic 'Do we need a new Barmen Declaration for the present situation in American church and society?'" Ibid., 26.

career was his role in the resistance of the "Confessing Church" to Hitler. Indeed, Dayton recalled that Barth was, in effect, the author of the "Barmen Declaration." It was a significant confession that proved to be the backbone of the Confessing Church's response to the "German Christians." Furthermore, Dayton put forward that the Barmen Declaration "epitomizes Barth's theology." Indeed,

> Jesus Christ, as he is attested for us in the Holy Scripture, is the one Word of God which we have to hear and which we have to trust and obey in life and in death. We reject the false doctrine, as though the church could and would have to acknowledge as a source its proclamation, apart from and besides this one Word of God, still other events and powers, figures and truths, as God's revelation.[50]

In February of 2004 Dayton certainly endorsed this. He further observed that Barth still played "an important role in canonical criticism and the Yale School," facilitated many to enter "contemporary theological dialogue," in the revival of Trinitarian theology, and as an important source for the construction of theology in a post-Christian era.[51] As well as the changing perceptions of Barth in North America, Dayton studied the relationship between Barth and evangelicalism.

THE RECEPTION OF KARL BARTH IN NORTH AMERICAN EVANGELICALISM: REFORMATIONAL AND PIETISTIC EVANGELICALISM

Dayton has argued that "there have been three primary periods in the history of Protestantism that have provided content to the word 'evangelical.'" He believed that those who use this term gravitate towards one or other of these periods.[52] The first of these is the Reformation. Those who identify with this group emphasize the great *sola's* (*sola fide, sola gratia, sola Christie, sola Scriptura*). Dayton observed that this also reflected the German use of the *evangelisch*, which essentially means "protestant."[53] The second period is predominately found in the Anglo-Saxon world where the word *evangelical* is more likely

50. Ibid., 25.

51. Dayton, pers. comm. (February 23, 2004) 2.

52. Dayton, "Karl Barth and Evangelicalism," 18.

53. Ibid., 19.

to connote the "evangelical revival" and "great awakenings." The third period is associated with a growing split in American Protestantism that culminated in the twentieth-century fundamentalist/modernist controversy. The word *evangelical* "in this context refers to a mixed coalition of a variety of theological and ecclesiastical traditions that have found common cause against the rise of 'modernity' and the erosion of older forms of orthodoxy."[54] Dayton believed that it is the first period, that of the Protestant Reformation, that is most congruent with Barth's most fundamental commitments. Dayton supported his claim by quoting John McConnachie's suggestion in 1947 that "no one has done more to interpret, transform, and illumine the issues of the Reformation for our day as Karl Barth."[55] Dayton further contended that it was Barth's rediscovery of the Reformation that launched him in his new theological direction.[56]

Barth himself was very much aware that his new direction emerged out of his own rediscovery of the theology of the Reformation. Dayton showed this as he alluded to Eberhard Busch's observation that it was in Göttingen, between April 1924 and October 1925, that Barth felt that his previous theological view amounted to his pre-Reformation position. However, at that point he believed that his eyes had become open to the Reformers "and their message of the justification and sanctification of the sinner, of faith, of repentance and works, of the nature and the limits of the church and so on."[57] Furthermore, Dayton noted that Barth echoed this view at his retirement when, in his final lectures, he used the word *evangelical* to describe his theology. Indeed, Dayton also contended that Barth's basic theological intention was "to recover and restate the Reformation recovery of the New Testament gospel."[58] However, Dayton was also aware that Barth sought to revise parts of the Reformer's theology. He noted that while Barth saw the need to revive the theology of the Reformation he also saw the need to go beyond their conclusions by continuing to find the meaning of Scripture. Barth understood that whenever he brought changes to the Reformers theology the basic reason for his reformula-

54. Ibid.

55. Ibid. Dayton quotes McConnachie from J. McConnachie, "Reformation Issues Today," 103.

56. Dayton, *Karl Barth and Evangelicalism*, 19.

57. Ibid., 19. Here Dayton quotes Busch, *Karl Barth*, 143.

58. Dayton, *Karl Barth and Evangelicalism*, 19.

tions were the same: "the pressures of what he called his 'Christological concentration.'"[59] In this Dayton concurred with Colin Brown that the basic difference between Barth and traditional Protestantism lay in his understanding of the significance of Christ. Barth's belief was that Christ was the sum of the Gospel, the true revelation of God, electing God and elected man. However Dayton, as an evangelical, was not deterred by Barth's development of Reformational theology. On the contrary, he believed that this move of Barth was not only appropriate, "but a necessary revision of the patterns of thought in Reformation theology."[60]

Dayton's second period is "expressed most fully in the pietist and awakening traditions."[61] While noting a lacuna of literature discussing Barth and pietism he does make reference to the important contribution of Donald Bloesch, who "has engaged Barth from issues that arise from the pietist vision."[62] Dayton also believed that an important early discussion is to be found in the 1978 publication of Eberhard Busch's *Karl Barth und die Pietisten*.[63] Busch's work is primarily concerned with the early Barth, including his critique of pietism in the earlier editions of his commentary on Romans and his responses to various journals of the *Gemeinschaftsbewegung*. Dayton makes his own contribution to this discussion by pointing out that Barth's interaction with pietism can also be found later in the fourth volume of his *Church Dogmatics*. Here Barth set himself against the pietist tradition as he "attacks what he sees as the individualistic tendency of pietism in which the experience of God's grace *pro me* obscures the priority of the *pro nobis*."[64] Barth was clearly concerned that pietism was grounded in subjective experience. He believed that they laid too much emphasis on the experience of conversion and the Christian life and too little on an objective doctrine founded on the Word of God. The main concern for Barth was in the possible theological distortions that would ensue. "As Barth put it in dialogue with Methodist

---

59. Ibid., 19.

60. Ibid., 20.

61. Ibid.

62. Dayton notes that this "can be seen particularly in his book *Jesus is Victor: Karl Barth's Doctrine of Salvation*." Ibid.

63 "Busch has deep family roots in the leadership of the *Gemeinschaftsbewegung*," which was a "fellowship" and "higher life" movement with links to the "Keswick movement." Ibid.

64. Ibid.

pastors: 'I do not deny the experience of salvation [. . .] But the experience of salvation is what happened on Golgotha. In contrast to that, my experience is only a vessel.'"[65] The influence of Wesleyanism in Dayton's thinking clearly led him to have difficulty with the critical manner in which Barth often commented on the pietists. Indeed, Dayton believed that Barth seriously misrepresented them in his portrayal of their theology as being so subjective that contended that an individual can appropriate their own salvation. However, despite these observations Dayton also found pietistic strands in Barth's work.

The Wesleyan theologian points to Busch's observation of pietist influences that dated back to Barth's early years. Dayton noted:

> [In] Barth's appropriation of and praise for pietist exegeses [. . .] (o)ne can also discern Barth's growing appreciation of Zinzendorf and his piety. Indeed, Barth discovered several of his basic themes in Zinzendorf, and came to see him as perhaps the only genuine Christocentric of the modern age. Also, in dialogue with Moravians, Barth shared Zinzendorf's linking of Christ as Savior and Creator, his tending to speak of our sanctification as fulfilled in Christ, and his tendency to polemicize against lessChristocentrically oriented representatives of pietism.[66]

Dayton also alluded to the influence of the Blumhardts and Leonard Ragaz in the religious socialist movement. The influence was clearly pietism's "strong doctrine of regeneration that soon overflows into culture and society."[67] Furthermore, Dayton suggested that Barth may have been more dependent on the influence of pietism than he may have realized. If so, Dayton contended, "Barth's relationship to this form of evangelicalism is more dialectical than his polemics would at first suggest."[68]

In the preface to the English translation of Busch's *Karl Barth and the Pietists* Dayton revealed that he took his first sabbatical leave in Tübingen

65. This aspect of Barth's theology has often led to accusations of Universalism. However, Dayton is convinced that Barth is often caricatured on the issue of universalism, and that his denials that he was a universalist "need to be taken more seriously than they often are." Indeed, Dayton, after several readings of IV/2, was convinced that "Barth posits more difference between believers and unbelievers than the awareness of the former of the salvation wrought for all." However, Dayton observed a "slipperiness" in Barth's language has created something of an issue between Barth and Pietists. Ibid., 21.

66. Ibid.

67. Ibid.

68. Ibid.

in the spring of 1980, less than two years after the publication of *Karl Barth und die Pietisten* (1978).[69] In the years since his time in Germany Dayton became increasingly convinced that in the English-speaking world the influence of pietism in Barth's theology had not been given the attention it has deserved.[70] It would seem that Dayton's period of study in Germany significantly influence his theological development.

Searching for an alternative, and already having had a positive encounter with Barth while at Yale, Dayton "fell in with a group of 'left-wing evangelicals' in the SMD (Studenten Mission Deutschland, the German counterpart of the Inter Varsity Christian Fellowship)."[71] One of the benefits of engaging with this group was the opportunity for Dayton to learn from their more advanced experience in dialogue with the theology of Karl Barth. Dayton revealed that this experience was a determinative moment in his life that reorientated his thinking at a number of points.[72]

His most important observation was the marked distinction he was able to make between evangelicalism in North America and Germany.

Dayton correctly observed that the American evangelical experience had been dominated by the "conservative/liberal" paradigm. This had resulted in evangelicalism being equated with protestant orthodoxy. In contrast, Germany had witnessed a reaction against pietism.[73] Dayton discovered an evangelicalism that "spoke of a contrast between 'academic' theology (*Universitätstheologie*) and 'church' theology (*Gemeindetheologie*). He found that German Evangelicals, instead of taking their cue from the 'fundamentalist/modernist controversy,' turned their attention to the earlier 'pietist' currents of the seventeenth and eighteenth centuries 'as they were reshaped in the nineteenth century by various *Geminschaften*.'"[74] Consequently Dayton found himself in quite a different theological culture. It was a form of evangelicalism that "actually assumed that Søren Kierkegaard was a Christian and took seriously Schleiermacher's claim to be a 'Herrenhutter (the center of the pietism of Count Zinzendorf) of a higher order.'" Dayton rightly concluded that this kind of evangelicalism

69. Dayton, "Preface" in Busch, *Karl Barth and The Pietists,* 1.

70. Ibid., 1.

71. Ibid., 1–2.

72. Ibid., 2.

73. Ibid.

74. That is, "fellowship groups in the Lutheran national churches." Ibid., 3.

would have been unthinkable in America.[75] However, the issue Dayton sought to investigate was the influence of pietism in Barth's theology.

Dayton believed that there is a strong case to be made that the mature Barth, in the fourth volume of his *Church Dogmatics*, had mellowed in his criticism of pietism. Dayton saw this in Barth's positive references to Bengel's *Gnomon*, the great pietist commentary, and a more sympathetic treatment of Zinzendorf than had previously been in evidence. Indeed, Barth appreciated Zinzendorf's "Christocentrism and linking of Christ and 'creation' as well as other themes."[76] Dayton further observed that Barth even began to ground his thought in the slogan "Jesus ist Sieger" (Jesus is Victor), which was used by the radical pietists in south-western Germany.[77] As a result of these observations Dayton contended that by the fourth volume of his *Church Dogmatics*, Barth was "making a positive appropriation of the pietist tradition that is quite unexpected in light of the earlier criticisms."[78] Indeed the influence of pietism strengthens Dayton's claim that Barth was indeed an evangelical. Dayton concluded that many of Barth's critics had been more Calvinistic than evangelical.

In his preface to Busch's book, Dayton asked if Barth's doctrine of Scripture "might not have more affinity with 'pietism' than 'orthodoxy' in the post-Reformation era."[79] He clearly believed this to be the case. Indeed, many pietists warned against the inerrancy doctrines so dear to orthodoxy and contemporary evangelicalism. According to Dayton the pietists understood orthodox evangelicalism's theology to have "too close a dialogue with philosophy." Alternatively, the "pietists advocated a sort of 'bible piety' that pulled the Scripture out from under the control of the creeds and put it to 'devotional' use, founding bible societies and other agencies to bring the Bible into the life of all Christians."[80]Dayton concluded that if one were to view Barth from this perspective, and consider pietism to be an influence in Barth's theology, then more sense could be made of Barth's radical (and anti-philosophical) biblicism and

75. Ibid., 3.

76. Ibid., 5.

77. Ibid.

78. Dayton provides an astute reflection when he states that Barth's earlier criticisms of pietism may well have been due to the his own struggle with his family's pietistic roots. Ibid.

79. Ibid., 6.

80. Ibid.

his "non-inerrantist, but genuinely authoritative, doctrine of Scripture."[81] Therefore, Dayton concluded that if his analysis was true then Barth should be considered a friend of evangelicalism, even if not to Calvinists. Indeed, if Barth is to be considered an enemy, then it is only on the basis of a view of evangelicalism that has a total disregard for the influence of pietism.[82] Finally, Dayton turned to a form of evangelicalism he describes as the defense of orthodoxy.

Dayton contended that the paradigm of "Evangelicalism as the Defense of Orthodoxy" is probably today's most common use of the word "evangelical." Indeed, it can more easily be defined by its opposition to liberalism than any positive attributes or commitments. Here Dayton noted the frustration that Barth evoked among many evangelicals. "He seems to veer toward them and to share fundamental commitments, but at the last moment he moves off in a new direction that is beyond their comprehension."[83] Dayton illustrated this in Barth's recollection of his reading of Heppe's *Reformed Dogmatics* in the spring of 1924. On the one hand, Barth came to the conviction that "the road by way of the Reformers to Holy Scripture was a more sensible and natural one to tread, than [. . .] the theological literature determined by Schleiermacher and Ritschl." At the same time Barth affirmed that he had no intention of returning to orthodoxy.[84] Barth's early determination is clearly expressed in his doctrine of the Word of God.

BARTH'S THEOLOGY OF THE WORD OF GOD

Dayton observed that one of the main issues to have led to a clash between Barth and many evangelicals amounted to a clash between a pre-critical reading of Scripture, in the case of the evangelicals, and a post-critical use, as adopted by Barth. However Dayton clearly indicated that many evangelicals, caught up in the fundamentalist/modernist debate, misunderstood Barth's approach to reading Scripture. Indeed, "(a)s Barth comments in the first preface to his commentary on Romans, if forced to choose between the older doctrine of verbal inspiration with accompanying modes

81. Ibid., 6.

82. Ibid., 8.

83 Dayton, *Karl Barth and Evangelicalism*, 21.

84. Dayton takes these words from Barth's forward to Heinrich Heppe, *Reformed Dogmatics*, v–vi. Ibid., 21 and 23.

of interpretation and the products of modern critical interpretation, he would go with the former." However, there are issues that continued to put Barth at odds with sections of the evangelical world. Again, Dayton put this down to a misunderstanding of Barth's actual theology. Dayton noted one accusation as being that the Bible is not the objective Word of God, but only becomes the Word of God when it is read under the inspiration of the Holy Spirit, or according to the subjective whims and predilections of the person reading it. Dayton found this description to be an inaccurate caricature and one-sided understanding of Barth since it did not take into account Wesleyan exegesis, which emphasizes a once-for-all process of inscripturation in the past wedded to the present 'inspiring' work of the Holy Spirit.[85] Important to this are the implications of Barth's Christological concentration.

The difficulty Dayton had with classic evangelicalism is found in its epistemology devoid of Christology. It ran with the dictum that truth is found in Scripture because "God wrote a book." For Barth, however, "this generates the 'irremediable danger of consulting Holy Scripture apart from the centre, and in such a way that the question of Jesus Christ ceases to be the controlling and comprehensive question.'"[86] Consequently Dayton found Barth's formulations to be "vastly superior" and agreed favorably with Bolich's suggestion that "it is at the point of Scripture that Barth has the most to contribute to modern evangelicalism."[87]

CONCLUSION

Donald Dayton has made a substantial contribution to the reception of Karl Barth in North American evangelicalism. This appreciation of Barth came about from his agenda to develop a theology that was different to the holiness and fundamentalist theology that he had abandoned as a young adult. Searching for a new approach to his faith Dayton found in

85. Ibid., 22.

86. Dayton quotes the *Church Dogmatics, IV/1*, 368. Ibid., 22. Indeed, Barth strongly contended that the older Protestant Orthodoxy's doctrine of verbal inspiration of Scripture was a product of rationalistic thinking—"the attempt to replace faith and indirect knowledge by direct knowledge, to assure oneself of revelation in such a way that it was divorced from the living Word of the living God as attested in Scripture . . . making it readily apprehensible as though it were an object of secular experience, and therefore divesting it in fact of its character as revelation." Barth, *Church Dogmatics: IV/I*, 368.

87. Dayton, *Karl Barth and Evangelicalism*, 22.

Barth a worthy partner in dialogue. The outcome for Dayton was to cause him to recast his most fundamental assumptions of evangelical theology. Dayton's primary contribution was as a commentator and interpreter of North American theology and the positive place Karl Barth has had in the development of new evangelicalism. Indeed, Dayton looked forward to future engagement by evangelicals with the Barth's work. Furthermore, Dayton explored Barth's political writing and favorably reported on their convincing theological foundations. In this respect, he also discovered in Barth a mature theologian of the Word who had thoughtfully engaged with leftist politics. Therefore this new evangelical Wesleyan elucidated the theological motifs of evangelicalism, socialism, the Word of God, Christology, and pietism, all as a consequence of his encounter with Karl Barth.

This chapter has also noted three significant influences in Dayton's theological development: The influence of reading Barth's work while at Yale University, the influence of Dayton's Wesleyan heritage, and his subsequent experience in Germany with the SMD. The influence of Barth led to the production of significant studies and reflections on evangelicalism in North America and how its various sub-movements have interacted with Barth's theology. Dayton's Wesleyan heritage also led to a much-needed study of the influence of pietism on Karl Barth. Dayton's conclusion was that this connection helped clear up many misconceptions and makes Karl Barth a true friend of evangelicalism. He was clearly an ideal mentor who can assist evangelicalism to construct a post-fundamentalist approach. Dayton also discussed Barth's theology of the Word of God. He found that many evangelical objections have arisen out of Calvinistic presuppositions. This was in contrast to Pietist evangelicals, who shared Barth's basic assertions.

After having studied each response to Barth, the thesis now seeks to draw the threads together in the form of concluding comments and comparisons.

10

Conclusion

IN TEASING OUT THE main features of Barth's reception by such a variety of scholars it will be most useful to divide the conclusion into two parts. Firstly, a number of comparisons will be made between the different theologians who used Barth as a significant source in their theological approaches. It is important to note that these theologians did not comprise a distinct school that gathered to share common ideas or goals. On the contrary, they largely worked independently of each other. However, the result has been an interesting mosaic of thought that is both simple in its conception, yet complex in much of its detail. The second section will highlight the interpretative tools of influence, source, motif, agenda and common agenda. There will be a comparison of the various influences that led to Barth becoming a significant source in their works. How Barth was used as a theological source in the writing of their motifs will also be discussed, along with the different agendas pursued. Finally, an attempt will be made to identify a common agenda they all shared.

We begin by comparing Donald Bloesch and Bernard Ramm. Both these theologians incorporated Barthian themes into their work and both developed approaches to theology after the pattern of Barth. However, the Swiss mentor became a significant influence in their theological thinking in quite distinct ways. Bloesch warmly accepted Barth as a valuable source for the construction of his own theology during his student days at Chicago University. Indeed, the Barthianism of the Niebuhr brothers was a significant presence in the denomination of Bloesch's childhood. The moderate European evangelicalism of Bloesch's upbringing fitted easily with Barth who guided him on an alternative path between liberalism and fundamentalism. Ramm, on the other hand, discovered Barth much later in life. This discovery followed a crisis moment that resulted in Ramm looking for a new beginning under Barth's guidance.

In a similar fashion to Bloesch, Ramm found in Barth a mentor who guided him towards an "alternate path." Consequently the influence of Barth has resulted in distinct marks of similarity. In this comparison three motifs are seen as being associated with their approaches to doing theology.

Firstly, one notes an orthodox engagement with modernity. Like Barth, both espoused the notion of the objectivity of the Word of God, and yet both advocated a use of the tools of critical study that modernism had produced. For this reason one may speak of a new kind of orthodoxy, or neo-orthodoxy within the context of North American Protestantism.

Donald Bloesch clearly followed Barth in believing that there was such a thing as the authoritative Word of God, while he also conducted a dialogue with modernity as essential to enable the Gospel to be received in the modern world. This clearly led Bloesch to follow Barth in seeing the Bible as a human book that bears the imprint of the divine revelation without actually being the revelation itself. Consequently, Scripture was a human product that while containing error, still had authority that has the potential of being a vehicle of divine grace.[1] The result was that Bloesch saw the need to recast orthodoxy through meaningful dialogue with new cultural situations. He dismissed fundamentalism in its rejection of old approaches and theological formulations, as a mistake. The belief that past positions, embedded in their rigid rationalism, could stand as a viable alternative to seekers after meaning and truth, had to be discarded. As Stanley Grenz has observed, Bloesch was by no means a backward looking confessionalist. Indeed, he sought "to interface the gospel with the contemporary situation." The result was a theological approach with a burning desire to engage constructively with culture.[2] As Bloesch put it in his *Theology of Word and Spirit*, "Theology [. . .] is both biblical and contextual. Its norm is Scripture, but its field or arena of action is the cultural context in which we find ourselves."[3] Bloesch's conclusion was that one must view Scripture with the paradox that the Bible is both fallible and infallible. Ramm's argument was similar, yet stated in a different way.

Bernard Ramm, with his scientific background, used the argument of language to convey his point that there could be no such thing as a perfect

---

1. Bloesch, *A Theology of Word and Spirit*, 32.
2. Grenz, "Fideistic Revelationalism," 53.
3. Bloesch, *A Theology of Word and Spirit*, 114.

communication between God and humanity in written form.[4] Following Barth, and with similarity to Bloesch, Ramm insisted that God had revealed himself perfectly in Christ and that this could not be equated with any subsequent expression of revelation in written form. Indeed, Ramm maintained, in contrast to Hegelianism and fundamentalism, that there is no such thing as a pure conceptual language. That is, a kind of perfect divine language devoid of any linguistic defect. As Ramm wrote in his earlier *The Pattern of Authority,* the voice of humanity cannot be substituted for the voice of God. In agreement with Barth, Ramm maintained that since the Bible is a human book,[5] it is quite impossible to sustain the argument that the truth arising from the actual revelation of God is somehow trapped within its pages. He followed Barth in affirming that God's Word has been revealed in Christ, God incarnate. Consequently, the Bible is a human historical record, and therefore to be described as only a witness. This does not mean to say, however, that the Bible lacks authority. Ramm asserted that Scripture has it in its unique capacity to bear witness to God's actual revelation.[6] As he said in *The Pattern of Religious Authority,* "the final authority in religion is God Himself . . . There is only one authority—God; and only one truth—divine revelation."[7] Indeed, inerrancy can only be found in "the Triune God in self-revelation."[8] Therefore, Ramm did not challenge the evangelical doctrine of inspiration, but rather evangelicalism's approach that confines God's revelation to a text composed by humans. Consequently, Ramm, like Bloesch, advocated an orthodox engagement with modernity. New ways of studying languages and texts, together with fresh philosophical perspectives, had led to advances in biblical scholarship that could not be ignored, less still derided as ungodly. In addition, Ramm and Bloesch display a high regard for Barth's Christological focus.

Secondly, one must note that both pursued Christological motifs in which Barth's proposal that Scripture has authority in its ability to bear witness to God's self-revelation in Jesus Christ, is reiterated. As has been seen, Barth's proposition was that God has revealed himself in Jesus

4. Ramm saw Barth's hermeneutic motif in theology as one of his most significant contributions to modern theology. See Ramm, *After Fundamentalism,* 10.

5. Ibid., 102.

6. Barth, *CD, I/2,* 541.

7. Ramm, *Pattern of Religious Authority,* 21.

8. Ibid., 21.

Christ. Scripture only has authority in that it is in a unique position to bear witness to that revelation. Following Barth, both Bloesch and Ramm contended that Scripture is a human word uniquely bearing witness to a divine Word and that the authority of Scripture derives from its authentic account of the revelation that has already taken place in Jesus Christ. This orientation has a direct bearing on their approaches. Consequently, they both revealed an allegiance to Barth in espousing the importance of a Christological approach to theology. As has been stated, Bloesch, in the opening chapter of his *Jesus Christ: Savior and Lord*, clearly set forth his Christological orientation by asserting that Christology constitutes the heart of his theology.[9] Ramm also asserted the importance of constructing theology on the basis of a Christological approach, found in the title of his first chapter in *An Evangelical Christology*: "Christology at the Center." He began this chapter by asserting that "(t)he Christian faith is based upon the person and work of Jesus Christ."[10] Consequently, Ramm promoted a Christian theology founded on and centralized in Christology, which stands as the pivotal foundation and basis of all other theologies.[11]

Thirdly, it is to be observed that both Bloesch and Ramm adopted motifs concerned with Scripture and the tradition of the Church. This followed Barth's assertion of a theology of the Word of God as proclaimed in the Church. Bloesch referred to this approach to his theology as *catholic evangelicalism*, while Ramm preferred the term *biblical and historic*.[12] This motif, after the pattern of Barth, resulted in both Bloesch and Ramm constructing theologies that drew heavily on historical sources and biblical references. In contrast to the simplistic approach of fundamentalism both authors applauded Barth's biblical and historical approach which has produced theologies in open and rich dialogue with the wider church. The result is a more honest and realistic approach to theological thinking. A similar approach was taken by Geoffrey Bromiley.

While it is true to say that Bromiley did not produce much in the way of a theological system, he did engage thoughtfully with Barth as both a translator and interpreter of his work. It is asserted here that similarities are to be found in the works of Bromiley, Ramm, and Bloesch. Bromiley

---

9. Ramm, *An Evangelical Christology*, 15.

10. Ibid.

11. Ibid., 16.

12. Ramm, *An Evangelical Christology*, 18.

shared Ramm's and Bloesch's agenda of an evangelical theology with Barth as a significant influence. He also saw Barth as a means to construct an evangelicalism freed from the rationalistic constraints of fundamentalism and the subjective abstractness of liberalism. Bromiley appeared to share Bloesch's and Ramm's motif of an orthodoxy engaged with modernity. Furthermore, it noted here that Bromiley shared with Bloesch and Ramm Barth's Christological focus and respect for theological history. Bromiley's conception of the Word of God, read and understood Christologically, and his historical focus, fitted well with Bloesch's *catholic evangelicalism* and Ramm's *biblical and historic* theology. However, differences are to be noted between these theologians and the contribution of David Mueller.

Barth would seem to have had a greater and more profound influence upon Mueller in his early years of theological formation than the theologians mentioned so far. He was born into a household appreciative of Barth and maintained this appreciation throughout the rest of his life. Consequently, Mueller's contribution was unique in that he continued the work of his father. He is also to be distinguished by his doctoral dissertation on Barth's theology. This is different from Bloesch, who came to an appreciation of Barth while writing his PhD, but did not write about Barth at that time; from Ramm, who studied metaphysics and science at postgraduate level; and from Bromiley's doctoral work, which was on German intellectual trends from Herder to Schleiermacher.

No major work on Barth's utilisation of historical theology is found in Mueller's writings. Consequently, his interpretation differed from Ramm and Bloesch in that there was no description of Barth's work as *biblical and historical* or *evangelical and catholic*. To this extent Mueller's work was also to be distinguished from Bromiley's, who also interpreted Barth's work in biblical and historical terms. The most likely reason for this can be seen in the similarities between Mueller's *Karl Barth* and the works of Thomas Torrance (*Karl Barth: An Introduction to His Early Theology, 1910–1931*), and Hans Urs von Balthasar (*The Theology of Karl Barth*).[13] These early significant and influential works emphasized Barth's theology of the Word and his Christocentrism. Balthasar considered that the "central concept," or *Denkform*, of Barth's theology is Jesus Christ[14] and Torrance followed this path as he described Barth's theology as a theology

---

13. Hans Urs von Balthasar, *Theology of Karl Barth*.

14. Hunsinger, *How to Read Karl Barth*, 8.

of the Word and a positive Christian dogmatics centered in Jesus Christ.[15] Clearly Mueller concurred with these interpretations and, in a similar fashion to these two early influential interpreters, did not make much of Barth's dependence on historical theology. However, while these discernible differences have been noted there are significant similarities.

Mueller clearly shared with Bloesch, Ramm and Bromiley an agenda to construct a new evangelical theology influenced by Karl Barth. He also asserted along with these theologians a common appreciation of Barth's motifs of a theology of the Word and Christocentrism. This theology upholds the authority of the Word but rejects the modernist rationalism of fundamentalism and the subjectivism of liberalism. It is also to be observed that Mueller's contribution had similarities with Bromiley's, since both sought to educate their readers about Barth's theology and present him as the basis for a new alternative for North American Christian theology. While Ramm's agenda cast the vision for a new theology and produced some examples of this; and while Bloesch continued to produce the results of that vision in a thoroughgoing way, Bromiley and Mueller both produced many of the tools for this enterprise to take place.

Similarities are also to be found between Geoffrey Bromiley and James Daane. Both sought an agenda to promote Barth as invaluable to the future construction of a vibrant evangelical theology distinct from fundamentalism, yet resonant with the theology of the Word and Reformation. Daane also engaged extensively with Barth's doctrine of election. This was his most dominant motif. In this one finds a similarity with David Mueller. Both were impressed by Barth's Christocentric approach to this doctrine. However, Daane's treatment was more extensive. None-the-less Barth's doctrine of election as election *of* Jesus Christ and the believer's corporate election *in* Jesus Christ was important to both their discussions. Both theologians also believed that Reformed theologians of the past had not developed the doctrine well, and consequently saw Barth's doctrine of election as correcting this fault. Indeed, Daane believed that God's election of Jesus Christ is the core of Christian truth and Mueller agreed with Barth's decisive affirmation of Jesus Christ as electing God and elected man. Bromiley also appreciated Barth's understanding of election as a *corporate* decree while Barth was appreciated by Bloesch for his doctrine of predestination which finds all of humanity predestined in Christ. A

15. Ibid., 10.

slightly different approach has been taken by Ray Anderson. A study of Anderson's theology has shown that like Bloesch, Ramm, Bromiley and Mueller, he had an agenda of constructing and promoting the theology of Karl Barth as a valuable source in the construction of an alternative evangelical theology. Indeed, it would seem that Anderson benefited from Bromiley's earlier work of translation and interpretation, and that he heeded Ramm's call for an evangelicalism "after fundamentalism." He was close to Bloesch in producing a thoroughgoing theological system influenced by Barth and yet differed from Bloesch in his agenda for a theology of praxis as distinct from Bloesch's systematic theology. Also, whereas Bloesch interacted with Barth on the basis of "appreciations and reservations," "Anderson manifests a degree and kind of appropriation that can only be described as operating *within* the Barthian paradigm" that closely reflected the influence of Torrance.[16]

It was found in this thesis that Bromiley, Bloesch and Ramm all shared the determination to retain their orthodoxy while they engaged with modernity. They also reveal the common motif of Christology and a respect for theological history. However, in Mueller's writing there was no major utilization of historical theology. Consequently, Anderson was closer to Mueller in emphasizing Barth's Christology while being less concerned with an historical approach. However, Anderson's reasons for adopting this approach were different from Mueller's. It was asserted that Mueller's Christological emphasis was a matter of interpretation for the purpose of describing Barth's approach to a new audience. Alternatively, Anderson's reason for emphasizing Barth's Christology arose out of his agenda for a theological praxis. In his parish setting he sought to develop theologies that applied to ministry. It is with Anderson's theology of the Word of God that most comparisons can be made with other theologians studied here.

Anderson's work, in common with Bloesch, Ramm, Bromiley and Mueller, reveals Barth's motif of the Word of God as God's self-revelation in Jesus Christ mediated through the written word. It was found that Anderson also believed that God's proclamation has already occurred in Jesus Christ, the Word made flesh. However, Anderson did not apply Barth's theology of the Word of God to a systematic theology, as in the case of Bloesch, but to a theological anthropology that served as a tool for

---

16. Thorne, *Evangelicalism and Karl Barth*, 117.

pastoral care. Anderson was primarily concerned with the Christian life and its meaning in the context of life with others. Finally the contribution of Donald Dayton was considered.

It is firstly to be observed that there are a number of similarities between Donald Dayton's experiences and those of Bernard Ramm. Both were raised in fundamentalist churches, both were profoundly affected by reading Barth's *Church Dogmatics* and both charted new theological courses with Barth as their primary guide. Each sought to construct and advocate for an evangelicalism beyond what they believed to be the impossibilities and restrictions of fundamentalist rationalism, as they looked for a post-fundamentalist theology engaged in constructive dialogue with modernism. There are, however, some notable differences. Bernard Ramm had a crisis experience of inward panic as, "like a drowning man" who sees parts of his life flash before him, so he saw his theology pass before his eyes, with his doctrines picked up here and there, "like a rag bag collection." As Ramm sought to rebuild his theology he found Karl Barth to be the one theologian who had the most to offer. Dayton, on the other hand, went through a process of discarding his Christian heritage, rediscovering his faith, and then seeking to build a new theological structure on his new foundations. As he did so, he was consciously guided by concepts derived from Barth's theology. However, like Ramm, Dayton found Barth to be a theologian who, in contrast to all others, had the most to offer. Here one finds their strongest point of convergence. One can also find similarities between Dayton and Mueller.

Both Dayton and Mueller sought to inform the American evangelical community about the theology of Barth and the positive lessons that could be learnt from him. Mueller focused on the nature of Barth's theology. In doing so he proposed an evangelical theology exploiting Barth's Christology and his theology of the Word of God. He further sought to promote the significance and relevancy of Barth to evangelicals since he was one who clearly stood in the heritage of the Reformation. Dayton has also been inspired by the fact that Barth's theology so firmly stands in the tradition of the Reformation era. Indeed, Barth appeared to be one who, more than any other, continued the work of the Reformation. Dayton particularly noted Barth's later conviction that he was best described as being a genuine evangelical and found Barth's theology resonating with the revivalist wing of the evangelical movement. Furthermore, Dayton, like Mueller, found Barth's theology of the Word of God and his Christology to be vastly superior to anything American evangelicalism had produced. Consequently Mueller and Dayton advanced convincing arguments that Barth not only fitted well into evangelicalism, but also has the potential to rid evangelicalism of its fundamentalist distortions and reorientate it into a vibrant movement in the heritage of the Reformation.

CLOSING OBSERVATIONS

Karl Barth has been received by North American evangelicals in a number of ways. Fundamentalist, for example, objected to Barth's theology of the Word of God and his theological approach, as we have noted. The charge laid was that rather than being a theologian of the Word Barth was a captive of Kantian philosophy. This group warned that Barth was a dangerous pseudo-evangelical who had to be avoided. Cornelius Van Til, for example, believed that Barth's theology was patterned after Kant's critical philosophy, since the modern dialectical philosophy that had been adopted by Barth was a product of Kantian philosophy. Indeed, Van Til believed that Barth had not only gone far beyond the Reformers, but well beyond Kant in meeting the demands of pure reason. Fred Klooster also objected to Barth's work and claimed that it was clearly outside the realm of orthodoxy and therefore fundamentally flawed. Klooster sounded a common fundamentalist objection when he stated that Barth could not be considered a theologian of the Word of God since he did not assent to Scriptural infallibility.

Conservative evangelicals offered a different response. They warned against many of Barth's supposed subversion of orthodoxy and yet appreciated that he was a significant theologian from whom evangelicals had much to learn. Carl Henry believed, in contrast to Van Til and Klooster, that Barth's theology mirrored the theology of Augustine and Calvin. However, Henry remained a Reformed critic of Barth in his contention that Barth's theology of the Word of God derived from non-biblical presuppositions. In many ways, however, this group formed a valuable bridge between the antagonism of the fundamentalists and the acceptance of the new evangelicals.

It has been shown that a group of new evangelicals offered a completely fresh perspective in North American evangelical theology. Their critique was initially leveled at the fundamentalists and conservative evangelicals. According to the new evangelicals these groups were captives of modernism, or the thinking of the Enlightenment—as Ramm referred to it, and highly restricted in their approach. The impact of modernism on their thinking had led to a highly rationalistic and systematized theological approach that had distorted the theology of the Reformers and distilled biblical teaching into a series of logical propositions. In contradistinction Barth, for the new evangelicals, was seen to be a true theologian of the Word and a valuable student of the Reformation. Indeed, the new evangelicals felt the need to make further adjustments to evangelicalism's response to Barth. They contended that Barth was a worthy mentor who assisted them to construct a Reformational theology distinct from the cultural accommodation of fundamentalism and conservative evangelicalism. Barth was seen as the one to guide them through to a construction of a new evangelicalism in *constructive dialogue* with modernism. Consequently, the new evangelicals believed that Barth was not to be criticized for his theology of the Word of God, but praised as a true student of the Reformation who sought to rescue the Bible from logical axioms and rationalistic propositions. These, they believed, had come to dominate the character of evangelical theology, confining it to an imprisonment of prescribed sequences of chapter headings, sub-headings and discussions of truth guided that were more guided by the rules of science than a living encounter with Christ. In contrast, Barth elevated the Word of God to an encounter brought about by the agency of the Holy Spirit and centered on God's revelation in Jesus Christ. Consequently it is contended that the new evangelicals found Barth to be a major arsenal of ideas and approach that enabled them to place evangelical theology in North America on a firmer basis, one that was solidly Biblical, theologically profound, and intellectually respectable.

This thesis has taken pains to establish that there were a variety of reasons why this group of theologians turned to Karl Barth in constructing their theological systems. It has been demonstrated that Bernard Ramm, Donald Dayton, and James Daane can be identified as theologians who represent a transition to new evangelicalism from fundamentalism. Ray Anderson represents a shift from conservative evangelicalism to new evangelicalism, while Donald Bloesch and David Mueller embraced new evangelicalism as a result of a taking on board a European evangelical appreciation of Barth's theology. Geoffrey Bromiley came as an English-born evangelical Anglican. The influences that led to these transitions have been identified and closely examined as have the motifs they pursued, as well as the agenda that drove them. Indeed, important here has been the contention that influences upon a theologian's thinking result in sources that the theologian uses as they pursue their theological motifs which in turn contribute towards the theologian's agenda.

Influences

It has been argued here that the approach taken by a theologian comes about as a result of the influences that have guided and shaped the theologian's thinking. Consequently, we have been able to demonstrate that there is a link between biography and theology. We have clearly shown that biography provides the rationale for the presence of sources in the theologian's work. Indeed, theological influences which present themselves at key moments of a theologian's development become the storehouse from which theological works are produced. This was especially true of Bernard Ramm during his crisis experience while lecturing in theology. His knowledge of theology collided with his scientific understanding in a dramatic way. Barth provided the needed resolution and way forward that Ramm so keenly sought.

Dayton was influenced in his reading of Barth, which enabled him to quite dramatically to reassemble his theology. Ray Anderson was influenced by Barth's work as a pastor as he sought a more satisfactory theology of ministry and also as a post-graduate student under the guidance of a Barthian scholar. James Daane encountered Barth's work initially as a fierce critic. However, his harsh analysis later turned to an affirming appreciation as he grappled with the task of preaching the subject of election. Donald Bloesch and David Mueller were both influenced by their family backgrounds. Bloesch's denomination was sympathetic to Barth's thought, with his student years affirming his appreciation. Mueller's father, a German evangelical in North America, had been a keen advocate of Barth. The influence of Barth on Geoffrey Bromiley is seen in his work as a linguist, translating Barth's work and commentating on his theology.

Motifs

Given the varied backgrounds of these theologians it is not surprising that they pursued motifs that differed from each other but each employed them to serve meaningful objectives. They represented the concerns that drove the new evangelicals to pursue a different path. They embodied the problems seen to have been manifest in the rationalist driven theologies they sought to respond to with a resolute alternative. The various aspects of Barth that proved inspirational may be distinguished here. They include: Ramm's Word of God, preaching and Christology; Bromiley's Christology, the decrees of God, election and the Word of God; Daane's election and preaching; Mueller's Word of God, Christology, and inspiration; Bloesch's Word of God, Doctrine of God, Christology, and soteriology; Anderson's anthropology, ethics, theopraxis, natural theology; and Dayton's pietism, North American evangelicalism, politics, and Word of God. This list, while representing a degree of variety, points to the dominant motif of a theology of The Word of God understood Christologically. Clearly, this dominant motif was instrumental in dealing with the issues which the new evangelicals contended with.

Agenda

What needs to be observed by way of summing up is that each theologian discussed had a particular agenda specific to his situation. Each had a separate objective. Here agenda has also been seen to be linked to biography. Life situations led to struggles and tensions in need of resolution, or important gaps missing in the literature that needed filling. Ramm sought for an evangelicalism beyond fundamentalism, Bromiley's agenda was primarily to translate Barth's work into English and promote him as a valuable evangelical theologian, while Daane's agenda was seen in his concern for preaching the doctrine of election, which contrasted with Mueller's agenda to inform and educate and Bloesch's call for an evangelical renaissance. Anderson's agenda to develop a theological praxis and Dayton's Pietistic agenda provide further contrasts. However, it is also true to say that they all share a common agenda, borne of an appreciation of Barth, a desire to learn from him, and an enthusiasm to use him as a significant source in the construction of their theologies.

Common Agenda

As well, the theologians considered here shared a common agenda to construct an evangelicalism free of the constraints and limitations of fundamentalism, conservatism and that other product of modernism, liberalism, while embracing an evangelicalism characterized by depth, sophistication, engagement and credibility; in short, a renewed new evangelicalism influenced by Barth. While fundamentalism, conservatism and liberalism were in the thrall of modernist rationalism, the new evangelicals, in contrast, engaged with modernism in a thoughtful and constructive manner. In so doing they sought to be faithful expositors of the Word, and true heirs of the Reformation. Not surprisingly they expressed this agenda in different ways. Ramm sought to stay clear of both the dangers of liberalism and the perils of rigid conservatism. Bromiley sought a path between liberals and conservatives, while Daane envisaged a progressive orthodoxy distinct from both fundamentalism and liberalism, which Mueller also saw as constraining and limiting. Bloesch aimed to construct a theology liberated from the absurdities of fundamentalism, and at the same time preserved from the subjectivity of liberalism. Anderson looked to move beyond the conservative Calvinism of his seminary education while remaining loyal to his evangelical identity. Likewise, Dayton sought after a moderate pietistic evangelicalism freed from the constraints of fundamentalism. The result over all is a new kind of North American evangelicalism that stands beyond the accommodation of modernist theologies. Indeed, all these movements were seen as negative products of modernist rationalism. Under Barth's influence these theologians sought an orthodoxy engaged with modernism; a new moderate evangelicalism rooted in the past yet finding its place in the present.

Finally, in the context of the history of Protestantism in the United States, characterized as it is by a multitude of fundamentalist groups on the one hand and the existence of traditional mainstream Reformation orientated churches on the other, the emergence of this "new" evangelicalism must be regarded as having considerable intellectual-historical and political significance. In the light of the fundamentalist upsurge that has accompanied the United States' foreign policy crises, exemplified by the Iraq war in particular, religion has become an unprecedented politicum. The forces of conservatism are unequivocally, and even polemically, fundamentalist. In this situation, that has world-political implications, the existence of a vigorous new evangelicalism inspired by Karl Barth, that has been investigated here, must take on significance beyond mere professional debates confined to the seminar rooms and lecture theatres of American universities and colleges. In the struggle for American hearts and minds the new evangelicals are playing a role which most of them initially would not have envisaged.

Bibliography

Adams, D. J., editor. *From East to West: Essays in Honor of Donald G. Bloesch* (Washington: University of America Press, 1997).

Ammerman, N. *Bible Believers: Fundamentalists in the Modern World* (New Brunswick: Ruters University Press, 1987).

Almond, P. C. Fundamentalism, Christianity, and Religion, The Fourteenth Sir Robert Madgwick Lecture delivered to the Faculty of Arts, The University of New England, Armidale, on Thursday, 25 October, 2001, University of New England, Armidale, NSW, March, 2002.

Anderson, A. "Karl Barth and New Directions in Natural Theology" in *Theology Beyond Christendom—Essays on the Centenary of the Birth of Karl Barth* (Allison Park, PA: Pickwick Publications, 1986).

———. "The Man Who is for God," in *Theological Foundations for Ministry*, R. Anderson, ed. (Edinburgh: T. & T. Clark, 1979b).

———. *On Being Human: Essays in Theological Anthropology* (Grand Rapids: Eerdmans, 1982).

———. *The Shape of Practical Theology: Empowering Ministry with Theological Praxis* (Downers Grove, IL: InterVarsity, 2001).

———. "A Theology for Ministry," in *Theological Foundations For Ministry*, R. Anderson, ed. (Edinburgh: T. & T. Clark, 1979a).

Barr, J. *Fundamentalism* (London: SCM, 1980).

Barth, K. *Anselm: Fides Quaerens Intellectum*, I. W. Robertson, trans. (London: SCM, 1960b).

———. *Church Dogmatics, I/1*, G.W. Bromiley and T. F. Torrance, eds., G. T. Thompson, trans. (Edinburgh: T. & T. Clark, 1936).

———. *Church Dogmatics, I/2*, G.W. Bromiley and T. F. Torrance, eds., G. T. Thomson and H. T. Knight, trans. (Edinburgh: T. & T. Clark, 1956a).

———. *Church Dogmatics, II/1*, G. W. Bromiley and T. F. Torrance, eds., T. H. L. Parker, W. B. Johnston, H. Knight, and J. L. M. Haire, trans. (Edinburgh: T. & T. Clark, 1957a).

———. *Church Dogmatics: II/2*, G.W. Bromiley and T. F. Torrance, eds., G. W. Bromiley, J. C. Campbell, I. Wilson, J. S McNab, H. Night, and R. A. Stewart, trans. (Edinburgh: T. & T. Clark, 1957b).

———. *Church Dogmatics, III/2*, G. W. Bromiley and T. F. Torrance, eds., H. Knight, G. W. Bromiley, J. K. S. Reid, and R. H. Fuller, trans. (Edinburgh: T. & T. Clark, 1960a).

———. *Church Dogmatics, IV/1*, G. W. Bromiley and T. F. Torrance, eds., G. W. Bromiley, trans. (Edinburgh: T. & T. Clark, 1956b).

———. *Church Dogmatics, IV/2*, G. W. Bromiley and T. F. Torrance, eds., G. W. Bromiley, trans. (Edinburgh: T. & T. Clark, 1958).

———. *Der Römerbrief, 1919*, Hermann Schmidt, eds. (Zurich: TVZ, 1988).

———. *Der Römerbrief*, 1927 (Zurich: TVZ, 1940).

———. *Die Christliche Dogmatik im Entwurf*, Gerhard Saunter, ed. (Zurich: TVZ, 1982).

———. *The Epistle to the Romans*, Sixth edition, E. C. Hoskyns, trans. (London: Oxford University Press, 1933).

———. *The Gottingen Dogmatics: Instruction in the Christian Religion*, H. Reiffen, ed., G. W. Bromiley, trans. (Michigan: Eerdmans, 1991).

Belgic Confession (1561, Art. XVI), and the Thirty-Nine Articles (1563, Art. XV11).

Berkhof, L. *Systematic Theology* (Oxford: The Banner of Truth Trust, 1939[1988]).

Berkouwer, G. C. *The Triumph of Grace in the Theology of Karl Barth*, H. R. Boer, trans. (Grand Rapids: Eerdmans, 1956).

Bloesch, D. G. *The Christian Life and Salvation* (Colorado Springs: Helmers and Howard, 1991a).

———. *Essentials of Evangelical Theology—Volume 1* (San Francisco: Harper Collins, 1982).

———. *The Evangelical Renaissance* (Grand Rapids: Eerdmans, 1973).

———. *The Future of Evangelical Christianity: A Call for Unity Amid Diversity* (New York: Doubleday, 1983).

———. *God the Almighty: Power Wisdom, Holiness, Love* (Downers Grove, IL: InterVarsity, 1995).

———. *Holy Scripture: Revelation, Inspiration and Interpretation* (Downers Grove, IL: InterVarsity, 1994).

———. *Jesus is Victor! Karl Barth's Doctrine of Salvation* (Nashville: Abingdon, 1976).

———. "Karl Barth: Appreciation and Reservations," in *How Karl Barth Changed My Mind*. D. K. McKim, ed. (Grand Rapids: Eerdmans, 1986b).

———. *The Last Things: Resurrection, Judgement, Glory* (Downers Grove, IL: InterVarsity, 2004).

———. "The Legacy of Karl Barth," in *Theological Studies Fellowship Bulletin* 9.5 (May–June, 1986a).

———. "The Lordship of Christ in Theological History" in *Southwestern Journal of Theology* 33:26–34 (Spring 1991b).

———. "Sin, Atonement, and Redemption," in *Evangelicals and Jesus Christ in an Age of Pluralism*, M. H. Tannenbaum, M. R. Wilson, and A. J. Ruden, eds. (Michigan: Baker, 1984).

———. "Soteriology in Contemporary Christian Thought," in *Interpretation* 35.2 (April, 1981).

———. *A Theology of Word and Spirit: Authority and Method in Theology* (Downers Grove, IL: InterVarsity, 1992).

Bolich, G. G. *Karl Barth and Evangelicalism* (Downers Grove, IL: InterVarsity, 1980).

Bradley, J. E. and R. A. Muller. *Church, Word, and Spirit: Historical and Theological Essays on Honor of Geoffrey W. Bromiley* (Grand Rapids: Eerdmans, 1987).

Bromiley, G. "Barth: A Contemporary Appraisal," in *Christianity Today* (February 2, 1959).

———. "Barth's Doctrine of the Bible," in *Christianity Today* (December 24, 1956).

———. "The Decrees of God," in *Christianity Today* 5 (April 10, 1961).

———. "Fundamentalism-Modernism: A First Step in the Controversy," in *Christianity Today* (Nov. 11, 1957).

———. *Introduction To The Theology of Karl Barth* (Edinburgh: T. & T. Clark, 1979).

———. "The Karl Barth Experience" in *How Karl Barth Changed My Mind*, D. McKim, ed. (Grand Rapids: Eerdmans, 1986a).

———. "The Karl Barth Centenary," in *Anvil*, 3:1, 1986b.

Brown, W. H. "Bernard L. Ramm: An Appreciation," in *Perspectives in Religious Studies* 17.4 (Winter, 1990).

Busch, E. *Karl Barth: His Life from Letters and Autobiographical Texts* (Philadelphia: Fortress Press, 1976).

Chopp, R. *The Power to Speak: Feminism, Language, God,* (Crossroad Publishing, 1991).

Coates, T. "Barth's Conception of the Authority of the Bible," in *Concordia Theological Monthly* (August 25, 1954).

Confroy, M., and D. A. Lee, editors. *Freedom and Entrapment: Women Thinking Theology* (North Blackburn: Dove Publication, 1995).

Colyer, E. M. "Donald G. Bloesch and His Career," in *Evangelical Theology in Transition*, E.M. Colyer, ed. (Downers Grove, IL: InterVarsity, 1999).

———, editor. *Evangelical Theology in Transition* (Downers Grove, IL: InterVarsity, 1999).

———. "A Theology of Word and Spirit: Donald Bloesch's Theological method," in *Journal for Christian Theological Research*, [http://apu.edu/~CTRF/articles/1996_articles/colyer.html] 1:1 (1996) Accessed: August 3, 1999.

Cross, T. "A Proposal to Break the Ice: What Can Pentecostal Theology Offer Evangelical Theology?" in *Journal of Pentecostal Theology* 10.2 (2002).

Dayton, D. "An American Revival of Karl Barth? (I)," in *The Reformed Journal* (October 24, 1974a).

———. "An American Revival of Karl Barth? (2)" in *The Reformed Journal* (November 24, 1974b).

———. "Breaking Down the Barriers to Faith: Karl Barth's Determinative Influence on My Life," in *Sojourners* 7:12 (December, 1978).

———. "Karl Barth and Evangelicalism: The Varieties of a Sibling Rivalry," in *Theological Students Fellowship Bulletin* (May-June, 1985).

———. "Karl Barth and the Wider Ecumenism," in *Christianity and the Wider Ecumenism*, Peter C. Phan, ed. (New York: Paragon House, 1990).

———. "Preface" in E. Busch, *Karl Barth and The Pietists: the young Karl Barth's critique of pietism and its response*, D. W. Bloesch, trans. (Downers Grove, IL: InterVarsity, 2004).

———. Review of G. Hunsinger, "Karl Barth and Radical Politics," (Westminster Press, 1976) in *Sojourners* 15 (December, 1976).

———, editor. *New Dimensions in Evangelical Thought: Essays in Honor of Millard Erickson* (Downers Grove, IL: InterVarsity, 1998).

Dollar, G. W. *A History of Fundamentalism in America* (Greenville: Bob Jones University Press, 1973).

Dorrien, G. *The Remaking of Evangelical Theology* (Lousville, KY: Westminster John Knox Press, 1998).

Douglas, J. D., editor. *The New International Dictionary of the Christian Church* (Exeter: Paternoster, 1974).

Dulles, A. "Donald Bloesch on Revelation," in *Evangelical Theology in Transition* (Downers Grove, IL: InterVarsity, 1999).

Elam, D. *Romancing the Postmodern* (London: Routledge, 1992).

Erickson, M. *Christian Theology*, 2nd ed. (Grand Rapids: Baker, 1998).

————. *Concise Dictionary of Christian Theology* (Grand Rapids: Baker, 1986).

Ford, D. F. "Barth's Interpretation of the Bible" in *Karl Barth: Studies in his Theological Method*, S.W. Sykes, ed. (Clarendon, 1979).

————, editor. *The Modern Theologians: An Introduction to Christian Theology in the Twentieth Century* 1 (Oxford: Blackwell, 1989).

Forde, G. O. "Does The Gospel Have a Future? Barth's Romans Revised," in *Word and Worlds* 14.1 (Winter, 1994).

Fox, R. W. *Reinhold Niebuhr: A Biography* (New York: Pantheon, 1985).

Frei, H. "The Doctrine of Revelation in the Theology of Karl Barth, 1909–1922." PhD diss., Yale University, 1956.

Grenz, S. *A Primer on Postmodernism* (Michigan: Eerdmans, 1995).

————. *Renewing The Center* (Grand Rapids: Baker Academic, 2000).

Hart, T. "The Word, The Words and the Witness: Proclamation as Divine and Human Reality in the Theology of Karl Barth," in *Tyndale Bulletin* 46:1 (1995).

Healy, R. M. "Arthur Cochrane and the Church-Confessing," in *Scottish Journal of Theology* 49.4 (1996).

Hendrix, S. "Luther" in D. Bagchi and D. Steimetz, ed., *The Cambridge Companion to Reformation Theology* (Cambridge: Cambridge University Press, 2004).

Henry, C. "Barth's Turnabout From the Biblical Norm," in *Christianity Today* 7 (January 4, 1963b).

————. "The Dilemma Facing Karl Barth," in *Christianity Today* 7 (January 4, 1963a).

Heppe, H. *Reformed Dogmatics* (London: Allen and Unwin, 1950).

Hicks, S. *Explaining Postmodernism: Scepticism and Socialism from Rousseau to Foucault* (Arizona: Scholargy Publishing, 2004).

Hubbard, D. A. "Geoffrey W. Bromiley: An Appreciation," in *Church, Word and Spirit: Historical and Theological Essays on Honor of Geoffrey W. Bromiley*, J. E. Bradley and R. Muller, eds. (Grand Rapids: Eerdmans, 1987).

Hunsinger, G. "Beyond Literalism and Expressivism: Karl Barth's Hermeneutical Realism," in *Modern Theology* 3:3 (1987).

————. *How to Read Karl Barth: The Shape of His Theology* (Oxford: Oxford University Press, 1991).

————, editor and translator. *Karl Barth and Radical Politics* (Louisville: Westminster Press, 1976).

Isherwood, L. and D. McEwan, editors. *Introducing Feminist Theology* (Sheffield: Sheffield Academic Press, 2001).

Jenson, R. W. "Karl Barth," in *The Modern Theologians: An Introduction to Christian Theology in the Twentieth Century* 1, D. F Ford, ed. (Oxford: Blackwell, 1989).

Jüngel, E. *Karl Barth, a Theological Legacy* (Philadelphia: Westminster, 1986).

Kaplin, L. *Fundamentalism in Comparative Perspective* (Massachusetts: University of Massachusetts Press, 1992).

Kepel, G. *The Revenge of God* (Cambridge: Polity Press, 1994).

Keylock, L. R. "Evangelical Leaders you Should Meet: Meet Donald Bloesch," in *Moody Monthly* (1988).

Klooster, F. "Aspects of the Soteriology of Karl Barth," in *Bulletin of the Evangelical Theological Society* 2:2 (1959).

————. "Karl Barth's Doctrine of Reconciliation," in *Westminster Theological Journal* 20 (May, 1958).

———. "Karl Barth's Doctrine of the Resurrection," in *Westminster Theological Journal* (October 24, 1962).

———. *The Significance of Karl Barth's Theology* (Grand Rapids: Baker Book House, 1961).

Lane, D. *The Experience of God: An Invitation to Do Theology* (Dublin: Veritas Publications, 1981).

Lewis, J. Review of D. Bloesch, "The Church: Sacraments, Worship, Ministry, Mission," in *Reformation and Revival Journal* 12.2 (Spring, 2003).

Little, F. H., editor. *German Church Struggle and the Holocaust* (Wayne State University, 1974).

Loewen, J. H. "The Anatomy of an Evangelical Type: An American Evangelical Response to Karl Barth's Theology." In *Church, Word, and Spirit: Historical and Theological Essays in Honor of Geoffrey W. Bromiley.* Edited by James Bradley and Richard A, Muller (Grand Rapids: Eerdmans, 1987).

———. "Karl Barth and the Church Doctrine of Inspiration: An Appraisal for Evangelical Theology." PhD diss., Fuller Theological Seminary, 1976.

Lohse, B. *Martin Luther's Theology: Its Historical and Systematic Development*, R. A. Harrisville, trans. (Edinborough: T. & T. Clark, 1999).

Macquarrie, J. *Jesus Christ in Modern Thought* (London: SCM, 1993).

———. *Principles of Christian Theology* (London: SCM, 1966).

Marsden, G. M. "Fundamentalism," in *Variety of American Evangelicalism* (Downers Grove, IL: InterVarsity, 1991).

———. *Fundamentalism and American Culture: The Shaping of Twentieth-Century Evangelicalism 1870-1925* (New York: Oxford University Press, 1980).

———. *The Fundamentalist Phenomenon*, N. Cohen, ed. (Grand Rapids: Eerdmans, 1990).

Marty, M. "Fundamentals of Fundamentalism" in *Fundamentalism in Comparative Perspective*, L. Kaplin, ed. (University of Massachusetts Press, 1992).

———, and S. Appleby, editors. "Conclusion: An Interim Report on a Hypothetical Family," in *Fundamentalism Observed (The Fundamentalist Project Volume 1)* (Chicago: University of Massachusetts Press, 1991).

———, and S. Appleby, editors. *"Fundamentalism Observed (The Fundamentalist Project Volume 1),"* (Chicago: University of Massachusetts Press, 1991).

———, and S. Appleby, editors. *Fundamentalisms Comprehended* (Chicago: University of Massachusetts Press, 1995).

———, and S. Appleby, editors. "Introduction: The Fundamentalist Project: A User's Guide," in *Fundamentalism Observed (The Fundamentalist Project Volume 1)* (Chicago: University of Massachusetts Press, 1991).

McClendon, *Biography as Theology: How Life Stories Can Remake Today's Theology* (Philadelphia: Trinity Press, 1990).

McConnachie, J. "Reformation Issues Today," in *Reformation Old and New: A Tribute to Karl Barth* (London: Lutterworth Press, 1947).

McCormack, B. L. *Karl Barth's Realistic Dialectical Theology: Its Genesis and Development, 1909-1936* (Oxford: Clarindon, 1997).

———. "The Unheard Message of Karl Barth," in *Word and World* 14.1 (Winter) 1994.

McGrath, A. *The Making of Modern German Christology: 1750-1990* (Apollos, MI, 2nd ed, 1994).

———. "Evangelical Theological Method: The State of the Art," in *Evangelical Futures: A Conversation on Theological Method*, J. G. Stackhouse, ed. (Grand Rapids: Baker, 2000).

McKim, D. K, *How Karl Barth Changed My Mind* (Grand Rapids: Eerdmans, 1986).

Miller, D. W. "The Theological System of Bernard L. Ramm." PhD diss., Southwestern Baptist Theological Seminary, Texas, 1982.

Mohler, R. A. "Bernard Ramm: Karl Barth and the Future of American Evangelicalism," *Perspectives in Religious Studies* 17.4 (1990).

———. "Evangelical Theology and Karl Barth: Representative Models of Response." PhD diss., Southern Baptist Seminary, 1989.

———. *Evangelical Theology and Karl Barth: Representative Models of Response* (Ann Arbor, MI: UMI, 1990).

Morgan, D. D. "The Early Reception of Karl Barth's Theology in Britain: A Supplementary View," in *Scottish Journal of Theology* 54.4 (2001).

Mueller, D. L. "Changing Conceptions of "Christian Experience" in Representative Contemporary Protestant Theologians," in *Perspectives in Religious Studies* 1:2(4) (1994).

———. "The Contributions and Weaknesses of Karl Barth's View of the Bible" in *The Proceedings of the Conference on Biblical Inerrancy* (Nashville: Broadman Press, 1987).

———. "Foundation of Karl Barth's Doctrine of Reconciliation: Jesus Christ Crucified and Risen," in *Toronto Studies in Theology* 54 (New York: Edwin Mellen Press, 1990).

———. "Karl Barth" in *Makers of the Modern Theological Mind*, B. E. Patterson, ed. (Waco: Word Books,1972).

———. "Review of Jesus is Victor! Karl Barth's Doctrine of Salvation," in *Review and Expositor* 74.4 (Fall, 1977).

———. "The Theology of Karl Barth and the Nineteenth Century" in *Religion and Life: A Christian Quarterly of Opinion and Discussion*, XXX14, no. 1 (Winter, 1964–65).

———. "The Whale and the Elephant: Barth and Bultmann in Dialogue," in *Perspectives in Religious Studies* 15:3(4) (1988).

Nicholson, L. *Femisnism/Postmosernism (Thinking Gender)* (London: Routledge, 1990).

Noll, M. A. "Old Princeton Theology," in *Evangelical Dictionary of Theology*, W. A. Elwell, ed. (Grand Rapids: Baker, 1984).

Oden, T. *Life in the Spirit: Systematic Theology* 3 (San Francisco: Harper, 1992).

Paul, S. *Humanism and Postmodernism* (Minneapolis: KIMM Printing, 1994).

Penner, M. B. *Christianity and the Postmodern Turn: Six Views* (Grand Rapids: Brazos Press, 2005).

Phan, P. C., editor. *Christianity and the Wider Ecumenism* (New York: Paragon House, 1990).

Parker, D. Fundamentalism and Conservative Protestantism in Australia, A Thesis Presented to the Department of Studies in Religion of The University of Queensland in fulfilment of the requirements of the Degree of Doctor of Philosophy, June, 1982.

Pinnock, C. H. "Bernard Ramm: Postfundamentalist Coming to Terms with Modernity," in *Perspectives on Religious Studies* (October 17, 1990).

———."New Dimensions in Theological Method," in *New Dimensions in Evangelical Thought: Essays in Honor of Millard Erickson*, David Dockery, ed. (Downers Grove, IL: InterVarsity, 1998).

Preus, R. "The Word of God in the Theology of Karl Barth," in *Concordia Theological Monthly* 31 (Fall, 1960).

Ramm, B. *After Fundamentalism: The Future of Evangelical Theology* (San Francisco: Harper and Row, 1993).

———. "An Appraisal of Karl Barth," in *Eternity* 20 (February, 1969) 36–38.

———. "Biblical faith and History," in *Christianity Today* (March 1, 1963).

———. "The Continental Divide in Contemporary Theology," in *Christianity Today* (October 8, 1965).

———. "Europe, God, and Karl Barth," in *Eternity* 10 (April, 1959) 10.

———. "An Evaluation of Karl Barth," *Southern Presbyterian Journal* 7 (May 4, 1959).

———. *An Evangelical Christology: Ecumenic and Historic* (Nashville: Thomas Nelson, 1985a).

———. *The Evangelical Heritage: A Study in Historical Theology* (Grand Rapids: Baker, 1973).

———. "Helps From Karl Barth," in *How Karl Barth Changed My Mind*, D. McKim, ed. (Grand Rapids: Eerdmans, 1986).

———. "Karl Barth: The Theological Avalanche," in *Eternity* 8 (July, 1957) 4–5, 48.

———. "The Major Theses of Neo-orthodoxy," in *Eternity* 8 (June, 1957) 18–19, 33.

———. *Offence to Reason: The Theology of Sin* (San Francisco: Harper and Row, 1985b).

———. *The Pattern of Religious Authority* (Grand Rapids: Eerdmans, 1957).

———. *The Witness of the Spirit* (Grand Rapids: Eerdmans, 1959).

Roberts, R. H. *A Theology On Its Way: Essays on Karl Barth* (Edinburgh: T. & T. Clark, 1991.

Reid, D. G., H. S. Shelly, and H. S. Stout, editors. *Dictionary of Christianity in America* (Downers Grove, IL: InterVarsity, 1990).

Riesebrodt, M. *Pious Passion—The Emergence of Modern Fundamentalism in the United States and Iran* (University of California Press, 1993).

Rohrer, J. R. "The Theologian as Prophet: Donald Bloesch and the Crisis of the Modern Church," in *From East to West: Essays in Honor of Donald G. Bloesch*, D. J. Adams, ed. (Washington: University of America Press, 1997).

Rumscheidt, H., editor. *Karl Barth in Review* (Allison Park, PA: Pickwick Press, 1981).

Sandeen, E. R. *The Roots of Fundamentalism: British and American Millenarianism, 1800–1930* (Chicago: University of Chicago Press, 1970).

Schelling, D. "On Reading Karl Barth from the Left" in *Karl Barth and Radical Politics*, edited and translated by G. Hunsinger (Louisville: Westminster Press, 1976).

Schnucker, R. V. "Karl Barth" in. *Evangelical Dictionary of Theology*, W. A. Elwell, ed. (Grand Rapids: Baker, 1984).

Schwobel, C. "Theology" in *The Cambridge Companion to Karl Barth*, J. Webster, ed. (Cambridge: Cambridge University Press, 2000).

Shelley, B. *Church History in Plain Language* (Waco: Word, 1982).

Shepard, W. "Fundamentalism Christian and Islamic," in *Religion* 17 (1987).

Shepherd, D, and K. Arisian, editors. *Humanism and Postmodernism: Essays from the Humanist Institute* (Minneapolis: KIMM Printing, 1994).

Sivan, E. "The Enclave Culture," in *Fundamentalisms Comprehended*, M. Marty and R. S. Appleby, eds. (Chicago: University of Chicago Press, 1995).

Spiceland, J. D. *Barmen, Declaration of,* in W. A. Elwell, ed., "Evangelical Dictionary of Theology," (Baker Books, 1984).

Spring, B. "Carl F. H. Henry dies at 90," in *Christianity Today* (February, 2004).

Steinmetz, D. C. "Evangelical and Reformed Church," in *The New International Dictionary of the Christian Church*, J. D. Douglas, ed. (Exeter: Paternoster, 1974).

Sykes, S. W., editor. *Karl Barth: Studies in his Theological Method* (Clarendon, 1979).

Tannenbaum, M. H, M. R. Wilson, and A. J. Ruden, editors. *Evangelicals and Jesus Christ in an Age of Pluralism* (Michigan: Baker, 1984).

Thorne, P. R. *Evangelicalism and Karl Barth: His Reception and Influence in North American Evangelical Theology* (Allison Park, PA: Pickwick Publications, 1995).

Torrance, T. F. "Bloesch's Doctrine of God," in *Evangelical Theology in Transition*, E. M. Colyer, ed. (Downers Grove, IL: InterVarsity, 1999).

————. *Karl Barth: An Introduction to His Early Theology, 1910–1931* (London: SCM, 1962).

————. "Theology of Karl Barth" in *The Scotsman* (April 14, 1952).

Vanhoozer, K. L. "Bernard Ramm," in *Handbook of Evangelical Theologians*, W. A. Elwell, ed. (Grand Rapids: Baker, 1993).

Van Til, C. *Christianity and Barthianism* (Philadelphia: The Presbyterian and Reformed Publishing Company, 1965).

————. *The New Modernism: An Appraisal of the Theology of Barth and Brunner* (United States: James Clark and CO. LTD, 1946).

Ward, G., editor. *The Blackwell Companion to Postmodern Theology* (Oxford: Blackwell, 2004).

Webster, J. "Introducing Barth," in *The Cambridge Companion to Barth*, J. Webster, ed. (Cambridge: Cambridge University Press, 2000).

Wilshire, L. E. "The United Church of Christ," in *Dictionary of Christianity in America*, D. G. Reid, B. L Shelly, and H. S. Stout (Downers Grove, IL: InterVarsity, 1990).

www.ingramcontent.com/pod-product-compliance
Lightning Source LLC
Chambersburg PA
CBHW060333100426
42812CB00003B/983